D1622144

WITHDRAWN
from the
MANITOWOC PUBLIC LIBRARY

# GAMERS

## WRITERS, ARTISTS & PROGRAMMERS
## ON THE PLEASURES OF PIXELS

WITHDRAWN
from the
MANITOWOC PUBLIC LIBRARY

# GAMERS

## WRITERS, ARTISTS & PROGRAMMERS
## ON THE PLEASURES OF PIXELS

## Edited by Shanna Compton

SOFT SKULL PRESS
BROOKLYN, NEW YORK

794.8 GAMERS
Gamers : writers, artists &
programmers on the
Manitowoc Public Library
3312800612829

©2004 by Shanna Compton.

Excerpt from *Plowing the Dark*, ©2000 by Richard Powers. Reprinted by permission of the author.

<www.shannacompton.com/gamers.html>

Cover design by Charles Orr.

Interior design by Shanna Compton.


Soft Skull Press

71 Bond Street, Brooklyn, NY 11217

<www.softskull.com>


Distributed by Publishers Group West.

1-800-788-3123 | www.pgw.com

Printed in Canada


Library of Congress Cataloging-in-Publication Data

    Gamers : writers, artists & programmers on the pleasures of pixels / edited by Shanna Compton.

        p. cm.

   ISBN 1-932360-57-3 (alk. paper)

   1.  Video games—Social aspects. 2. Video games—Psychological aspects. I. Compton, Shanna.

GV1469.34.S52G37 2004

794.8—dc22        2004019899

The editor wishes to thank Richard Eoin Nash, Sarah Groff-Palermo, David Janik, Kristin Pulkkinen, and everyone at Soft Skull; Charlie Orr for the cover design; Susanne Reece for copyediting the essays; Matthew Sharpe for his help; her husband Shawn Hollyfield for their ten-year two-player game; and of course, all of the contributors included here.

"If a typewriter could talk, it probably would have very little to say; our automatic washers are probably not hiding secret dream machines deep inside their drums. But these microchips really blow you away!"

—Charles Bernstein, "Play It Again, Pac-Man," 1991

# insert coin

## SHANNA COMPTON
## Walkthrough: An Introduction

In 1950 in Corpus Christi, Texas, Harmon Dobson opened the first Whataburger hamburger stand. Bigger is better in Texas, as you know, and these two-handed burgers were a hit. By the company's thirty-fifth anniversary, the Whataburger chain had expanded to just shy of 400 stores, spreading across the state and even as far as Florida. Millions of their caramel-and-cream colored nickel coffee mugs were refilled again and again with caffeinated promise. Country-music star Mel Tillis performed virtuosically stuttered slogans on their television and radio ads. I was fifteen and a part-time cashier.

The décor of the franchise in our local mall reflected Whataburger's Texas roots, complete with faux split-rail fencing and genuine leather saddle seats at the tables up front, horseshoes and farm implements on the pine-board walls. The leftover late '70s orange-and-brown color scheme carried over into our double-knit polyester uniforms, naturally, and even the manager wore a pearl-snap Western shirt, short-sleeved with a W-print tie. Whataburger was not the first place I'd applied, but they were the first to call, and this was my first job. I lied and said I was sixteen. If there was one thing I thought I could do—how hard could it be?—it was "Build a Better Burger." For the last three years, I'd been obsessively playing *BurgerTime* for

Intellivision.

*BurgerTime* features Peter Pepper, dressed in chef's hat and smock, who runs from level to level of a *Donkey Kong*-like structure dodging not thrown barrels but animated wieners, fried eggs, and pickles. Peter Pepper's objective is to build giant burgers by knocking their parts—bun, lettuce, patty, bun—into stacks on the floor below. I think some levels also featured sliced tomatoes and American cheese, and a squeeze-bottle of ketchup. Personally, I like pickles on my burgers, but I couldn't have it my way in *BurgerTime*. Mr. Pickle was the enemy, as much as Mr. Wiener and Mr. Egg; they all caused trouble for Peter Pepper. My options were two—hit these rogue foods with shakers of pepper, or squish them with falling burger parts.

My burger-building mastery notwithstanding, that job at Whataburger sucked. My friends routinely came by with their skateboards to taunt me about my uniform and demand free cokes. The other employees were much older than I was, and kept telling me if I'd just smile I'd be right purdy. When it was time for my lunch break, to avoid making conversation, I changed my shirt (no help for the brown elastic-waist trousers) and headed for the arcade around the corner, just past the fountain.

The Gold Mine. Like the Whataburger, this place was tricked out with evocative set design. It was pretty dark in there, but I recall mining carts and tracks, a mine-shaft entrance, a sign with picks and shovels and California panhandler-style lettering. I'd slink in smelling of fries to play *Centipede* (whee! a trackball!), *Asteroids, Pac-Man, Q-Bert* (I was hopeless but loved it regardless), or *Pole Position*. *Pole Position* particularly appealed back then. I'd qualified for a "hardship license," meaning I could drive at fifteen (though legally only to school, work, or to help Mom shuttle around my younger sisters), and I'd already bought a car; that's what the stupid job was for. But the driving in *Pole Position* wasn't like real driving; it was fast, reckless, and completely without practical purpose. No parking lots, no traffic tickets, no errands. I guess pretending to be sixteen, flipping burgers at a faux ranch, and dropping quarter tips into slots in a faux gold mine, meant there wasn't much about those days in the mid-eighties for me that didn't add up to fantasy, really.

Like many of the contributors in this book, I grew up playing video games. The first video game I ever played was *Pong*. My cousin had an Atari 2600, complete with the ideal suburban "game room" and his own game-dedicated television at his house across town. I had a

Commodore 64 on which I played some early text games (and programmed and printed "locker signs" for my friends: STEPH LOVES NICKY LOVES STEPH LOVES NICKY, ad nauseum). I even took a computer class at the local community college when I couldn't have been more than eleven or twelve. We learned BASIC, and simple word processing, and surveyed the history of computers. I remember being handed a sample punch card by the teacher and thinking what a pain in the ass it must have been to have to communicate with a machine via a stack of slotted cardboard. (*Whew, sure glad all we have to do is type GOTO 10.*) Even so, the Commodore 64 soon lay filmed with dust and my programming skills never progressed beyond locker signs—we got Intellivision for Christmas and that was that. I played *Donkey Kong, Astrosmash* (a knockoff of *Asteroids*), *Truckin'* (I'd once answered my second-grade teacher Mrs. Lancaster that I wanted to be trucker when I grew up), *Auto Racing, Major League Baseball* (the only sports game I liked—it talked: "Yer out!"), *Frog Bog* (I asked for *Frogger,* but…), and *Snafu* (a completely weird game of writhing, crashing snakes which I'm sure my mother had no idea was named after the military slang for "Situation normal: all fucked up"). I loved my Intellivision; my middle sister, not so much. I sometimes had to beg her to play.

By the time I started working at Whataburger, Intellivision's "Blue Sky Rangers" were confronting layoffs and competition from up-and-coming companies. My youngest sister is ten years younger than me though, and she kept our games and home system fresh. She traded in the near-obsolete Intellivsion and *BurgerTime* for a Nintendo and *Super Mario Bros.,* etc. I played off and on with her through high school, and still couldn't resist the cocktail-table *Ms. Pac-Man* or *Space Invaders* at the pizza joint, until these familiar machines began gradually disappearing, replaced by games I'd never played, and which often cost more than a quarter.

I played some in college too, once I started going to bars, because the games where there and we were bored and playing video golf or *MegaTouch* sex trivia even was better than being hit on by frat boys. But it wasn't the same; not until 1995 when I first played *Myst*.

Holy mother Catherine, that game was cool. And completely absorbing. My husband and I put the CD in our new Bondi Blue iMac one Friday night and played till it was time to call in sick on Monday. I dreamed the music. I was amazed by the graphics and gasped at the surprise cut-scenes. I adored the 3-D gameplay and first-person perspective. All these years I'd given up playing games and now I couldn't stop. Between playing *Myst* and its sequel

*Riven,* we hunted up more games: *Necronomicon* (horrible interior monologues, but oddly compelling with decent graphics), some disappointing game in which we were supposed to capture demons in jars, *Return to Zork* (based on the earlier *Zork* text-only game, but with graphics) and *Zork Nemesis* (not really based on the original at all), and I got hooked on MacSoft's *Scrabble.* We were twenty-five and twenty-four—grownups—regressing into complete gaming dorks. We didn't care. We got a subscription to *Game Informer* with our membership to GameSpot (good for skimming the ads). We made excuses to our friends for not going out on the weekends. We decided not to admit in public we played video games.

But then one day at the bar, my husband made a joke about Atrus and his linking books, and someone else at the table laughed. We were outed. Turns out we weren't alone.

When I started thinking about an anthology of personal essays about video games, I hadn't read *The Video Game Theory Reader* (Mark J. P. Wolf & Bernard Perron, eds. Routledge, 2003) or *Supercade* (Van Burnham, MIT Press, 2001), or seen the recent PBS documentary *Video Game Revolution* (Greg Palmer, KTCS Television, 2004). I hadn't heard about the American Museum of the Moving Image's exhibit *Hot Circuits: A Video Game Arcade* (the first-ever museum exhibition on gaming back in 1989), though I did catch wind of *BLIP: Arcade Classics from the Museum's Collection* earlier this year. And I didn't realize so many people I knew played video games, had always played video games, would never stop playing video games. But the more I asked, the more I learned.

"So, do you play video games at all?"

This question was met with either one of two responses. "Oh man, I love video games, especially _____. Have you played that?" Or, "Uh, not since I was a kid." But sometimes "Not since I was a kid" turned into "Well, I do have a PlayStation," which turned into rhapsodic narrations of a recent trip to Oddworld with Abe to rescue the Mudokons from slavery. Some folks, mostly "intellectual types," seemed reluctant to admit their penchant for play. Witness Salman Rushdie.

According to David Cronenberg, Rushdie was the inspiration for the film *eXistenZ,* in which game designers are celebrities and their games are indistinguishable from real life. "It wasn't perhaps the meeting itself with Rushdie but his situation, the reality of his situation, and the strangeness of it," Cronenberg said. "I was intrigued and horrified and in particular how it related strongly to the Burroughsian concept; the terror of having to live with what you have created, because it goes away and develops a life of its own and comes back to haunt you."[1] When Cronenberg met Rushdie in 1995, he interviewed the exiled novelist for *Shift Magazine*. In a section of the interview called "Super Mario Meets Two Great Artists," they briefly discussed video games.

**Cronenberg: Do you think there could ever be a computer game that could truly be art?**
Rushdie: No.

**There's a beautiful game called *Myst*. Have you seen that?**
I haven't seen that.

**They say this is democratic art, that is to say, the reader is equal to the creator. But this is really subverting what you want from art. You want to be taken over and you want to be—**
Shown something.

**Exactly. Why be limited by yourself? But they say, "No, it's a collaboration."**
I like computer games. I haven't played many. At the *Super Mario* level I think they're great fun. They're like crosswords because once you've beaten the game, you've solved all its possibilities.

**There's nothing left.**
Whereas this is not true of any work of art. You can experience it over and over. And if you come back to it in five years it's a different work, it's a different thing. There's a different thing between a puzzle and a book. These are just very clever puzzles and they are very enjoyable and they require certain skills, which are quite clever, useful

---

[1] "David Cronenberg talks about *eXistenZ* and reality," by Wyndham Wise in *Take One*, Spring 1999.

to develop. Sometimes they make you use your mind in very interesting ways because it requires natural steps. You have to think in ways you wouldn't expect in order to find the solution. But it's just a game.

**You would say, then, that a game designer could never be an artist?**

Never say never. Somebody could turn up who would be a genius. But if one thinks about noncomputer games, there are many which people say have the beauty of an art form. People say that about cricket, people say it about every game.

But actually, they're not art. You can have great artists playing games. You can think about a great sports figure as being equivalent to an artist. I could see that there could be an artist of a games player, a kind of Michael Jordan of the Nintendo.

**They have those competitions internationally.**

In the end, a work of art is something which comes out of somebody's imagination and takes a final form. It's offered and is then completed by the reader or the viewer or whoever it may be. Anything else is not what I would recognize as a work of art.[2]

Just a few years later, speaking to Webster Hall curator Baird Jones, Rushdie admitted with more enthusiasm that during the time he was hiding from Ayatollah Khomeini's fatwa-faithful, "[m]y main pastime was playing Nintendo games. I devoted so much time to mastering *Super Mario* that I must have been the world champion by the end of my seclusion."[3]

Never say never. The writers, poets, programmers, visual artists, cartoonists, game testers, and championship gamers interviewed by myself and the contributors to this anthology aren't ready to. Video games have provided each of us with reasons to love them, whether as a nostalgic link to our budding independence in childhood, an imaginative escape from the worka-

[2] "Cronenberg Meets Rushdie," by David Cronenberg in *Shift Magazine* 3.4, June-July 1995.

[3] "Whitney Developing a Cult Following?" by George Rush and Joanna Molloy, *New York Daily News,* May 20, 2003.

day world, a competitive challenge to be met and conquered, or as a vibrant, promising new art form. From the creation of *Spacewar!* in 1962, through the golden age of the video game arcade in America, to the console-in-every household proliferation today, games have provided us with something books, music, the plastic arts, and even film have not. We get to act as well as react. We get to play.

Rushdie's definition of art is useful here, and I'd argue that since the time of that interview games have come a long way toward being something "offered and…then completed by the reader or viewer," the goal becoming more than to simply beat them. Rushdie shifted from plain "no" to "never say never" in a single, short, can-video-games-be-art chat with Cronenberg back in 1995. I wondered what he'd think of games today. I also wondered what my friends, other writers, artists, anybody who would listen thought about them, too. So I asked.

## Walkthrough: Summaries of the Essays in this Book

Novelist **Richard Powers** takes a fictional look (in an excerpt from his novel *Plowing the Dark*) at the staying power of the 1970s classic text game *Adventure,* finding that Memory Lane leads back to the Colossal Cave for just about everybody working for a Silicon-Valley "realization lab" called TetraSys.

**Whitney Pastorek** revisits her past life as a full-blooded fantasy geek and, humming along to tunes of a certain '80s-era pop star, makes a modern-day journey to the Dark Castle, old-school style. No emulators for this girl.

**Drew Gardner** prefers the simplicity and elegance of vector graphics to 3-D rendering or raster graphics, and says he learned some Newtonian physics from his favorite games besides.

**Ernest Hilbert** puts down his joystick long enough to remember the heyday of the arcade, when he battled enemy ships on scrolling screens and provided his own dialogue and supplementary off-screen stories.

**Joseph Housley** recalls his first Nintendo, the magical machine complete with light gun that seemed to him and his brother better than snow forts or basketball or anything the outdoors of Maine had to offer, at least at first.

**Mark Lamoureux** takes a look at the graphics of the 8-bit Atari 2600 through the lens of primitive art and discovers not only totem animals and spirits, but also object lessons in dental hygiene and a couple of randy characters acting out their baser instincts in early erotic-themed games like *Beat 'Em and Eat 'Em.*

**Katie Degentesh** gives a nod to another iconic presence of the early 1980s in the title of her essay, "Playing Material Girl," and examines what young Americans are taught about capitalism even in their games. Nevertheless, she concludes she wouldn't give them up to be the Princess of Persia.

Professional-wrestling enthusiast **Marion Wrenn** suggests that like the "smart marks" of her favorite sport, gamers enjoy being duped by the inauthentic authenticity of the games they play, and she's got WWE's Brock Lesnar to back her up.

**Luis Jaramillo** grapples with virtual bloodlust, despite being raised among meetings of the Beyond War group in his living room. "It's called hunting, not killing," when he plays *Big Buck Hunter II: Sportsman's Paradise.*

Cartoonist and game developer **K. Thor Jensen** conquers *Double Dragon* and never looks back, at least until he grows up and has to get a job.

Obsessive record-nerd **Daniel Nester** goes on a quest with Steve Perry and the boys, playing the late-great rock band Journey's video game *Journey Escape,* only to find himself making friends with the legendary gamer Todd Rogers who has obsessions of his own, as well as sage advice to impart.

**Jim Munroe** explores the physical pleasures of gaming and the ways in which reality can bleed, with *MoCap Boxing, Dance Dance Revolution,* and the work-related injuries of poor Mario.

**Laurel Snyder** goes from greasy spoon to dive bar and beyond, lit by the glow of *Boxxi* on the multigame bar console *MegaTouch,* exploring allure, addiction, obsession, and eventually maturity.

Lawyer and poet **Maureen Thorson** plays back-seat driver and her thug's main squeeze as she and her beta-tester boyfriend get up to no good in Vice City.

**Thomas Kelly** hates golf, especially the clothes, and the snooty attitude, and the sudden popularity of the so-called sport among even blue-collar types, and…the list goes on. So how, then, did he become addicted to *Golden Tee*?

A self-described "mild-mannered, reasonably well-integrated lesbian New York poet,"

**Shannon Holman** gets in her little pink *Moon Patrol* buggy and drives until she's as close as virtually possible to the pixilated hotness of Laura Croft and reflects that sometimes queer culture can feel a lot like perpetual high school.

**Aaron McCollough** plays football. Fake football, that is. And during halftimes he takes a look at coach-cum-sportscaster John Madden and masculinity through the screen of the best-selling football game of all time, *John Madden NFL Football.*

**Bill Spratch** might just be a conspiracy nut, but he does raise a couple of interesting points: why does *SOCOM: U.S. Navy SEALs* include a recruitment video on the game disc, and are we, in fact, hard-wired to cheat in life, as in our games?

Novelist **Shelley Jackson,** author of the award-winning hypertext fiction *Patchwork Girl,* raises a family of Sims. They walk like us, have sex like us, and talk like us—sort of. But if Sims played video games, what would theirs look like?

**Roland Kelts** takes us on a tour of a pinging, bleeping, flashing section of Tokyo called Akihabara with his childhood hero, Ultraman Toro, and describes the pivotal moment when for him, reality became just a little too real.

**Jim Andrews**, the creator of a poetry-based game called *Arteroids,* shares the history of his work on the game, which is an example of a hybrid form between art and game, as he leads us on a quest to rewrite our "id entities," battling boredom as we go.

**Nic Kelman** compares the history of film to that of video games and wonders what's missing. Where are the games we *should* be playing? Where are the designers and programmers—the artists—who should be making these games? He leaves us with a Video Game Arts Manifesto.

Just as all movies or books or examples of visual art aren't classified "fine art" (though I'm less much less concerned about that distinction than some), there's no reason that *Grand Theft Auto: Moons of Jupiter* can't be shelved alongside the future video game we can someday all agree to bless with fine art status. What will it be like? And will we still call it a game, or will it be something else?

Much the same way those faux split-rail fences graced the décor of my Whataburger, and those real leather saddles stood out among the fakery, some resemblances to and even genuine moments of "art" may be found in video games from past to present. But let's not stop there. Perhaps the often-quoted Eliot line could serve here: the one about borrowing and stealing.[4] Once video games progress from borrowing from other mediums like film, once they fully incorporate what technologies and palette tools they need, and have moved beyond, then they've matured. And so have we as gamers.

As Nic Kelman and others have pointed out, films and video games already share certain palette tools, and have followed up to a point a similar evolutionary path. At least one critic has turned the descriptive tables when attempting to fill in the video game to art (in this case film) comparison. Wayne Bremser, in a recent feature piece for *Game Girl Advance,* compares Matthew Barney's *Creamaster 3* to a video game, suggesting Barney borrowed directly from— get this—*Donkey Kong,* which itself borrowed from the classic film *King Kong.*[5] Yeah, like, full circle.

"The plot of *Cremaster 3* is taken from the Masonic order and the myth of Hiram Abiff [...], but the narrative center of the film is found in its architectural spaces. Before being populated with adversaries, spaces in *Cremaster 3* and video games are transformed sculpturally to create an arena for action," Bremser explains. "Barney and game designers look for strong visual landscapes that are ripe for a character's running, jumping, smashing, and climbing." Bremser then goes on to outline the following pairings: Barney's Entered Apprentice (the name of *C3*'s protagonist) equals Mario. The innards of the Chrysler Building and later the spiral entrails of the Guggenheim (both locations in the film) equal the multiered construction sites of *Donkey Kong.* Hiram Abiff (played by sculptor Richard Serra) equals Donkey Kong, throwing gobs of melted Vaseline at the Entered Apprentice in place of the barrels the giant ape threw at Mario. There's more. Whereas *Donkey Kong* has four "degrees"—ramps, girders, elevators, and conveyor belts—the Guggenheim in *Cremaster 3* has five—the Order of the Rainbow Girls, the battle of the bands between Agnostic Front and Murphy's Law, Aimee Mullins who transforms into a deadly cat, the Five Points of Fellowship, and Richard Serra. Finally Bremser reimagines the film as an actual video game:

---

[4] "Immature poets imitate; mature poets steal." *The Sacred Wood: Essays on Poetry and Criticism* by T. S. Eliot, Methune, London, 1920.

[5] "Matthew Barney Versus *Donkey Kong,*" May 23, 2003.

"A game adaptation of *Cremaster 3* could include all of its characters, sculpture, mythical elements, and action. You could climb the rotunda, pick up objects and toss them. You could confront punk rockers and legless felines. Why would a designer want to create this game? The effort could be the first game recognized as a relevant piece of contemporary art. It could be more compelling than the film or the exhibit. It could even be a great game."

By choosing an "art film" instead of a blockbuster hit or classic Hollywood-heyday picture for his comparison, Bremser makes a headway, I think. In fact, his tracing of the possible lineage from *King Kong* to *Donkey Kong* to *Creamaster 3* is one I find quite useful to think about. It's exciting, really. I heard a rumor a few years ago that one of my favorite directors, David Lynch, was set to collaborate on a DVD-ROM video game; I couldn't wait to play, but it never happened. The iconography and technology developed for video games have already slipped into other mediums such as film (in which computer-generated special effects have been de rigueur since George Lucas's *Star Wars*), painting and sculpture (as in the work of the incognito Parisian artist who calls himself Space Invader).[6] Even fashion designers have borrowed from video games; for her fall 2004 collection, Miuccia Prada's research included observing gamers in arcades. In her words, her resulting designs were inspired by a combination of "eighteenth-century painting with video games," (even if Jane Pinckard of *Game Girl Advance* thinks Alexander McQueen and John Galliano capture the video game aesthetic better in their clothes).[7] So the slippage goes both ways, as Art dunks its chocolate into Video Game peanut butter.

Are we closer than we think to creating games that are also art? As flash poems, and hypertext fiction, and art-based games like Jim Andrews' *Arteroids* have hinted, there are more ful-

---

[6] The artist known as Space Invader, or sometimes simply Invader, makes tile sculptures of the invaders from his favorite game and affixes them to bridges, buildings, sidewalks, and other structures from Paris to New York. You can read more about Space Invader's artistic invasions of cities around the world at his website, <www.spaceinvaders.com>, which even includes maps to help you find his handiwork. He'll also sell you an Invasion Kit, so you can make and install your own.

[7] "Video Chic," April 15, 2004.

gent ways for video games to borrow from, and to inform, other artistic mediums than most designers/programmers are currently pursuing. But maybe it won't be the programmers who make that final step, turning video games into art—unless they stop thinking like programmers and start thinking like artists. And some of them have.

Video game auteurs like Rand & Robyn Miller (the *Myst* games), Lorne Lanning (the *Oddworld* games), and Benoit Sokal (*Syberia*) have created games that can affect as powerfully as the imagery in Barney's *Cremaster 3* or the bold abstractions of a Robert Motherwell painting. The Schulman Combo duo of Stephan Schulz and Johannes Büneman have created *99 Rooms,* a virtual gallery of their art, photography, music, and sound effects that incorporates familiar first-person game navigation and Flash animation; the viewer "plays" through it.[8] Morton Subotnick, when I saw him a few years ago at the Kitchen, showcased a demo computer program for composing music that very much resembled an interactive, changeable abstract painting with a live soundtrack. Haruhiko Shono, creator of *Radical TV,* has experimented in award-winning multimedia projects such as *Alice, L-Zone,* and the breathtaking *Gadget* (which combines a CD-ROM and full-color art book for an immersive experience like nothing else I've seen) in ways that convince me that the intersection of art and games, if we haven't entered it yet, lies just ahead.

Truthfully, I have no idea what else today's game designers and programmers have up their sleeves, what will be in store, literally, for us in the near future. But I hope it's something like art, something that takes the gamer beyond her role as mouse-clicking virtual explorer or joystick-wielding soldier, or even a motion-capture dancing fool—as cool as those roles are to play. Come on guys. We're ready.

---

[8] *99 Rooms* is online at <www.99rooms.com>. Check it out.

## RICHARD POWERS
### FROM _PLOWING the DARK_

**You are standing at the end of a road before a small brick building.**

Stark words flashed across the network's broadcast channel, like that annual decree going out from Caesar Augustus. Like the first four measures of "Auld Lang Syne." Like the face of a friend bobbing out from a crowd just clearing International Customs, lit in familiarity's halo.

Jack Acquerelli, his day's work put to bed and his night's fantasies brought up in a foreground window, laughed to himself at the phantom text. Similar bursts of recognition must have passed through everyone still logged in at this hour. The sender was good. The message carried no header, no time stamp, no originating workstation ID. Just a raw text stream, plopped down on a hundred screen status lines, like a writ coming straight from God, Gates, or some other upper-echelon SYSOP.

Jackdaw ran a quick check to see who was on. Eighty-six users, not counting concurrent sessions. Folks at all six facilities, from the Sound down along the coast, as far south as the Valley. Seven people right here at the RL. Night and prototypes: something about 2 A.M. rendered it the perfect hour for wire-wrapping.

Any dozen of these guys were good enough to have managed the stunt. A few of them had written the damn operating system. There were too many wizards for Jackdaw to trap the identity of the sender. The words were best treated as a collective artifact.

Jackdaw killed the user check and popped back to the OS prompt. In just those few seconds away, some feel-fingered soul—a certain arjrao 1, working on a TG Graphics box over at the mother ship—had already managed to dispatch a follow-up any one of these late-night acolytes could have supplied:

**Around you is a forest. A small stream flows out of the building and down a gully.**

The words filled Jackdaw with a great sense of well-being. Happiness flowed in its own small stream out of Jackdaw's chest and down into his typing digits. It felt like a snatch of last year's plaintive progressive-rock waif bleeding out of the radio of a car that tracked up a mountain road in the dark. Like a drug maybe, though Jackdaw had never partaken. Like first love. Like learning, word of mouth, that your first love loved you back.

His eyes took in the summons of the words. His hands on their keys felt the fingers of that seventh-grader still inside them. He stared at the sentences and saw his father, one Saturday morning in 1977 when young Jackie had been acting out, taking him to the office and parking him in front of a gleaming Televideo 910, hooked up to a remote mainframe through the magic of a Tymeshare 300-baud modem.

All a trick, Jackdaw saw in retrospect, an elaborate diversionary tactic to fool a boy into— of all things—reading. The screen had glowed at him then, each letter a phosphorescent worm made up of a couple of dozen discrete pinpricks of green light. You are standing at the end of a road. Before a small brick building.

"So?" eleven-year-old Jackdaw had pouted. "So what?" But half-enthralled already, half-guessing that this place might be vastly more interesting than the larger one that was good for so little except disappointment.

"So," his father mocked. "So type something."

"Type something? Type what?"

"Anything. You're standing in front of a building. What do you do?"

"Anything? You mean, like…anything?"

"For heaven's sake. Just try something and see what happens."

Belief, at eleven, was still wide. And those words were even wider. Boy Jackie read the sentences on the screen again. This time the road, and the small building, and the forest, and the stream flowing out of the building, and the gully it flowed into jumped out at him in all dimensions, cobbling up some temporary, extensible, magic scratchpad valley expressly created for getting lost in.

The idea of walking through this valley lifted him out of that morning's misery and set him loose along that small stream. He found himself split over two locales: at the end of the road and in the middle of a chorus line of letters, though which he hunted, with escalating excitement, for the key *e*.

**Enter building,** Jackdaw typed into the broadcast dialog box and let it rip. The message echoed on his screen's status line, amid a hail of identical messages bouncing around the wide area network all over the North Coast.

His was not the only private raft out on this nostalgic cruise. Most of late-working TeraSys, apparently, remembered the archaic incantations, the geographies of pleasure buried in the mists of a dozen years back. Like calls to a radio contest, the responses flooded in. Exhortations to **Enter building** and **Go building** piled up along the bottom of his screen. Even a simple **Building** and a simpler **Enter**.

*Get outta my life,* Jackdaw howled. *You gotta be kidding me.*

Spider Lim, dozing on the cubicle couch, shot up, spilling the bag of Sun Chips balanced on his sternum. *What is it? What's happening? Something crash?*

*Original Adventure?*

*Huh? What about it?*

*You could just type "Enter" to go into the building?*

*Oh yeah. Sure.*

*I played that thing for over twenty thousand minutes, and I still have all the logs and hand-drawn maps to prove it. Two years, on and off. And I never knew you could get into the building without typing "Building."*

*That's all right. I never got past the dragon sleeping on the carpet.*

*The dragon? You just kill it.*

*With your bare hands?*

*Yes.*

*Damn.* Spider fell back prone on the couch, palm-butting his forehead. *Idiot! That never occurred to me.*

**You are inside a building, a well house for a large spring.**

**There are some keys on the ground here.**

**There is a shiny brass lamp nearby.**

**There is food here.**

**There is a bottle of water here.**

Once in a lifetime, if lucky, a soul stumbles onto pure potential. Young Jackie, on the end of a road, felt himself transported in the blink of an electronic eye into this building, this well house for a large spring. Some patient genie in this molded box—circuits too complex to imagine—promised to act upon Jackie's every demand. You are inside a building. You are inside a book. Inside a story that knows you're in there, a tale ready to advance in any direction you send it.

Eleven years of existence had already wearied the child. The world was no more than a monotonous, predictable tease, a limited reward with unlimited restrictions. TV was a sadistic trick, one he's seen through at age nine. He failed to grasp the appeal of cars, which only served to move human stupidity around a little faster. Sports were beyond him, girls incoherent, and food a bore.

But this: this was something he'd given up on ever seeing outside of his own, private theater. This was salvation. This was where he'd always hoped to live.

He stood at the base camp of pure possibility, his remote puppet free to roam the universe at will. He looked up at his father, helpless with deliverance. His father mistook his crumpled smile of bewildered arrival. "Try going west."

Too blissed out even to be irritated, the boy typed: **Go west.**

**It is now pitch-dark. If you proceed you will likely fall into a pit.**

Of course it was dark. Why else was a lamp sitting in the foyer? His father was senile, pitiful, a liability on this unprecedented journey. Without thinking, the boy doubled back, got the lamp, and lit it. Get lamp, light lamp: somehow, the machine knew. Objects existed, as did actions. Things had the qualities they embodied. He moved about in this terrain, changing it with everything he chose to do, leaving the land and its pilgrim sprite forever updated.

The light came on, revealing a debris-filled room. A low cobbled passage blocked up with mud.

"What's this called?" he pleaded with his father.

"*Adventure*."

"No," he said, panicked with impatience. Pointing at the screen. "What's *this* called?" This latitude. This venue. This concept.

"Oh. The place, you mean? Colossal Cave."

A simple Telnet session could now give Jackdaw the entire original classic, FTP'd from any of several hundred UNIX boxes where the solution, like some fire-breathing beast, now lay curled and dormant, guarding its ancient hoard. Five minutes would have brought up the full walk-through on his screen, scripture to be cut and pasted from the editor window into his tiled message buffer. But Jackdaw had no time to cheat. The real-time gauntlet had been thrown down.

Comments began to fly, faster than he could read them. Choruses of **Plugh you, too!** and **Fee, Fie, Foe, Foobar,** the inside jokes of pioneers queued up and blazed their brief transmission. One-meg-per-second whispers of **Wave wand** and **Go west**, the hushed remembrances of those who were at the beginning, the first generation of celestial navigators ever to look upon this cosmology, ever to take the fabulous new orrery out for a test spin cast off into the unmapped depths all over again.

**You have crawled around in some little holes,** Jackdaw typed, **and wound up back in the main passage.**

He hit the Send key four times. Four copies of these words meandered out over the night's mazed network. Thirty seconds later, someone down in San Jose echoed back:

**Thanks a brickload, ja-aqul. Like I really needed to be reminded of that part.**

It had been clear to little Jackie, from the first Return key, just what he was facing. This game was nothing less than the transcendental Lego set of the human soul, its pieces infinite in both number and variety. He scoured that room, the well house for a large spring. He got the keys, got the food, got the water bottle, and never looked back. He left the building. He wandered outside, into the virgin forest. He followed the gully downstream, where the water entered a little grate. He toyed tirelessly at the grate's slit, trying to pry away its stubborn secret.

"What on earth are you doing?" came his father's fatherly dismay.

"Nothing." Exploring. Sampling utter open-endedness, nibbling the full fruit of possibility down to the core.

"The cave's back in there. In the cobbled passage. You were right at the entrance dum-dum."

But there were too many possibilities already overlooked. Too much to investigate before Jackie could allow himself the luxury of the cave entrance. He stood in the great outdoors, that raw expanse of valley, typing **Look trees, look leaves, look rock, look water.**

It took only an hour to discover just how small the adventure really was. What had seemed wider than the whole of California was, in fact, largely a cardboard prop. He could not, for instance, climb a tree in the forest and look out from its crest. He could not scoop soil up into his bottle and pour it down the little grate. He could not spread food pellets in the woods to coax out wild animals. If he walked too far in one direction, the newfound continent simply stopped. **You cannot go in that direction.**

The machine replied with a paralyzed **Huh??** more often than it acted upon his command. The machine, it turned out, was nearly as brain-dead as his father. Weight, containment, edge, resonance, extension, heft: one by one, the qualities that the cave's strewn treasures promised fell away into chicken wire and pâpier-maché. Infinity shrunk with each primitive property that this universe shed.

Infinite, instead, were the things this machine would *not* let you do. Colossal Cave was just a come-on, a tricked-up fox-farmer-hen puzzle that dealt successfully only with the answers it already expected. But the place it mocked lay too close to the Northwest Territories deep in Jackie's head for the resemblance to be anything short of real. He didn't fault the idea of the game, but only this particular work-up: this flawed, first-run parody of the land that this land really wanted to become.

A further hour of bumping against the program's limits, and disillusionment turned to challenge. Another hour, and challenge became obsession. Jackie had at last found a place on this forsaken globe where he might live. He crawled around in the cobbled passages that computing threw open, the tunnels blasted through with a further update, another thousand lines of code, the next implementation.

For all that it lacked, Colossal Cave was still endless. However deterministic, however canned the script or pointed the narrative, it still promoted him from victim to collaborator. You are in a room, with passages leading off in all directions. The room itself was still an experiment, still a lab more richly stocked with prospects than any that the rest of waking San Jose had to offer.

Jackie begged his father to get a terminal at home. Thereafter, whole days passed, unmarked except for the ghostly pencil lines spreading across his expedition's graph-paper map. He spent days in a blocked gallery, dislodging himself in a rush, on an aha, a dream inspiration as exhilarating as anything life had to offer. Free up for further caving.

And while he collected his crystal rods, his gems the size of a plover's egg, his journey pushed forward on another plane, down channels more wonderfully insidious. The quest for arrival, for the perfect score, left him tunneling through a maze of chambers with passages leading off in all directions, filaments no more than a fraction of a micron thick.

*Know what? That program taught me how to type.* The voice from behind Jackdaw shocked him out of the network relay chat. Spider, eyes closed, cheek to the cushions, playing ventriloquist in his own throat, exercised that Vulcan mind link he enjoyed with anyone stroking a keyboard within a twenty-meter radius.

Jackdaw nodded, his gesture invisible. *That program taught me how to hack the operating system. Huh?*

*Serious. I started by learning how to do a hex dump of the game file, peeking into its guts for any text strings that might give me a clue. Anything to nail down another twenty points. Then I taught myself assembly language so I could disassemble the entire program. Follow the logic. Finally see how to beat it.*

*Oh sure. I tried that too. Only I got sidetracked somewhere in the ALU. Hooked by exactly what was happening in those registers when they added the contents of two memory addresses. Somehow forgot all about the sleeping dragon and his damn Persian carpet.*

But Jackdaw had not forgotten. Nor had any of these eight-six users scattered around the eastern Pacific rim. A distributed horde of boys attacked the cave with a fierce single-mindedness that mathematicians reserve for intractable proofs. They exchanged clues by electronic bulletin board, by satellite uplink, posting their discoveries through their technocrat fathers' primitive e-mail accounts. They formed clubs, networks of the estranged and ludicrous, their membership only waiting to inherit a future they knew to be solely theirs…

**Anyone ever figure out the Hall of Mists?**

**Anybody still have his back issues of *Spelunker Today*?**

An incalculable expenditure of time. A colossal waste of his life's potential. And yet Jackie's life: the vapor trail of narrative left simply from playing the game. Time-sharing, pirating, paying out extortionate prices to secure each spin-off, each latest extension to the great underground empire, the next, hot upgrade of the ongoing adventure, each more tantalizingly realized than the last. Worlds within a two-thousand-word vocabulary, then four thousand, then eight. Interactive novels that grew to parse whole sentences. Places where glass bottles broke and food molded. Where trees could be cut down and formed into planks or paper, boats or battlements. Lands where your accumulated actions changed your own stamina and strength and wisdom, where these changing numbers altered the further paths allowed you. Lands that allowed actions and responded in ways that surprised their very programmers.

Inevitably, there arose graphics. At first the pictures were a rush, each panorama ever more glorious than the last. But the pretty picture adventures came, within a year or two, to sadden Jack past saying. He could not explain it, explanations only saddening him all the more. Some richness, some open-endedness had been crushed under the inescapable visible.

His father sympathized. "I felt the same way when TV killed off radio. Hearing about creatures from the eighth dimension beat having to look at them." His father's wisdom rating had somehow soared in the years since Jack was a kid.

Whatever else they spoiled, graphics threw open portals all their own. The visual interface launched habitations faster than anyone could click through them. Any eleven-year-old who'd ever touched a video game was way out in front of the scientists on that score. Scientific visualization was born in the first wave of *Space Invaders.*

They came in rapid succession, games neither adventure nor role-playing, creatures unique to this infant medium. The sandbox games, with their feedback growth and their open-ended tool chests. The God games, with no victory except survival, no goal but to steep yourself in ever more elaborate playing.

Adolescent Jack governed his own surging metropolises. He assembled whole utopian societies of shifting, conflicting needs. He hauled hops across the British Midlands, returning to London with trainloads of finished beer. He nursed branching ant colonies and interplanetary mining enterprises. He hired quarrymen and masons and carpenters to build him a castle that allowed him to cultivate the surrounding countryside, then tax it for every turnip he could squeeze out of it.

He sailed his sloops and pinnaces around the Caribbean, raiding Nevis and St. Kitts, buttressing the economy of Curaçao. He trained botanists and missionaries and game hunters and sent them up the Nile in makeshift canoes. He brought a peace-loving subcontinental Stone Age tribe up through the Renaissance, into the Industrial Revolution, and on into space. Then he repeated the journey in another neck of the random earth, spewing carnage and mayhem as he advanced.

He spent his teens alone, sealed in his bedroom, voyaging. All the while, he held on to that first hint, hoping to locate the fecundity that he's wrongly thought already inhabited that first adventure. Each new release, each innovation of design, produced in him the sliver of recovery. But Closer only stoked the fire of Not Quite.

Life's turn-based games led Jack Acquerelli into programming, less to make ends meet than to bring about those playgrounds that did not yet exist. College provided him with the silicon sandbox of his dreams. He worked alone and in teams, the line between the two progressively blurring. He collaborated with coders he never met, people he wouldn't have known had he passed them on the street, guys who went by tags like SubClinical, TopX, and BotTot. He built his share of dungeon crawls, each populated with increasingly more anatomically correct homunculi. He helped write a primitive multiuser talk channel, code that allowed his fellow undergrad designers to collaborate at all hours and paved the way for multiplayer spaces.

His senior honors project was called *Development,* a resource management game with a twist. Randomly generated world maps laid down reserves of various resources—coal, iron, gems, and soil. The Hittites, Cretans, and Phoenicians of this archaic Earth set to the usual task of discovering, extracting, and refining the hidden treasure, then selling off the finished goods. The capital they amassed they plowed back into new technologies, new levels of goods created from out of the storehouse of further raw finds.

But then came Jack Acquerelli's special contribution to smart games. The available research paths—the papyrus you could press from your fibers, the metals you could smelt from your coal and ore—varied from game to game, depending on the proficiency and research of the pursuing tribe. All skills expanded, contingent on their honing. No two races ever followed the same path. No two games of *Development* ever developed the same way. And of course— the holy grail of strategy gaming—no session of *Development* ever needed to end. It could spin itself out forever, unpredictably, to any of an infinitude of never-to-be-reached outcomes.

In the spirit of the digital age's gift economy, Acquerelli gave his masterpiece away, free for the downloading. The cheaper the game, the more players it gathered. And the more players that played, the more ingenious the strategies. Strategies proliferated, each one a complex program in its own right. And the more unanticipated strategies that poured into his game, the closer Jackdaw came to that sense of total liberty he hadn't felt since the age of eleven.

The game went cult, producing its own spin-offs. In his act of hacker's generosity, Jackdaw lost his chance to retire by the age of twenty-two. But the success did write him a ticket to any of the game-design outfits just then capitalizing on the housebroken PC. TeraSys discovered his work just as Jackdaw began sending around his résumé. In the summer of 1987, a rash of *Development* addiction at TeraSys brought in-house applications productivity to a standstill. The game had exactly that deep, replayable economics that all good simulation craved. TeraSys put in a bid for Jackdaw's services, one that, as always, preempted the competition.

From the instant that Jackdaw stood in the first prototype of the Cavern, no other bids existed. For the second time in one lifetime, he'd stumbled upon pure potential. Here was a story one could walk around in, only life-sized, this time for keeps. He would have signed on for half of what they offered him. He would have given everything to be able to fly his father up to this mountain, stand him inside this play fort strung from blank white sheets. Would have given the world to tell him, You're standing in front of the sky-blue future. *Here's the wand. Do something. Anything. What do you want to do?*

But his father was through with doing. His father was six months beyond wanting anything. Adventure had taken him beyond the need for machines. His father had ported off somewhere where parsers weren't required, over a border where all the checkpoints of disembodied imagination stood flung wide open.

And Jackdaw had lost all chance of ever repaying the man. Now way to thank him aside from submersion in the new project. Even among colleagues who slept and breathed the Cavern, Jackdaw stood out. Steve Spiegel joked about having the kid's mail forwarded here. Sue Loque suggested he go on a monthly pizza plan. Jon Freese rode him about stepping into the sunlight now and then, if only to refresh his personal hit points.

But the truth was, no outward life compelled Jackdaw half as much as the life inside. In a footrace against the hardware clock, every real-time hour counted. He endowed the Crayon

World with depth. He scented its flowers as a labor of love, one that left him with more energy than he expended. He taught the paper bees their acts of floralocation, showing all the patience of a Trappist honey farmer. He worked with biochemist Dale Bergen, tirelessly parking massive 3-D enzymatic molecules with all the skill of a veteran valet tearing down the corkscrew ramp of a multideck car park.

He lived to breathe life into the Cavern. The lamp, the food, the brass keys, all led him deeper into the labyrinth, from one state-of-the-art implementation to the next. Each line of his code inched toward that higher library of manipulable Forms. Each control structure and array assignment further eked out the shape of this new biome's indigenous life.

He felt himself out on the leading edge of the thing that humanity was assembling—this copious, ultimate answer to whatever, in fact, the question was. How much time had passed, how many Saturdays since the one when his father had led him here? No time at all. A day. Yet here was this wide-area token ring connecting scores of users up and down the coast, assembled from hardware that made the Televidoe and Tymeshare look like the crudest flint. Here was this community of visionary cavers, hours past midnight, hacking away on whatever sequel to discovery that discovery allotted them, shooting off nostalgic messages into the broadband, their elegies for the end of *Adventure's* opening chapter. He'd watched the leapfrogging machine design itself, every year more potent and incredible. He'd turned his bootstrapping algorithms beyond the best debugger's ability to backtrace until at last he found himself here, in pitch-darkness, not at the end of that valley road but at its start, reading the semaphore sent by his circle of colleagues, few of whom he'd ever met face-to-face, typing out his own contribution to the group quest into the compliant keyboard—**Go north, go north, go north**—the joint goal receding Zenoesque in front of them, down vistas twisting in all directions.

Somewhere over the course of playing, the underground adventure had gone mainstream, had come aboveground, warlocks taking to the surface without a single, unsuspecting non-gamer quite knowing the shape of the new rules or the size of the global coup. Digital toys came alive, every living soul's life history and health and bank account now a comprehensive Save Game file. Moore's law—performance doubling every eighteen months—fell from civilization's pace rabbit to a drag on the exploding system. Some days, the digital revolution seemed to poke along too slowly ever to bring Jackdaw into his inheritance. He and his people rode a geometric increase that outpaced all things except the appetite for more performance, the need to reach escape velocity.

Boys who came alive on a fantasy game had launched an entire planet-shattering industry. Boys solitary and communal, dispossessed and omnipotent: remote avatars in a wizard's romp of their own devising. Each month, the combined anarchy of invention made more brute headway on the final ascent than had all of history up until Hollerith. And still the revolution had not yet filled more than a thimble of its potential. The latest virtual engines were still nowhere near to delivering what the terrified, yearning boys' collective needed them to deliver.

Yet out of these walk-in caves had come a game as attentive, as robust, as responsive as life should have been. At long last, in this lucky lifetime, coders would succeed in constructing the place that the brain had first mistaken the world for: the deep, accountable, pliant, original adventure that Jackdaw, for his eager audience, now labored to complete.

He perched over the wan light of his terminal, as over the heat of a desert campfire. He tapped out his private contribution, as yet a secret kept from everyone else on the Cavern project. Across the wires, his remote, ghostly fellowship continued to recite its litany of lost landmarks:

**You are in the Hall of Mists...**

**You are in a complex junction...**

**You are on the edge of a breathtaking view...**

Lured out by the topic, the contributors perched over their workstations as distant as six hundred miles and as near as just down the hall. But each participant might as well have been in another galaxy far, far away. Filled with commemorative desire, Jackdaw typed:

**Anybody ever make it through to the end?**

Silence flashed across the broadband. Silence turned into more silence, a coaxial glitch, a pileup in the packet traffic. Then the lag grew too long to be anything but these faceless agents, each deferring to the others to go first. Eighty-six boys—give or take the stray girl who'd stumbled in among them—each waited for someone to send back word of the ultimate solution.

Comic, then embarrassing, the silence lengthened into strangeness. Like one of those lulls in the party conversation that snaps all the diners into an embargoing self-consciousness. Like the silence of shipboard refugees, out on the top deck, looking up at the hollow stars. Your night is so great and our network so small, O Lord.

**You kidding?** someone typed, followed by a spurt of expletive-laced negatives. **A hundred points short. Fifty. Ten.** The confessions poured in, and the broadband conference drifted into state, releasing its system resources, relinquishing the moment of brief coalescence, dispersing all participants to chip away at their various private galleries, their maze of tunnels spreading through the unmappable hive.

# WHITNEY PASTOREK
## I AM TELLING YOU THIS BECAUSE I TRUST YOU
## NOT TO USE IT AGAINST ME

In junior high, I was a complete and total loser. Here is how I know that this is true: Once a month, I would make a pilgrimage to Memorial City Mall, the shopping center that sat at the end of my street and was therefore easy for a twelve-year-old girl to reach by sprinting across busy Bunker Hill Drive, past the seedy apartments where people kept getting shot, over the asphalt parking lot rippled with Houston heat, and into the meat-locker air conditioning behind the glass doors. I would head straight past the food court and to the right, to a little smoke shop, where the smell of pipe tobacco reminded me of my father and the salesmen watched my sticky preteen fingers carefully for signs that something had stuck. Towards the back of that store, amidst the cigars in their brown boxes and the Zippos glinting with naked women and Harleys, was a tall glass case filled with knickknacks. I would scan past the puppies, past the cars, past the unicorns, even—I would scan the knickknacks until my eyes lit upon the one, the perfect one, the perfect one for a loser like me. I would have the salesman unlock the case and place it in my hand and I would feel the cool, perfect weight and hold the obligatory attached crystal or glass ball up to the light and watch it glisten, I would breathe deeply the tobacco warmth and say, "I'll take it." And then on the counter I would spill my allowance from the month, and into a bag would go the sculpted essence of my mis-guided passions: in junior high, I collected pewter dragons, castles, and wizards.

I was, okay, fine, yes, I was a fantasy geek.

In junior high, I read books with titles like *Magician: Apprentice* and rattled off Welsh and Gaelic mythology with ease. I loved the way the a and the e were reversed in the word *Gaelic.* I obsessively rented *Willow,* wishing more than anything that I could be beautiful, mysteri-ous, red-haired Joanne Whalley—not, like normal girls, so that I could marry Val Kilmer, but so that I could dispatch evil warriors with a broadsword while riding an enormous black stal-lion and wearing a mask made from a skull. I am fairly certain that one year I dressed as Lloyd Alexander's Horned King for Halloween. And on a shelf of my bookcase, next to the Ford Mustang hood ornament I had painted red in anticipation of my impending high school mascot—the high school where, very quickly, I learned that I needed to keep all of this infor-mation here a secret or I would be forced to eat lunch in a very forlorn corner of the cafeteria—on that shelf of my bookcase where I'd put my hopes for my future, I put my drag-ons, my castles, and my wizards. I may have bought *one* unicorn. I'm not sure that matters, really, in light of the rest of it.

But there is one part I'm not ashamed of: during this unfortunate time and even after, I played a video game called *Dark Castle.* And it was spectacular.

I'd grown up in a household, well documented now, run by a pair of symphony musicians. They were somewhat adverse to pop culture that lacked educational value, and so our tele-vision watching was relegated to *Sesame Street* and our music to classical and our home com-puter, purchased sometime in the mid-eighties, was not a Commodore 64 or an Atari or even an Intellivision, but rather a Texas Instruments 99-4A, the world's geekiest geek machine ever invented, a silver, boxy thing that ran 99-4A percent educational software, "games" that "helped" with "math" and other terrifying things programmed in Basic with blocky text and muddy colors. (Its one redeeming game, *Munch Man,* was little more than a rip-off of *Pac-Man,* with the titular hero leaving a trail of dots behind him rather than eating his way clear of the maze, which always made the name of the character exasperatingly contradictory to me and had I known the word at the time I'm sure I would have nicknamed him Shitty Man, but that's not what this story is about.)

So, because of the educational computer at home, I was somewhat retarded in joining my generation's progress towards developing a set of super-powerful Nintendo-controller-button-pushing thumbs (I would create the most exquisite excuses for why I needed to visit Nintendo-owning friends after school and on weekends, however, so that I could try and catch up on the thumb-strength thing and also watch MTV). And because of my lack of pop-culture knowledge—because my brain was not filled with *Punky Brewster* or *Top Gun* or Duran Duran or sugared cereal—it could be argued I was almost destined to become a fantasy geek by default, as many strange things have been created in vacuums from which nothing good can emerge. By junior high, I'd tired of *Munching Shitty Man* and the TI 99-4A (which I did not, by the way, at any time, try to break on purpose or program to do nothing but scroll the phrase "piece of crap" continuously). I passed the district's required computer literacy class in summer school with flying colors after developing a choose-your-own-adventure-type game that I like to think of as an early forerunner of *Myst,* and I was super bored. I sat grumpily on my bed, paging through *The Black Cauldron* for the millionth time, and whined about how useless everything was and how I wished I could travel back in time/become invisible/train to be a powerful wizard, etc.

Into this fertile nerd ground, then, was cast my first Macintosh computer. My parents were enticed by Apple's long-time presence in the school system (insert rhapsody about the glories of the old Apple IICs here, especially where they concerned *Oregon Trail,* a game we would fight like dogs to play during our free period in the elementary school library, sometimes teaming up three or four to a computer, taking turns hitting the space bar to shoot wolves and deer and stressing over how much grain to dump when the rains made the wagon too heavy to ford the flooded river, and if it was OK to leave the four-year-old daughter behind because we were sick of dealing with her stupid cholera) and in a move so very uncharacteristic in our why-should-we-do-that-just-because-someone-else-did-it family, they trotted out and came home with a Macintosh SE, a beige, boxy thing that smelled of something I now can only identify as "New Macintosh SE Smell" and featured a black and white screen with resolution that made the Texas Instruments monitor look like a Lite Brite.

It was beautiful, that first Macintosh, wasn't it?

We started with very little software, just MacWrite, I think, and maybe *Solitaire,* whatever came with the thing, with the amazing new computer, which we set up on a desk in the family music rehearsal studio and thrilled to the possibilities of Hypercard and the amazingly realistic detail of Clip Art and the ability to print something just by pushing the little button that looked like a printer. And the monthly allowance trip changed from a walk to the mall to a car ride to the software store. Luckily, the only place in the neighborhood that carried Mac programs was conveniently located near the public library and so I think the driving route was somehow reassuring to my mother, allowing her to convince herself that she was not leading her daughter towards a future of pixilated brainwashing but rather towards the safe, proven brilliance that only books could bring, but then one day we drove to the software store and came home with *Dark Castle,* and I walked into the studio and sat down at the Mac and I don't think I got up for about three years.

Released by Silicon Beach Software in 1987, *Dark Castle* opens on a title screen that I swear could challenge anything the Xbox wants to bring. It's a grayscale rendering in clear, crisp lines—an etching, almost, a woodcut made by binary fairies—of a path up to a castle with this icky vulture in the foreground and if you hover there long enough to appreciate the grain of the rocks and the moon on the water, lightning will flash with that great Macintosh *crrackk!* and an organ will play Bach's "Toccata & Fugue in D minor"—*duh-nuh nuuuuh...duhnuhnuhnuh nuh-nuh,* a.k.a. that scary organ song—and the lightning will keep flashing, turning the whole screen to its negative for a brief, brilliant second that, as a child raised by Lite Brites, absolutely blew my mind.

Next up is an instruction page packed with stuff like, "A year ago a wandering minstrel sang about a brave warrior who battled the Black Knight with only the rocks he had brought in many little bags. He failed, though he did find that there is a key at the bottom of the dungeon that will unlock the door back into the Great Hall." Knights! Dungeons! I was hooked! Sure, it would have been better (and more accurate, really) had they said "bard" instead of "minstrel," but this really was a game that I was prepared to play until my fingers bled. It was the summer of '88, Paula Abdul was on the radio, and I was busy staying up all night trying to kill rats with rocks and remembering to duck when the flaming eyeball came flying by and fighting the wizard in his tower with the lightning *crrackking* around me. It's seriously all about those sound effects, this memory of mine: the rats with their tinny *mee-meep,* the wheezing noise they make when they die, the incessant fluttering of the bats, the *yeah!* the little man you're controlling utters every time he picks up a bag of rocks or a bottle of elixir or whatever, the *nyah-nyah-nyahs* of the pygmy troll things that run around shaking their hands in the air. The best sound is when the little man—it's weird, I never gave him a name—falls off something or gets hit in the head: he gets dizzy, spins on his heels with lines swirling around his face and says, *woooah, woooah, woooah, brrrr!* It's better if you hear me do it out loud. I know every one of these sounds the same way I know every word to "Straight Up" and "The Way That You Love Me" and "Opposites Attract." I am, as I said, not ashamed of any of this. Paula Abdul used to be a very respectable artist.

My penchant for nostalgia being what it is (and having decided that three years of one's life is nowhere near enough time to lose to a singular, geekish hobby), I recently decided that I needed to bring *Dark Castle* back into my life. Video games have once again passed me by—these games today, with their grand theft autos and their graphic sex, my god, I have no interest in shooting people or racing cars or, well, shooting people but what else are video games about these days, exactly, and could I sound more like my mother?—and anyway, my thumbs are still horribly underdeveloped, and so I found I had returned to sitting on my bed grumbling about how everything is useless and I wanted to travel back in time. So I did.

A perfectly functional Macintosh SE—the same exact computer that set my parents back $3,700 in 1988—costs $20 (plus shipping) on eBay. Paula Abdul's *Forever Your Girl* was a dollar at a Brooklyn stoop sale (where, for good measure, I also bought a VHS copy of *Flatliners,* because that movie rules). *Dark Castle* took a little longer to find, because Silicon

Beach went out of business long ago and the company that bought the license is busy rereleasing the original software in fancy color and with fancier sounds, I bet, although I can't imagine who would want to play this game if the bats sounded like anything other than someone throwing a stack of cardstock against a ceiling fan, so, apparently unable to buy the original program, I did a little internet research, wandering down the dark Google path to some underdesigned websites that told me there are "emulators" out there, programs that let you run the old software on modern computers (and that's about the extent of my understanding of emulators) but who wants to play a black-and-white game on a color laptop? I wanted the real thing, I wanted to play it on the nine-inch screen of my brand new ancient Macintosh, and so I butted into a vintage Macs listserv thing where I asked if anyone could help me and thanks to a very nice man in Sweden I found and downloaded a copy of the game onto my old iMac, plugged in a 3.5 inch floppy drive, copied the game onto a floppy, took the floppy out into the living room where the SE was sitting on the coffee table, put the disk in the drive, put "Straight Up" in the CD player on repeat, used the square tacky mouse to click on the little castle icon and:

*crrackk! duh-nuh nuuuuh... duhnuhnuhnuh nuh-nuh. crrackk! crrackk! duh-nuh nuuuuh... duhnuhnuhnuh nuh-nuh.*

And I started to cry.

When the sobs subsided, I found myself addicted to the notion of sucking my past off a computer monitor, through wires, and onto squares of fancy plastic, then projecting it onto another monitor in the other room and bringing it back to life. The continued Brilliance-slash-Terrifying, All-Consuming Evil of the internet allowed me to find a whole slew of programs I'd thought were gone forever: *Déja Vu* (a sort of noiry murder mystery thing with a decidedly antifeminist bent where all the women are hookers or double-crossers and the only thing a man can count on is the gun he swiped out of the hooker's purse after he punched her), *Scarab of Ra* (something having to do with an Egyptian temple but I have to be honest and say I never have figured out the point of this game and I wish the monkey would quit stealing my gold), and, of course, *Zork* (MAC: **You are in a forest.** ME: **Go west.** MAC: **You are in a forest.** ME: **I want to kill myself.** MAC: **What do you want to kill myself with?**). It's like owning a giant retro GameBoy, and has in fact led me to consider purchasing a retro GameBoy on eBay where they're currently running for around thirty bucks, but I'm not sure I want to pay that extra ten dollars (plus shipping) just for the portability of *Tetris*, which I have for the SE now, in the great old-school big nine-inch screen version with the backgrounds of the Kremlin and the hockey players.

In junior high, there was nothing that made me happier than a Saturday spent reading a good fantasy novel, watching a little *Willow,* and then playing *Dark Castle* alone in my quiet house after everyone had gone to sleep. So please don't ask me why, now, I intermittently burst into tears while playing with my Macintosh. It's probably a healthy combination of reasons, not the least of which being my realization that, for all intents and purposes, I am still a fantasy geek, even though I swear that I don't even know where all my pewter figures are and that if my mother just happened to save them, each wrapped carefully in newspaper and laid gently in a box in the attic of her house in Houston, that certainly had nothing to do with me and is a decision she made on her own, undoubtedly fueled by the horrid memory she carries of the time she threw away my Big Bird doll when I was six because it stank and I never forgave her and she probably just *assumes* that I would have the same reaction to her throwing away the pewter figures which I would *not,* because I'm not *like* that anymore.

In fact, when I put that *Dark Castle* disk into the Mac for the second first time, the strangest thing happened. I started to play and although I could feel the muscle memory trying to scramble over the sixteen years of accumulated other nonsense in its path ("get this ability to drive a stick shift out of my way! when did she start playing darts?!?" etc), there was just no helping the fact that my hands no longer had the ability to work in tandem with my eyes in this context and I'd forgotten where all the tricky bats were hiding and every time I moved the mouse to throw a rock the little man's arm just went all wonky and I ended up either throwing at the ceiling or at the floor and no rats were dying, only my self-confidence. It took me two hours to get out of the easy warm-up room. After all those late nights in which I completely neglected to create a personal life in favor of a super-rich emotional one (and terrific aim when imaginary-rock-throwing), I was left, sixteen years later, with nothing. I jumped and fell. I hit my head and got spinny. The pygmy things killed me. The big man in the dungeon with the whip killed me. I fell in lava, I fell off ropes, an anvil fell on my head. I misspelled my name while entering my 568 points into the high scores as "Whiney." I now completely suck at *Dark Castle.*

But in other news, I have a boyfriend. And I can watch MTV whenever the hell I want. While drinking beer. It's like Paula says: two steps forward, two steps back. It's just a natural fact.

# DREW GARDNER
## Coin-op Physics: A Vector-Graphics Retrospective

In the mid-1970s several companies began putting coin-ops in the lobbies of restaurants, hoping that children would fill them with their parents' quarters while the food was being cooked. I was happy to oblige in this respect. The games immediately drew me in with simple but beautiful flashing shapes and lights, fascinating controllers, and richly detailed fantasy art on the cabinets.

The idea of feeding quarters into a machine to engage interactively in some excitement, fun and time-wasting was a no-brainer. The precedents were pinball and Skee-Ball, which I eagerly played every summer at the Jersey shore. Skee-Ball was a bowling game in which the ball jumped up a ramp at the last second and landed in variously scored pockets. Tickets were then given to redeem for valueless but appealing prizes. The real appeal was not in acquiring the prizes, but in the feeling of having generated value with one's own skill to get them—a feeling not often accessible to children. The tone set in these Skee-Ball/pinball arcades was similar to what I would experience later as a young teenager in video game arcades during the coin-op heyday in the early 1980s—a chance to explore different games and try out my skill in an adult-free darkened space with a slightly sleazy vibe that involved competition, vagrancy, and truancy etc., all appealing qualities to any self-respecting eleven-year-old boy.

The first video game I remember playing in one of these restaurant lobbies in the mid-late 1970s was Scott Bristow's *Tank* (1974), a simple black-and-white game that featured the first use of read-only memory to store graphical data. ROM allowed the images in the game to display just enough detail to represent objects, beyond the simple rectangles and lines that appeared in Atari's *Pong* (1972). *Tank* was a two-player duel-type game with a top-down perspective where the opponents would drive around a maze-like screen peppered with barricades, avoiding mines, shooting each other and trying to avoid being shot. The ultimate goal was racking up enough points within a set time limit to win the game. More quarters bought more time.

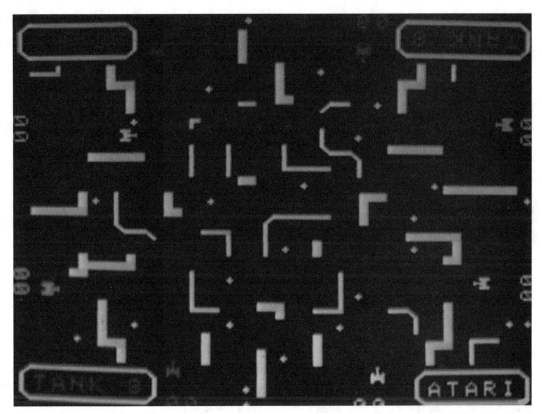

*Tank* by Scott Bristow for Atari

*Tank* was produced at a time when the processing power of affordable computers was not advanced enough to produce enemy artificial intelligence. Like *Pong,* the computer in *Tank* provided the interface and game parameters, but the competition had to come from another human. Winning points was certainly important in this game, but more important was entering the space of the game, developing the skills needed for controlling the little square globs of light, and of course the delights of destroying my sister's tank.

I would soon learn that there were other pleasures to be gotten from video games besides destroying my sibling's military equipment. It turned out that the laws of Sir Isaac Newton could be fun.

The first coin-op game I recall playing by myself against a simulation of the laws of physics was another Atari game called *Stunt Cycle* (1976), in which the player controlled an Evel Knievel-type character and jumped over buses. The idea of finding excitement by jumping over things with a two-wheeled vehicle was a concept I was already familiar with, growing up in suburban New Jersey. Inspired by Knievel, my friends and I had spent hours rigging

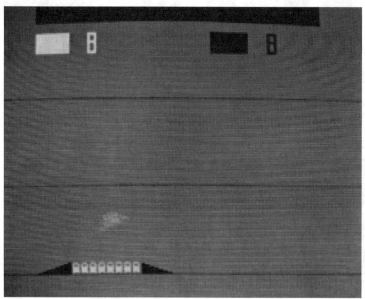

*Stunt Cycle* by Bob Polaro for Atari.

ramps from plywood and cinderblocks and jumping our bicycles over garbage cans, flaming scrap wood, and each other. This was our way of playing around with Newtonian physics.

The theme, controller, and cabinet art of *Stunt Cycle* drew me to the game, but it was the gameplay and physics engine that kept me there. *Tank* was fun and diverting, but *Stunt Cycle* was addictively fun. The controller for the game was a realistic-looking motorcycle handlebar that featured a rotating grip for acceleration and a brake. These were the only two inputs. Adjusting the motorcycle's speed based on accelerating force, friction, inertia, and time was the key to successfully jumping the buses and landing on the opposite ramp without crashing. Buses would be added as the player advanced. My absorption in the game came from the learning curve involved in gaining control of these simulated aspects of physics. It was about learning skills necessary for successfully interacting with the computer simulation, which was based on mathematical expressions of real-world physics under the likewise simulated game-danger of bodily harm. It was thrilling. Modern racing games with complex physics engines are the descendants of *Stunt Cycle*.

The games I would become most involved with over the next few years, as arcade gaming became more and more popular, would combine the basic elements from *Tank* and *Stunt Cycle*—simulated gravity/inertia/momentum, and shooting stuff.

Games based on computer simulation of the properties of physics have a much older history than most play-ers are aware. *Tank* was basically a land-based version of Steve Russell's *Spacewar!,* a game that preceded it by twelve years. *Spacewar!* (1962) is considered to be the first video game, sometimes along with William Higinbotham's *Tennis for Two* (1958). Inspired by the space-opera fiction of E. E. "Doc" Smith, *Spacewar!,* like

*Spacewar!* by Steve Russell at MIT.

*Tank,* involved two-player, two-object combat, but in outer space. The ships battled in around a central sun. The challenge was to duel while controlling the direction and speed of one's ship in the vacuum of space while avoiding being sucked in by the sun's gravity or shot by the other player.

*Spacewar!* was programmed as a demonstration for the room-filling DEC PDP-1 computer at MIT, long before it occurred to anyone to try to make money on video games. Had the PDP-1 been marketed as a home gaming system at the time, it would have retailed for $120,000. The game spread quickly through universities or research facilities that could afford the computer. It was the first shareware gaming hit—shared via punch cards. Later it came with the computer. The display of PDP-1 was a giant, modified oscilloscope that produced line-based, or vector graphics. Vector graphics systems would later reappear in the arcade game heyday of the late 1970s and early 1980s. This display technology, which facilitated some of most artistically distinct arcade games ever produced, had its origin in military radar-display technology used in World War II, reappropriated for the purpose of generating adolescent fun. A descendant of this graphics format is still in everyday use in the form of Acrobat files.

Vector graphics were basically line art, rather than continuous-tone art or raster graphics. The art in vector games was drawing rather than painting. A vector graphics system allowed for rapid animation and manipulation of the objects being represented, and the glowing segments had a very particular look—thin white undulating lines in reversal against a black background. Because these graphics were based on straight line sections assembled from plotted points, the objects used in the vector games tended to be composed of basic art forms—squares, triangles, and rhomboids assembled together to form objects. By the late 1970s, affordable technology capable of rendering vector graphics had caught up to the PDP-1. Some of the best designs in early videos games like *Asteroids, Tempest,* and *Battlezone* used this system.

The first a vector graphics game I encountered as a kid was Larry Rosenthal's *Space Wars,* a 1977 Cinematronics game. It was the first commercially successful arcade version of Steve Russell's original *Spacewar!*. My sister and I spent hours battling it out in *Space Wars.* The black-and-white graphics, created using Larry Rosenthal's Vectorbeam system, were spare but

*Space Wars* by Larry Rosenthal for Cinematronics.

beautiful, mostly negative space with objects composed of small, brightly undulating lines. The five-button controls were Rotate Left, Rotate Right, Thrust, Fire, and Hyperspace. As in Russell's game, the space of the game was finite but continuous, with the ships disappearing from one of the edges of the screen to reappear on the opposite edge. Occasionally an asteroid would streak past, possibly providing the inspiration for a later game based on similar parameters—*Asteroids*. *Space Wars* included a number of improvements over the original—smoother gameplay, crisper and more detailed graphics, several difficulty settings, and the ability to inflict partial damage to one's opponent. It was possible to blow half of a ship away, leaving the other player spinning around with a single engine, disabled, but still able to play. The cabinet was massive, and of all arcade cabinets, the most reminiscent of the vending machines they seemed to have been based on.

Tom Skelly's *Rip Off* (1979) was a Cinematronics game that took the *Tank* model of top-down rotate/move/shoot and transformed it from a duel into the first collaborative video game. Two people played against computer-controlled artificial intelligence. The object was to protect a central stash of undulating triangular fuel canisters from pirate tanks that were trying to steal them. These pirate tanks were some of the first AI ever used in a video game. They acted according to independent goals, simple rule-sets that dictated their individual behavior. When several pirate tanks appeared together, this was known as *swarming*. The game design and black–and–white vector graphics of *Rip Off* were not particularly unusual, but this swarming enemy behavior was something I'd never seen before. The tanks didn't follow scripted paths; they moved in graceful, unpredictable, and purposeful ways. They seemed alive. It was possible to play the game individually, but it was most interesting when two people joined forces and developed strategies for defending their fuel. Cinematronics created several different vector games with similar parameters and feel, including *Armor Attack* and *Demon*.

The prearcade, restaurant-lobby vector game I have the most vivid memories of is *Lunar Lander* (1979). Howard Delman developed a vector generator display system for Atari, and

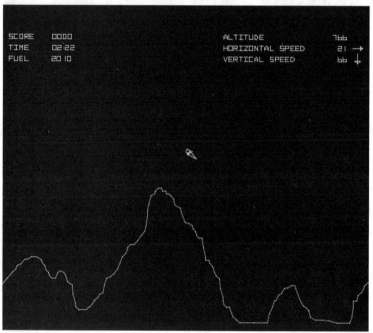

*Lunar Lander* was the first game to utilize it. As was true of *Spacewar!*, the *Lunar Lander* game design was public domain. All-text versions of the simulation game had been around for a long time. The first graphic version was written by Jack Burness on a DEC GT40 in 1973. Titled *Moonlander*, this vector-graphics game was controlled with a

Atari's *Lunar Lander.*

light pen and is said to have been quite difficult. The lunar surface in the game featured a McDonald's.

Atari's *Lunar Lander* featured four controllers, Rotate Right and Left, Abort, and a distinctive analog Thrust controller with a spring-resistance mechanism. This controller was incredibly satisfying to operate; it felt like operating a serious piece of equipment. Like *Stunt Cycle*, *Lunar Lander* was a single-player game in which the challenge was rooted in learning the physics simulation and in gaining enough skill controlling the vehicle to land it safely. The independent rotate-and-thrust control mechanism in *Space Wars* was combined with the gravity-based Newtonian world of *Stunt Cycle*, but with much more complex gamer input than just acceleration and breaking. The player controlled a lunar excursion module that started in free-fall over a mountainous landscape. The idea was to land the LEM on any flat surface without destroying or disabling it. The only enemy to be overcome was one's own lack of experience and skill. The game was about getting somewhere safely. Bonus points were given for landing on platform areas of various difficultly. The repeating one-screen world of mountains scrolled left or right as the ship approached either side, as did the sparse stars in the background. The text-based origins of the game were reflected in a text readout of speed, altitude, and remaining fuel at the top of the screen. It was possible to play through most of the game referencing only the text readout. Instead of a time limit, quarters purchased units of fuel. For those blessed with limitless quarters, the game could be played indefinitely without regard to fuel consumption. For the rest of us, it was necessary to develop an economy of fuel use. There was nothing more nerve-wracking than running out of fuel just as the ship was positioned perfectly for a final decent.

*Lunar Lander* was also the first multiple-perspective video game. As the descending LEM grew closer to any point in the mountain range, the perspective snapped into a close-up position, making all the elements of the game larger and faster for the final landing scene, adding dramatic tension and requiring a slight shift in response time. I remember getting a huge rush from this moment. The magnification effect intensified my focus, which was already concentrated on the limited parameters of the game world, just as the critical moment of the game arrived. The perspective switch also created a sense of depth in the space of the game. There was more to the spatial dimension of the game's world than what could be experienced at first. This sudden, additional power of vision created a feeling that was something like first

I COIN I PLAY

©1979 ATARI INC

*Asteroids* by Ed Logg & Lyle Rains for Atari.

seeing the scene in *Blade Runner* in which the main character uses a magnifying machine to see around corners in a photograph.

*Lunar Lander* was a popular game, but it was quickly superseded by another vector graphics game that proved to be so popular that it would help establish video games as a form of art and entertainment rivaling television and film: Ed Logg & Lyle Rains's *Asteroids* (1979). When Atari realized how popular the game was going to be, they stopped production on *Lunar Lander* and started shipping *Asteroids* in the remaining *Lunar Lander* cabinets.

I experienced the *Asteroids* phenomenon in the Space Port arcade in the Quakerbridge Mall in Lawrenceville, NJ. An entire wall of the arcade was reserved for the game. Adults were playing *Asteroids* to blow off stream on their lunch breaks. Players had to queue up behind games to get access, and anyone playing had a audience of other players watching from either side, taking notes on rock-destroying technique. The combined thruster rumbles and the pings and crashes of the games mixed in a beautiful, crazed cartoon-like experimental-music sound space in the resonating chamber of the arcade.

*Asteroids* was similar in design and look to *Space Wars,* but instead of dueling other players, it featured a single-player design in which the object was to destroy and avoid a swirling field of rocks that broke into smaller rocks as the player shot at them. Part of the game's unique feel came from the contrast of the player's constant active attack with the inert but chaotic momentum of the orbiting asteroids. No game had ever incorporated as many animated objects. It was possible to just watch someone playing *Asteroids* and marvel at the sight of multiple rocks of different sizes and shapes rotating and tumbling through the closed, continuous world of the game at different speeds. Quarters bought lives, not fuel, and points lead to extra ships, extending the gameplay. Since skill was rewarded with an extension of game-playing time, a good player could play for a long time, fighting the increasing speed and difficultly. Gaining skill, winning more game time, and achieving a high score became part of a reward system that made the game especially addictive. *Asteroids* was also the first game that allowed high-score players to distinguish themselves by entering their initials for permanent display.

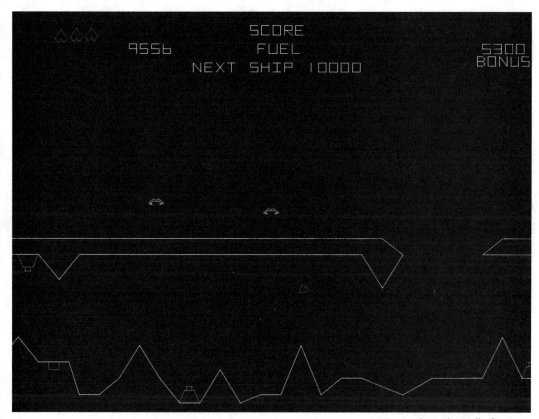

*Gravitar* by Mike Hally for Atari.

A color version of the Atari vector graphics system was eventually developed, leading to one of the most original and visually striking games of the time—*Tempest* (1980). Other vector games less related to the *Space Wars* model were also produced, including the original first-person shooting games, *Tailgunner* and *Battlezone,* and the World War I dogfighting game *Red Barron,* all of which I devoted significant time to. The game that most fascinated me, though, was Mike Hally's *Gravitar.*

*Gravitar* (1982) was a hybrid game that combined, refined, expanded, and improved on several games that had come before it. It merged the basic gameplay elements of *Lunar Lander* and *Asteroids,* added a number of new elements, and distinguished itself as being one of the most challenging arcade games ever produced. It was not a particularly popular game. The game's difficulty split the players into two camps: Those who wanted a quick blast of excitement tended to hate it, since its initial learning curve was steeper than most new games at the time. Players with more patience and an interest in a greater challenge found it highly rewarding.

The full-color *Gravitar,* like *Lunar Lander,* involved descent onto a planet, but instead of one lunar surface, the game featured eleven unique planets divided into three universes. Each planet had a unique landscape and a different level of gravity—the game featured true level design. The menu screen was itself a game, with gravity from a "Death Planet" dragging at the player's ship as he tried to reach each individual world. Once the player made it to a planet, his ship would appear in free fall over the planet's surface, but landing wasn't part of the program. Multiple gun emplacements peppered the landscape. Gameplay involved shooting out the emplacements, evading or shooting enemy ships, and using a tractor beam to get fuel from various locations on the surface. Fuel was a limited resource; it couldn't be bought with quarters. The tractor beam doubled as a shield for protection against enemy fire. The controller set-up was similar to that of *Space Wars* and *Asteroids,* and the gravity physics was similar to that of *Lunar Lander,* so players familiar with those controls could use skills they had already developed. Using the buttons separately was adequate for the first few planets, but as the difficulty and complexity of the game increased, more finger-independence on all five controllers was required. Different combinations of thrusting and rotating had to be mixed with toggling between shields and firing, which couldn't be done simultaneously. The finger-independence required to get good at *Gravitar* approached the level of skill needed for playing a percussive musical instrument.

In *Gravitar,* the close-up perspective switch of *Lunar Lander* was upgraded with real-time zooming animation. This combination gave the multiple perspectives a more dynamic quality, and, combined with several planets to be explored in the game universe, deepened and expanded the game unlike any that came before it. This quality of depth, combined with the patience and leaning curve leading toward mastery of the game, and the relative openness of the universe and freedom of approach, related *Gravitar* more closely to later console games that combined action with long-term resource management and strategy—like *Halo*—than to its precursor vector-graphics games. The fact that simpler gameplay and faster games made more commercial sense may have accounted for *Gravitar*'s lack of popularity in arcades.

Even more than that of *Asteroids,* the *Gravitar* scoring system rewarded skill with points that generated extra ships, increasing the player's odds of getting deeper into the game and exploring previously unknown landscapes. And that was really the central point of playing—getting deeper into the game.

*Gravitar* required unflagging concentration. A momentary drifting of thought or second of worry about something outside the game would quickly lead to disaster. This is an important part of the particular quality of the fully absorbed gamer—playing well requires forgetting about the rest of life, granting a welcome respite from the normal chains of thought, feelings, associations, and worries. Playing a half-hour of *Gravitar* left me energized and refreshed. This respite was mixed with the pleasure of learning motor skills through repetitive practice and developing various strategies for solving problems. I could go in any order though any of the planets in a given system, there was no forced linear path. The game balanced navigation skills with fighting skills, which would often come into conflict because of the design of the ship—it could only shoot up as its thrusters worked against gravity. Most of the enemy bunkers were below the ship, requiring complex shoot, rotate, and thrust and defend combinations.

The task-balancing in *Gravitar* amounted to patiently learning the artful management of inertia and limited resources, skills that extend beyond the gaming universe. Along these lines it could be said that the game also encouraged me to learn to use forces I couldn't control to my advantage. Luckily, it didn't take long to figure out that the gravitational field of the death star could be used to swing around to the planets. Far better than wasting fuel dumbly struggling against it.

Economy of time is an element of many video games that helps to create their unique feeling of drama. *You have gotten this far, don't die now or you'll have to start from the beginning. Gravitar* upped the ante on this basic video game dynamic by rewarding skill with a way to save time and skip to the good stuff, using a mechanism that was almost a minigame in itself. Since there was no way to save, the depth of the game created a problem—it was tedious to replay all the planets that had already been mastered in previous games just to get to a deeper level. To deal with this, Hally placed a Red Planet within each solar system, with a spiraling tunnel that lead to an exploding nuclear reactor that had to be activated. Successful activation was followed by a timed escape, like the last few minutes of *Alien*. When the Red Planet quest was completed, the entire solar system could be skipped. Once I got good at this, I could pick up the drama at its most interesting point. Starting the game by warping twice in a row with full fuel and many extra ships meant there was a lot to lose very quickly. It also meant that each time I might get deeper into the game than ever before.

The Red Planet concentrated the themes and dynamics of the game—depth, subtlety, and variation. There was no gravity, so I had to master new navigation skills, maneuvering precisely within new physics parameters. This pattern of new challenges created with limited graphic and memory resources repeated into the deepest levels of *Gravitar*. Once all three universes had been played, they repeated, but with their physics reversed and the number of bunkers increased. This cycle was followed by a stage in which the planet's surface was invisible, and finally by invisible landscapes with reversed gravity. Hally got around limited computing power with creative permutations of the rules of the game.

What made *Gravitar* engaging even by today's gaming standards was the drama created by the depth of the game design, combined with the subtlety of its gameplay. The ability to navigate the ship across many different terrains and situations was the central skill needed. *Gravitar* was about the joys of developing self-control and patience as a way of discovering new challenges.

# ERNEST HILBERT

## Flying Off the Screen: Observations from the Golden Age of the American Video Game Arcade

"Insert coin."

— *Galaxian,* Namco, 1979

We live in an era awash in nostalgia. It is harmless, for the most part, but it sinks many efforts to create things that feel new. It has become something of a wet security blanket, frayed and somewhat malodorous. The most negligible token of the past is confiscated and reproduced a thousand times over, generating a kaleidoscopic uproar of objects, noises, and images, an ever tightening spiral of retro credibility traded against whatever irony remains to be gleaned from such distant glances backward. Ever since baby boomers took it upon themselves to teach their high-school Bob Dylan albums in college courses, each successive generation has clung dreadfully, embarrassingly to the most obvious symbols and marks of its own youth. This trend has provided brief moments of balmy reminiscence, but it has done so at the inexcusable cost of cheapening memories as a whole. It is probably unnecessary to point to any one or even any ten examples of this cultural hoarding in clothes, music, hairstyles, films, and television. We have grown accustomed to preserving immense swaths of yesteryear's merchandise and general cultural detritus that would otherwise have sunk peacefully like silt to the bottom of our shared historical ocean. My generation is no different. In fact, the composer Daniel Felsenfeld once remarked: "Generation X constantly mistakes nostalgia for quality."

I am hesitant to add more coals to this seemingly unappeasable bonfire of sentimentalities, but I believe I may have alighted upon aspects of my experience as an arcade video gamer in the early 1980s that say more about me and possibly about my contemporaries than I first expected. Additionally, I have found that a wistful look back through passages grown murky with time is not only enjoyable but downright nourishing, on occasion. One need not be a Wordsworth to long for the exquisite glow and bright sense of wonderment that drains out of the world as we gain in years. The world remains vivid. We go dark. We should realize that what is lost in freshness and excitement is repaid in wisdom and accomplishment, even small virtues like patience. While trolling through my own bleary memories of zapping and zoning out to beams of colored light, I recovered something that might speak to the entire suburban experience, at least as it existed for some of us. My games of choice scrolled from top to bottom on the screen. Powerless to move my vessel in any other direction, I dreamed of breaking free and exploring. I would invariably master a game and then—while dutifully glued to the screen—begin imagining what was happening off-screen, in the rest of the game universe. We were permitted to see excruciatingly little of the worlds we were so intent on pummeling and blasting, so these untouched fields to the left and right of the screen developed an incredible allure. Who knew what challenges waited?

Born in 1970, reared in the sunny suburbs of southern New Jersey, between Philadelphia and Atlantic City, I happily lived through the remarkable rise and heart-rending decline of the arcade gamers' world. The Golden Age of the video arcade can be thought of as 1980 to 1985. During this period, commercial arcades spread to most corners of the country. They would hold sway for only a few years before home gaming systems began to render their ungainly arcade cousins increasingly redundant. There is no question that the astounding achievements of today's game designers, not to mention the dizzying dexterity of today's players, would have been absolutely unimaginable in the early 1980s. That is exactly why it was a Golden Age. It was not yet confused and corrupted by the sheen of adult sophistication. No one older than us played the games. They were for kids. The games seemed so threatening and so astonishing precisely because we were so innocent. The big game cabinets, smoky arcades, black lights, the rattling obsession with buttons and battles, these were genuinely new. No experience in history compared to the sudden onslaught of digital distractions at our disposal. The real world became peripheral as we stared absorbedly into the cabinets, rising for air only after the last ship had been blown apart, the last climber fallen from the skyscraper, the last yellow ball cornered by munching ghosts. They were exhilarating days, when chips of light could send us soaring to heights of inspired excess, transport us to other ages, other worlds. It was a rapturous experience. It is nearly impossible to understand this today. Young gamers cannot remember a world without affordable, compact, and convincing games. We have grown accustomed to incredible speed and convenience in all forms of entertainment. The screens we spend so much time staring into at work and at home require less and less of us.

It is instructive to think back a quarter century or so. I can only just remember playing *Pong* (1972, Atari, though I would not twist the paddles until at least 1977) while sprawled on the yellow shag pile at a friend's house, around the time I first saw *Star Wars* at the drive-in movie theater. By the time I was ten, I had played *Space Invaders* (1978, Taito) and *Pac-Man* (1980, Namco) in the back room of the local 7-

Gottlieb promotional poster, 1983.

11 convenience mart, which went out of business and was replaced by a 6-12 (I am not making this up). I also enjoyed the more whimsical games like *Q-Bert* (1983, Gottlieb) and *Donkey Kong* (1981, Nintendo), which produced the long-legged franchise of the *Mario Brothers*, largely via the later home system). Video games were not yet a legitimate business. There was something sordid about the whole enterprise. Once a week, on Saturday mornings, two men in suits and sunglasses would arrive in the dusty gloom with canvas bags to empty the week's quarters out, glancing furtively about to see if they were being watched by anyone other than a skinny kid with oily hair wearing a Bad Company T-shirt (me). I drooled at the silver pour of coins, never having seen so many quarters in all my life. Like many boys my age, I calculated all pricing in terms of the number of games I could play. Thus, a one-dollar large soda was four games of *Pac-Man*. A Snickers bar was roughly one game of *Wizard of Wor* (1981, Bally/Midway). A Big Mac represented about one hour of concentrated gameplay according to this economic conversion. This was hardly currency arbitrage or futures speculation, but it

shows how video games had already begun to change the way we saw everything around us. We were frenzied in our pursuit of high scores and extra men. We could not wait to press the Player One button one more time.

This particular back room also contained a *Defender* cabinet (Williams, 1980), which was hopelessly complex by my standards, with no fewer than five control buttons, including hyperspace and a smart bomb. I derived hours of enjoyment watching the teenagers play it, frantically smacking the buttons, as their disregarded cigarettes dwindled down to ash and melted the pictorial plastic façade of the console (later models would sometimes arrive with metal ashtrays attached, so gamers did not have to risk their cigarettes rolling off, the owners having their otherwise sturdy fortresses marred by miniature black lava flows). The room also had *Asteroids* (1979, Atari), a form of shoot-em game, which seemed bleak and desperate to me. There was simply no way out. It kept getting faster. Acceleration was a universal quality of games, but to make matters truly terrifying asteroids were hurled from every direction at once. It was too much. It made me queasy to watch someone play for any serious length of time. It eventually gave way to the slightly less threatening *Time Pilot* (1982, Centuri), which was full color and had pleasant clouds in the background to dispel the sense of deep-space isolation and terror of its predecessor.

This dreary gamers' grotto predated the widespread use of home systems or a proper mall arcade. We had only our converted janitor's closet, with no décor to speak of, aside from empty Yodel cartons and a defunct exit sign rusting off the cinder blocks. This was all about to change. I witnessed in contented awe as video games went from zero to a hundred in no time at all. I squatted in rapt fascination as friends manipulated the Commodore 64 text games, with such thrilling turns as "do you wish to go left or right?" to which they would respond by pressing L or R and learning that they were eaten by a dragon or found a hoard of gold pieces. Game over. No, it had hardly begun. Atari 2600 was probably the most popular home system of its day. My family's den featured the Sears knock-off version, called Tele-Games, which had a bogus wood finish, similar to that which graced some unfortunate station wagons of the era. The 2600 games demanded more imagination than radio plays or books had from earlier generations of Americans. In a primitive sequence of blocks— ("graphics, man") moving vertically and horizontally, accompanied by blips and beeps that would embarrass a microwave—we detected castles, battlefields, alien worlds, and carnivals. Games today are so sophisticated, and so damned fast, that I generally back slowly out of the room when I encounter one. Whatever their athletic merits, they do not seem to require much imagination at all. The game does all the work. All you have to do is play. Likewise, games have come so far in their home incarnations that arcades seem to be inching closer to extinction, along with table football (the vibrating sheet-metal affairs ordered from the back of the Sears catalogue) and eight-tracks (my favorite was the *Fame* soundtrack, because I fully planned to live forever).

But in the early 1980s, home games could not compare with the sophistication of the arcade versions, the large stand-up consoles. The arcade revolution was upon us. Not only did the arcade versions have more zest and zing, they did not compete for screen time with *Columbo* and *Benny Hill*. Also, no parent ever would have attempted to cross into the strobing darkness of the arcade. My mother recalls passing near a mall arcade and noting that it released an odor similar to that of a high-school gym, heavy with hormonal perspiration and other discharge brought on by the absolute thrill of scorching our way toward manhood via some interplanetary warfare. In order to give us a sense of accomplishment, the games awarded absurdly high scores. They registered in the tens of thousands, the hundreds of thousands. Each minor accomplishment was rewarded with hundreds of points. We felt rich. This made us very excited, and hungry for more. No board game had ever allowed me to enter my initials at the end next to some lavish score like 256,650. When we were hot, we were hot. It was better than gambling. This is why the management (which was largely invisible so far as we could tell) maintained the air conditioning at meat locker lows. When the crowd thinned, our skin-tight Diver Down T-shirts did little to prevent goose bumps. It was pirate cave and pulsating concert hall, our own corner of the world, a place for those sulking through the sad and frivolous days between childhood and a perpetually postponed adulthood.

It was a craze, much like disco before it, only with much less sex involved. Pop songs filled the airwaves. Friends loaned each other the 45 single of Buckner and Garcia's "Pac-Man Fever." The duo went on to release an LP with songs dedicated to *Frogger, Asteroids, Centipede, Donkey Kong, Space Invaders, Defender,* and even *Berzerk.* "Pac-Man Fever" climbed to number nine on the US *Billboard* charts in 1982 and was featured on the hit-making TV show *Solid Gold.* Paperback books soon arrived on shelves, offering tips and strategies for staying alive a bit longer in the reader's game of choice. Teachers appropriated them as contraband. Parents were concerned. They were worried. They became alarmed. Committees were formed and security guards briefed. As with heavy metal—also a relatively new fashion, one no less bizarre and adolescent—these new arcades were seen as legitimate threats to quiet suburban life. They attracted a bad element, much like juke joints, honkytonks, and pool halls had in previous generations. Kids played hooky to spend the day battling blocks of light. Arcade owners were instructed to check gamers for identification on school days, to ensure they were not truant in the shadowy zones roaring with *Pole Position* (1982, Namco) and *Rally X* (1980, Bally/Midway), games that implored you to grip the steering wheel and go absolutely nowhere.

When our local mall opened, it arrived with the requisite arcade, imaginatively named the Space Port. Predictably, it was designed to resemble someone's idea of a space station. Skylab

had fallen in 1979. It might well have been resurrected in our mall, across from the Friendly's restaurant franchise. Styrofoam portals and blue plastic screens aside, the clumsy attempt at set design fooled no one. We were in a mall, and we knew it. If we wanted to escape, we looked down into the game screens. It is difficult to express just how sub-Kubrick it all was, except to say that it was probably more like a truck stop than any kind of spaceport. Much to my disappointment, I would later learn that nearly every town in the northeastern United States had a Space Port of its own. This disappointment is assuaged somewhat by the knowledge that down south they had arcades called the Gold

Mine, which required gamers to pretend they were entering a place where their dads might well have worked in real life.

Finally we had access to all the games we could possibly want. The only arcades that could boast more games than the malls were the echoing caverns down at the New Jersey shore. On the seaside boardwalk we had Coin Castle, Lucky Leo's, Royal Arcade, and Big Top. I am happy to report that some of the games I played twenty years ago are still there, still functioning, still one quarter per play; long may they glow. (There are few things in the New Jersey countryside sadder than a video game cabinet with a dead screen, resting by a dumpster to be hauled off.) There were sports games, like *Track & Field* (1983, Konami). There were plenty of martial arts games, like *Karate Champ* (1984, Data East). There were cartoon games, which were thought to be the wave of the future, in which the joystick activated loops of film, *Space Ace* (1983, Cinematronics) and the immensely popular *Dragon's Lair* (1983, Cinematronics), which drew crowds of astonished spectators. These were the first games to require fifty cents per play. The champion player would line quarters up to reserve the game and ensure an afternoon's play. The quarters wedged into the head of the cabinet served as the mark of the serious player. At thirteen years old, I guarded my quarters fiendishly, and I would spread out my time at the arcade by watching others play, with no small tinge of envy.

There was always a bored, superior-looking man who ambled around in dark blue overalls wearing a chunky change belt. Aside from his role as the nominal adult on the premises, the change-giver was already obsolete in the first years of the decade. Gamers could just as easily use the change machines. In fact we usually felt more comfortable dealing with the machine, unless it spat the rumpled bill back out again. If you wanted change for a five-dollar bill, for instance, the change-giver might huff and incline his head just so. It meant he had to depress the change tube on his belt no fewer than twenty times. Machines did not roll their eyes or squint at you with a sinister, half-formed grin. The machine had the added bonus of not being an object lesson in what might well be your future if you did not stop playing the games and get some homework done.

Over the years, the robust old pinball machines were gradually edged out. They were the proud old ships, towed up the river one last time to be broken for scrap. In the early days, they still took up an entire wall of the arcade, but they already seemed to be dinosaurs left over from another era, namely the 1970s. Pinball wizards were usually older men with moustaches and Confederate-flag bandanas, who hung out in bars and listened to Foghat, downright hoary by our standards. Video games were for our generation. Eventually, pinball games would be relegated to three or four in the back by the unused water fountain (usually with petrified pink gum molded over the spout). They would ping and gong sadly. They would offer extra balls and free games. They shimmered in the lustrous dark. Some even had video screens embedded in them, in a rear-guard effort to keep up with the video games, but these hermaphrodites did little to slow the twilight of the pinball game. They were beautiful, and one day they were just gone. No one knows where they went.

Early on I developed a penchant for the military games, shoot-em games, known collectively as scrolling shoot-em games. The godfather of scrolling games did not actually scroll at all. It was the almighty *Space Invaders.* The player simply shunted a squat laser cannon back and

forth on a planet surface while squarish invaders flapped their stubby appendages and clomped ever nearer. The first time the backgrounds seemed to move, or scroll, was usually in the form of stars and constellations, as on *Galaxian* (1979, Namco) or *Galaga* (1981, Namco). By 1982, gamers had *Flying Shark* (Taito), in which a biplane would scour over what appeared to be lush Indochinese jungles and harbors. Why a biplane would be marauding in these climates was beyond me, but it was too much fun to really question (like just about everything good that came out of that decade). By 1983, we had *Xevious* (Namco/Atari), followed by *Two Tigers* (1984, Bally/Midway), *1942* (1984, Capcom), *Tiger-Heli* (1985, Taito),

*Flying Tiger* (1987, Taito), and *Twin Cobra* (1987, Taito). The ultimate triumph of the scrolling style came rather late, just as the whole genre was being supplanted by more pliable types of on-screen navigation. It was called *Raiden* (1988, Seibu). By that point, it was impossible to ram any more movement or color onto the screen. At times the entire screen became a swimming fudge of explosions and projectiles. In short, every aspect of the form had been pushed to its most extreme point, making it absurd. The same thing happened to heavy metal and hairstyles. It was a mark of the 1980s, this excess. It provided the illusion of progress, but it led only to a tedious cul-de-sac.

The scrolling battle game consisted of a steadily cascading landscape that appeared at the top of the screen and moved ever downward. This established the sensation of movement, as this scrolling was relative to your vessel, which was actually not going very far at all. You could perform circles and dodges within the bottom tenth of the screen, but that was it. The view was from above, what is often called bird's eye view, providing knowledge of the action that would have been entirely unavailable to the flyer in the actual plane. Regardless of whatever choices you might make regarding various maneuvers and evasions, the game scrolled on, insidiously. Your only duty was to survive, as endless missiles of various sizes and intensities continued to emerge from every corner of the landscape. The death toll for the opposing side would have been nothing short of catastrophic. Planes and saucers, tanks and bunkers were vaporized by the dozens, eventually the hundreds and even thousands. The losses would be unsustainable by any but the greatest, presumably most evil empire. Their resources would have to be as vast as they were incompetent. How else, why else would they hurl countless of their own planes to down a single one of yours? No war in modern history (barring, possibly the two American Gulf Wars) has been so terribly, unforgivably one-sided. You left untold wreckage behind as you scaled and gunned toward some goal, a boss, as they came to be known in the increasingly structured argot of the video game world, some magnificent hovering battle station or castle. You always seemed to be clearly attacking, invading the realm of the enemy. Insofar as one thought at all about the moral underpinnings of this murderous carnival, a strike into the enemy's heartland consisted of a dire and unavoidable preemptive strike. The only solace available to the machine's side of things was that regardless of your skill, stamina, sheer ingenuity and mastery, you would finally succumb. They would sneak up on you. They would overwhelm you. Your plane would detonate into scattering debris. Nonetheless, your war could be waged so long as you could fund it, in the form of the colossal quarter (this is when games were, without exception, one quarter per play). The quarter was your key back into the fray.

The battle was pitched, interminable and highly repetitive. For a tyro, every micron of available mind power was rallied to keep the biplane or jet from being knocked out of the air. After a while, perhaps a month and fifty-dollars' worth of quarters, the brain began to handle these small details on its own, on auto pilot, the details of dodging and bombing, sometimes looping and, if one were lucky, using a smart bomb to clear the skies ahead for just a moment before squadrons of foes filled it back up again. At this point, the once frantic weaving calmed into a master's steady arc of survival. As with most activities in the life of a teenager, the great majority of the mind was left unattended, unengaged, in short, bored. It became like a runner's high. In order to continue reeling in the cheap buzz of triumphal escape patterns, one devoted the higher, perhaps bookish portions of the mind to creating a more stimulating experience. I found it rather easy, and even a welcome challenge, to engage in a conversation with a bystander whilst storming the enemy's capital. It also provided a rare moment to seem actually busy while at a mall, to appear fraught and vital. When no one stood around, I imagined dialogue on my own, then the mind drifted to the unseen spaces off the screen. It was a state that took some time and money to achieve, but it was wonderful.

Upon reflection, I have come to realize that the odd, somewhat perverse act of imagining a world beyond that of the screen served several functions. It threw the mechanical repetitions of the actual game into some sort of almost historical, or at least strategic, relief. It lent meaning on a grand scale. It also alleviated the sense of loneliness that as a gamer I sometimes felt. I was part of a team, facing the same challenges, all along the front, on other fronts, other theaters of war, other planets! I was part of a great crusade (though if pressed I would never have been able to suggest just why any of it had to take place at all). It also fulfilled my need to imagine what was going on elsewhere, outside of an arcade in a mall on the edge of a small town in New Jersey. To be certain, there are more remote locales to be had, such as a dairy farm in North Dakota, but I still felt a terrible urge to know what was going on somewhere else, like Philadelphia or, my Oz, my Atlantis and ultima Thule, New York City. What went on beyond the frame became an obsession for me.

At first I would mentally layer dialogue over the crashes and whirrs produced by the game. As the game began, I would register distress, then panic, with headquarters: "Where are all these fighters coming from? There shouldn't be an enemy base anywhere near here! This was supposed to be a standard patrol run. Send reinforcements!" The extra men I had in reserve when the first life was lost would serve as those drastically needed reinforcements. Once I had raised the alarm, I needed to massage the state of crisis in order to keep it going. Stylistically speaking, my principal sources for dialogue were *Star Wars* and *Battlestar Gallactica* dogfights:

"Ernie, you've got a bogie on your tail."
"I know, damnit. I'm trying to lose him."
"Just hold tight. We're breaking formation and coming up to your left."
"You just watch the five bandits coming in out of the top right corner."
"Top right corner? Of what screen?"
"My screen."
"I'm not on the same screen as you, remember?"

Scrolling games no longer exist, so far as I am aware, and probably have not for some time. A side effect of advancing technology has been the ability of designers to create three-dimensional and point-of-view gaming perspectives, so it seems as if the player is actually engaging in the actions determined by the joystick. To someone weaned on more stable, downright inert, types of gaming, this has the unwelcome effect of inducing vertigo, as the fighter jet, skateboarder, or cartoon hero pivots and dives, and the whole world turns around it.

For hours, days, weeks, years, the screens emitted their eerie glow, reflected in the faces of the players and their followers. Aside from rare exceptions like *Dragon's Lair*—which if played properly could be viewed by an audience as if it were a movie—games of the Golden Age typically lacked any narrative bend or arc. There simply was not enough computer memory to tell stories. The action advanced through phases of increasing difficulties, sometimes interpolated by small vignettes of the characters at rest or celebrating. Sometimes you would receive menacing congratulations, something like "Good work, human fighter. But you still have not beaten the Solvalou Mother Ship. Are you ready for more?" Of course I was. Designers tried to add stories, but there was never much to them. The games were mental lozenges, to be sucked for minutes or even hours at a time. They replaced thinking. That is why they had such a strong appeal to adolescents, who might otherwise be worrying about a myriad of minor or major problems, from zits to abortions. They were therapeutic because they were escapist in more ways than one. It was possible to escape rational thought while entering a fantastic realm of battle. This is why it was necessary for some to add a few layers of dialogue over the blips or imagine breathtaking displays of heroism happening off screen.

For the record, permit me one final observation. It is difficult to exaggerate the exultation, the sheer bloody rush a twelve-year old boy can achieve by blasting Ozzy Osbourne's "Flying High Again" through foam orange headphones while committing mass murder. To make the experience even headier than it already was, I often believed girls, live girls, named Tammy or Debby might, just might, be watching. Add to all this the sugar-induced delirium most American kids are constantly working their way through, and it is a small wonder I did not simply pass out, overcome by the sheer grandeur of it all. Never mind that I erroneously believed these glorious mirages of teased hair and stonewashed jeans might be impressed by how hard I was trying to be a winner in a *video game*. The fact that there were girls in an arcade at all was a great thrill, undiluted, for a time at least, by the harsh fact that they would never be remotely interested in me. Never mind. Never mind any of it. Never mind that it was just a game, and that I was down five dollars. Ozzy understood.

Kris Kristofferson once grumbled into a microphone something about not knowing if the "going up was worth the coming down." He did not have *Xevious* in mind, I am certain, but just as I had scaled the heights of shimmering mayhem, down I would slide inevitably toward the sullen, domestic moment when my dad would pull up outside the food-court entrance in the sleeping-pill-blue Ford Escort station wagon, regal in a rumpled suit—my dad always commanded a measure of dignity just beyond what the suburbs could normally provide—playing the classical radio station a bit too loud, and off home to dark green carpets, a fridge with a half-full container of milk, all the safety of a suburban home. My father would ask how I had enjoyed my dissipation, my hours and quarters lavished on the brainless boxes at the mall. I would answer, "Dad, I didn't make the modern world. I'm just living in it." On summer nights I would dream of places where lights stayed on all night, past 9:00 P.M. at least. I imagined the humid sodium glow from the corner gas station multiplied a million times. I wanted to travel the broad realms of the world off my screen. I wanted to see the Pyramids of Giza and watch bars of sunlight fall through the Parthenon. Realistically, I would have been happy with anything on the other side of the turnpike. I wanted to get off the screen. I wanted to add more dialogue. Even while I lay with my ears ringing from AC/DC, hoping I would one day manage to leave the town and the old house, I knew it all had to wait. Everything had to wait. As I fell asleep, I drifted out into an advancing landscape, skies ahead teeming with thousands of enemies, the universe unbound and quarterless, and the big soft lights scrolling down on me all night long.

# J. BRANDON HOUSLEY
## Our Fingers & Thumbs

Romey's family got it first then the Lumbs then the Libbys and soon we, the Housleys in the wakewhite stead above the Railyard Creek, bought in and settled snugly with our first Nintendo set. The rectangular console came with two controllers, a booklet and a gun and we, not able to set it up ourselves, pointed the gun at each other and fired.

We were seven and ten, my brother and I, and the Nintendo was my father's idea. It was a Christmas gift to us both in the winter of 1987 and something of a rarity in a house that was technically kept low—only one TV in our four-story, twelve-room home. The house sat beside a stream running over old train-track beds and was used for years as a mainstay in the journeys of those in the Underground Railroad. The walls were hollowed out and my brother and I would enter into the lining through a small door in his bedroom closet, venturing through the inner byways to the attic where we'd step through a trapdoor, scaling down the inside of the backhouse, green-stair hallway that emptied out through a passage in my father's blue-hued den. It was a terrific house to grow up in and a marvelous spark for exploration. Sometimes my brother and I would draw charts of the inner walls and figure that we hadn't found a way leading around the Green Room doors, thence sending off again into the walls, equipped with flashlights and our paper maps. Sometimes we'd even come back with jewelry that, we were later told, was stashed in the various dark pockets within the walls and hidden by the house's former owner, an old woman paranoid about the theft of her riches.

At first, the Nintendo seemed an unneeded addition to our enormous home. My parents encouraged science and there was a row of chemistry sets in the basement as well as books with ideas for experiments and tests. Outside we had a tree house in a yard as long and wide as a football field, a basketball court of sorts, an abundance of toys, balls and games, and the gloss of the creek and its small fish and bugs. In the winter, however, things slowed down. We were in Maine after all, where life was cold. Snowball fights, snow-forts and sledding were physically exhausting and one could really only do that kind of thing once a day at most. What we needed was a Nintendo and for Christmas that year, we got one.

Later that day it was set up in the Green Room, a room overlooking our driveway playground and ball field. The rooms in the house were named after the color they were painted

—ones green, blue and red among others—with the Green Room most likely painted after its views of the lawn and the trees and the flowerbeds at the edge near the creek. Within the house, the Green Room bordered my parent's bedroom and sat down a snaking hallway from my father's study on the second floor of the southern, street-faced side of our home. My mother often sat at a window-view desk adjacent to this room and wrote music reviews for the local paper in Portland, where she was an arts critic. She also used this desk for her German and Russian translations as well as for grading the papers of her language students that she taught at a small, private school just off the ocean. Her desk was unwalled away from our TV sounds and hollers and less than a month after receiving the machine, she began to regulate our play.

For the first two or three days, however, we enjoyed it endlessly. There was *Double Dribble* in which our thumbs seemingly flicked the ball the length of the court, with the occasional basket banking in. Matching up with the canned sounds of the computer crowd, we screamed with delight or with anger, depending on who had shot the ball. There was *Blades of Steel* in which, apropos to whatever might end up in this otherwise banal game of hockey, the fights dictated who really won or lost. And, of course, we had the split game of *Super Mario Bros.* and *Duck Hunt,* the latter packaged with a gun that, even when the Nintendo was off, was included as a novel prop in our fun and generally existed as a new means to taunt each other.

Notwithstanding the holidays or the time of year when most were trapped indoors, my mother increasingly seemed incensed at the hours we spent transfixed with the TV screen in our eyes and the controllers in our hands. My brother and I had even lured my father into the gameplay once or twice, yet despite his natural dexterity and the professional quality of his hands and eyes (he was a dentist in his working life) he lost interest quickly and would hand the clickers back to us. After a while, my mother would climb the stairs and soon walk up to speak but stop, looking at the three of us, yet never staying long enough to talk. Oftentimes she would turn around, heading back from whence she came as if she had only, solely come to check on us instead of passing by and moving through the room to something else.

Though I didn't know it at the time, my parent's marriage was on the way out. They split on religion, though my father seemed to take little interest either way and generally let her raise us as she wished. He was an atheist while she was raised Episcopal and held strong and fast to her belief in Jesus. On Sundays she would take us to a Bible group that, in retrospect, seemed to have been run by a rather odd, cultish clan that inspected, under microscopes, the backs of dollar bills for tiny signs into their faith. The word of God was evidently everywhere, they said, and my brother and I played along, singing once a week about the joy joy joy joy down in our hearts that we weren't really sure about to begin with. I later found out that, on these Sundays, my father would go out to bars or sometimes stay at home and drink.

Ultimately, my father's drinking surpassed his interest in his work and his wife and his kids and shortly after Christmas that year, my mother and my uncle put him in a rehabilitation center that he wouldn't leave for over two years. In that time, in the months after my father went away, when the divorce was pushing through and when the snow fell regularly, my brother and I spent lots of time indoors in the Green Room, playing Nintendo while my mother talked on the phone and sobbed and would come out and finally watch us play with her face and eyes red from tears and salt. We were not going to be able to keep the home, not without my father's income, but my mother let on for a good while longer, taking on extra assignments and jobs and, generally, making ends meet.

For my brother and me, one of the most noticeable aspects of this new era was our mother's suddenly pressing evening obligations, reviewing concerts almost every night for the Portland Press Herald. These new nights out brought in a different line of babysitters, not the regular friends of the family we were used to. I later found out that Steve Prey, our customary sitter of over five years, and Katie Towle, our other mainstay when Steve was unavailable, were both friends from someone we knew through my father and that my mother no longer felt appropriate asking them for help. So on came the new line, mostly a gaggle from the local college, and they let my brother and me do whatever we wanted which was, nightly, shooting ducks and fighting on the ice.

Our previous babysitters were usually very active. Steve would encourage us to invite over the neighborhood kids for elaborate games of Capture the Flag that usually ended with a few people missing in the walls and no one knowing just how my brother or I made it from the downstairs kitchen to the upstairs, attic nook without passing by any of the guards or watchmen. Katie would set up basketball goals on the tops of doors and organize small games of Nerf two-on-two that lasted hours and became ritual, weekly competitions. Yet these new sitters were passive and drab and let my brother and me lie, letting them off the hook by letting us sit in front of the Nintendo while they fooled around downstairs with their boyfriends or ate through our cupboards of food.

It was easier that way, for us and for them, and the nights passed quickly without bother. There was an agreement between the sitters and us, a policy of unwritten rules stipulating that they wouldn't tell our secrets if we didn't tell theirs. Things went on like this for the first few weeks without incident, yet there were always new sitters which meant my brother and I had to keep up the game, the series of lies, but we usually won out to the sitter's general apathy and, in turn—after my mother's nightly departure—would run upstairs to play. Occasionally one of the sitters would challenge our claim, stating that he or she knew what we should and shouldn't do, but we resisted. Strung high through our tantrums and screams, they cowered and quivered and lost and generally left us alone to the clicks of our fingers and thumbs.

For the first few months, these were our nightly lives until a horrible, inevitable oversight changed everything. Like any other evening, my mother left around six, after introducing us to another new sitter. Before she had pulled out of the driveway, my brother and I had already and easily convinced the new dupe that, Really, Nintendo is a fine way to spend our time and Honest, do you really want to mix chemicals in our dark, quiet basement? She was pleasant and dismissive and responded that she didn't care so up we went to the Green Room until about a half-hour before my mother returned. Thereafter, we turned off the set and sat on the front-hall stairs, making sure the evening went as planned.

When we heard the door open, it was the same regular banter.

"How were things?"

"Things were great. The kids were great."

My brother and I smiled, but then the tone

of my mother's voice changed and we could hardly hear her talking. We descended slowly down another flight until we peered around the kitchen doors and saw a yellow legal pad in my mother's hand, her face quizzical and looking at the sitter. We didn't know it at the time but a small report of the evening had been written and, consequently, had given us up. The sitter saw us and my mother saw the sitter, quickly turning to see my brother and me scuttling back up the stairs. She called us by our full names and we came moping as she calmly led our fool out to her car.

When we returned to the house, after the good-byes, my mother turned to us.

"What did you boys do tonight?"

I looked at my brother and he, being the eldest, spoke. In that moment of concession, everything was crucial.

He told her we had played basketball for a while then gone to bed. That was it. I looked at him and he wouldn't look back, knowing he had let us down. It was a hard hit for our team, but we were wearing our pajamas, the uniform of bedtime, and that, in a small way, seemed like it could go the distance.

My mother was quiet and sternly asked us again yet, by then, we were too terrified to move. She visibly shook with ire and looked at us until we looked away. We had never seen her furious like this before and it was something dire and awful. Neither of us spoke. In stillness, we watched her turn from us and walk to the table, tearing off the top sheet of the legal pad and holding it high in front of our rapt eyes. I can perfectly recall her face then—red and angry and sad—and her eyes, two different sizes and two off-shades of green, were lightning from the horrors of divorce.

Quietly, she spoke.

"This. This does not say what you said."

Then she left, walking past us through the kitchen then up two flights to her bedroom where we heard the door close with force and knew that night we weren't being tucked in. The days after that were weekdays and my mother was gone for almost every hour, save breakfast and dinnertime. It had warmed up in the weeks previous and was now March. The snow was mostly melted and the after-school programs at our school across the street had begun and my brother and I, three grades apart, still managed to find each other on the fields. The programs weren't every day though and, on one of the warmer afternoons that week, we decided to skip them altogether to go home and play Nintendo.

Our doors were never locked and we went right inside after crossing between cars and the other students walking home. For the next three hours we played *Super Mario Bros.* with my brother continually trying to demonstrate how he could beat the game in a matter of minutes and yet he never could, saying "If I didn't just die just then I could've got that thing that gets me there" or something along those lines until we moved on to another game and forgot about his quests and crusades. We just played and played and forgot about time and the weather outside and the other things there were to do.

On that particular day, my mother came home early and walked right in on us. It was at least an hour earlier than she usually arrived and we looked up in awe as if our father had returned or as if we'd just been told the summer wouldn't come or if we had only six months left to live. It was a shock for the lot of us yet my mother calmly walked into the room and stood above my brother and me who had, by this point, dropped the controllers and moved a good few feet away from the television as if we had never been playing in the first place. Her dress was white, purple and blue and hung thin and long, making her uneven green eyes shine and her small bob of brown hair look perfectly kept with lustre.

She moved slowly towards the TV set and turned it off. Looking down at the two of us, our backs pressed against the Green Room couch, she abruptly shifted in a way that scared us terribly and then fully jumped with both feet off the ground and onto the Nintendo. The front swivel piece flew off under her weight and the middle of the machine sagged from the initial impact. Then, with her left foot on the ground, she took individual jabs at it with her right heel, plunging into the box while more pieces flew and the back dented down and in. She went at it with a few more thrusts then softly stopped, her breath hardly above a whisper. With the red light on the front of the box now blinking, she spoke:

"Get out of here and go outside. Look. You can finally see the ground."

And so we did, my brother and I running down the front-hall stairs and outside before saying a word to each other but making sure we were definitely not in that house near the TV.

After that, my mother gave the set away to the neighbors and, soon later, my brother and I began to share a room. For a little more income, our bedrooms were being used by students from the local college and within a year, the student who had been staying in my room introduced her father to my mother and they were married a few months afterwards. And in a year from then we had left New England and settled in Mississippi where life was wholly different. We never had a television again after that, certainly never had video games and, to top it off, we weren't allowed to eat foods with sugar or chocolate.

But things were good and even though the South lacked snow and the summers were too hot, I remember smiling the first time I rode a bike outdoors in December and when it slid around the corner of an evergreen on a sidewalk covered with sand, there's a picture of me to prove I looked up grinning with the blood running fast from my skinned knee.

# MARK LAMOUREUX
## 8-BIT PRIMITIVE: Homage to the Atari 2600

The contemporary world is lousy with texts, with continuums. The multiplicity of signs birthed by technology staggers the mind; our terminals are the magic notepads—notebooks—whereupon can be found the ceaselessly scintillating apparitions of our collective digital dream, our hyperconsciousness. The computer screen is a text, which can be read like any other, replete with its own historical narrative, its own lineage, and its own mythology. It is a canvas, a dialog and an entity, and, like any art form, dialog or entity, its infancy and adolescence are rife with latent myths and symbols, a language as pregnant and elegant as that of adulthood. I find my own adulthood haunted by those ghosts of my digital past, those bitmapped and parti-colored sprites of the Atari 2600.[1]

In this piece, I will compare the formal characteristics of primitive visual art and folk narrative to those of these Atari 2600 video games to demonstrate their striking similarities. Any system of representation, be it painting, sculpture, drawing or computer graphics, must learn

---

[1] Atari released the Atari Video Computer System (Model #CX2600) in October, 1977. It would be renamed the Atari 2600 by 1983. Van Burnham, *Supercade* (Cambridge, MA: The MIT Press, 2001), pp. 147-149.

in its early stages of evolution to stand on its damp and spindly mimetic legs, although from the moment of its genesis it wants to run. In primitive art we find merely a naiveté of technique, but not of intent or motivation. Primitive art applies elegant solutions to problems by using its rudimentary palette, displaying its own unique and vague logic; it is the playground of myth, of fairies, and demons. In his *Mythologies,* Barthes tells us, "everything can be a myth provided it is conveyed by a discourse."[2] And indeed in these early home video games we do find a discourse, a language. I will use the term "games" to refer to said texts for the purpose of brevity and clarity, though the texts themselves represent an amalgam of formal elements of relevance beyond said texts' conception as a form of entertainment. The games speak to us. As I will explain here, they help to reveal the demons of our present consciousness, the fears and anxieties of the human interacting with the machine, those infant terrors and closet monsters of the childhood of our symbiotic relationship with the machine on that most basic level of play. Insofar as the games represent a kind of mythology, human interaction with these texts constitutes a ritual whereby the "player" has commerce with those saints and devils of the digital world and the singular lens that world superimposes on our own. These games present us with proto-images, flattened two-dimensional landscapes, stylized spaceships, cars, and animals. In *Adventure,* one of the earliest games marketed by Atari, the hero is a simple square, the sword a crude arrow pointing at the target—a dragon that looks uncomfortably like a reptilian duck in profile.[3] The images are incomplete, standing upright only upon the crutches of context and metonymy. It is through those holes in the extremities of representation that the creatures of myth are allowed to enter:

> But in general myth prefers to work with poor, incomplete images, where the meaning is already relieved of its fat, and ready for a signification, such as caricatures, pastiches, symbols, etc. . . . Myth is a pure ideographic system where the forms are still motivated by the concept they represent while not yet, by a long way, covering the sum of its possibilities for representation.[4]

---

[2] Roland Barthes, (sel. and tr. Anette Lavers) *Mythologies* (London, UK: Jonathan Cape, 1972), p. 109.

[3] Atari. *Adventure,* 1978.

[4] Barthes, *Mythologies,* p. 127.

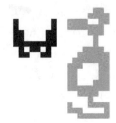

Figure 1

Figure 2

These games employ this ideography of incompleteness, the symbology of myth, and also the logic of the folktale. The world of these games is populated by sinister anthropomorphized and animate mundane objects, bizarre transformations, guardians, demons, magic swords and talking animals, chthonic underworlds and labyrinths: those tropes which have existed in primitive art and narrative throughout history.

Returning to *Adventure,* we find the landscape nearly saturated with such folktale elements: a yellow, black, and white castle and labyrinths that our square hero must navigate, some shrouded in mist, allowing the player to see only a small portion of the screen. There is a magic (and anachronistic) horseshoe magnet, which unfailingly attracts objects in its immediate vicinity. It has its trickster also, an impish bat that traverses the enclosed universe of the game picking up objects (or entities) and spiriting them off to remote areas of the playing field. This magic bat has no problem, even, lifting the "immense" dragons and carrying them off [*fig. 1*]. A magnet-bearing bat wreaks general havoc on the world. It is significant to note that the bat is as large as the hero him or herself, who is also the same relative size as the sword, the various keys to the castles, and the chalice. The largest object in this universe is a magic bridge that allows the hero to effortlessly breach the walls of the labyrinths as if they were insubstantial. In the flattened two-dimensional world of the game, said bridge functions more like a door, and is rendered by two unconnected purple bars like a large pair of brackets [*fig. 2*].

The labyrinth features prominently in countless other games, and each labyrinth is populated by its requisite monsters and beasts: the

Figure 3

5 Atari. *Pac-Man,* 1981.

6 20th Century Fox. *Alien,* 1982.

7 Atari. *Berzerk,* 1982.

8 CBS Electronics. *Wizard of Wor,* 1982.

ghosts of *Pac-Man*,[5] the creature of *Alien*,[6] the angry robots of *Berzerk*[7] and the demonic denizens of *Wizard of Wor*[8] [*fig. 3*].

Figure 4

As in a folktale, ordinary objects can become magical or sinister. In *Megamania*, a craft reminiscent of the Starship Enterprise is beset by waves of bomb-dropping hamburgers, cookies, bugs, radial tires, steam irons, and the like; though the representations of such are primitive enough that the game's manual is required, at times, to recognize them [*fig. 14*].[9] In *BurgerTime*, a tiny chef must tamp down various hamburger strata while avoiding animate hot dogs, french fries, and slices of American cheese [*fig. 4*].[10]

Additionally, there is no shortage of bizarre protagonists: in *Deadly Duck*, a bullet-spitting waterfowl battles hordes of brick-dropping crabs [*fig. 5*].[11] In *Kangaroo*, a boxing-glove-clad mama roo attempts to rescue her baby from a gang of apple-hurling monkeys.[12] When she is united with her child the machine belts out, inexplicably, a few bars of "Oh, Susanna." Inversely, in the somewhat alarmingly titled *I Want My Mommy*, an animate teddy bear ascends a series of magic ladders guarded by demons to be reunited with its mother.[13]

Figure 5

In Imagic's beautiful *Fathom*, a dolphin must collect purple seahorses who reveal yellow stars, which in turn grant him pieces of a magic trident that are then used to free a mermaid from her underwater cage. In order to secure the final pieces of the trident-key, however, the player must shift perspectives from the dolphin to a seagull (masterfully rendered with bands of gray and white) whose wing-

[9] Activision. *Megamania*, 1982.

[10] Mattel. *BurgerTime*, 1982.

[11] 20th Century Fox. *Deadly Duck*, 1982.

[12] Zimag. *I Want My Mommy*, 1983.

[13] Atari. *Kangaroo*, 1983.

Figure 6

Figure 7

Figure 8

beats are controlled by the press of the joystick button, to fly through ravens and clouds.[14]

In *Demons to Diamonds,* a horizontally scrolling cannon must alchemically transform correspondingly colored three-eyed demons into sparkling diamonds by way of a magic bolt [*fig. 6*]. Attempting to transform a demon of the opponent's color will result, however, in the creation of a skull and crossbones that fires upon the player.[15]

While these games borrow heavily from established mythic pantheons, they also create their own. In *Atlantis,* the player must protect the futuristic underwater city from attacking spacecraft.[16] When the game ends, an escape-saucer ascends from the ruined city; this saucer becomes the main character of the sequel game *Cosmic Ark,* in which the protagonist rescues exotic animals from strange planets (perhaps to repopulate the ruined underwater metropolis).[17] Borrowing narrative and images from the classic film *Jason and the Argonauts,* the game *No Escape* requires Jason to use a sling to knock bricks from the ceiling of Aphrodite's temple, causing them to fall upon and crush antagonistic skeletons and centaurs [*fig. 7*].[18] In *Riddle of the Sphinx,* the protagonist must offer a series of hieroglyphic objects to the sphinx to solve a series of riddles explained in the game's manual (an interaction between texts), while avoiding the god Anubis and accepting the assistance of Isis [*fig. 8*].[19]

Indeed, the games are obsessed with monsters, strange creatures, demons, and chimeras, all lovingly rendered in blocky bitmaps, looking like they've stepped from the walls of caves or

---

[14] Imagic. *Fathom,* 1983.

[15] Atari, *Demons to Diamonds,* 1982.

[16] Imagic, *Atlantis,* 1982.

[17] Imagic, *Cosmic Ark,* 1982.

[18] Imagic, *No Escape,* 1983.

[19] Imagic. *Riddle of the Sphinx,* 1982.

ancient woven tapestries. It is no coincidence that this manner of representation corresponds with that of the earliest artists, and that artists of the video game should have something in common with those of antiquity.

Franz Boas explains in his book *Primitive Art:*

> In an art, the technique of which does not admit the use of curved lines and in which decorative patterns have developed, there is no room for curved lines, and the curved outlines of objects are broken up into angular forms. The patterns, or as we usually say, the style, dominates the formal as well as the representative art.[20]

The style of representation in the games is unburdened by the constraints of realistic mimesis and revels in its blocky forms and garish colors. As Boas writes, "Neither primitive man nor the child believes that the design or the figure he produces is actually an accurate picture of the object to be represented."[21]

As programming technique was refined, individual companies began to develop signature styles. In particular, Imagic's use of bright colors, sophisticatedly bitmapped objects and figures and a sophisticated composition of space on the screen and Activision's use of bands of colors to suggest atmosphere (as on the horizon, in the sky or under the water) both stand out in their singularity and elegance. This manipulation of the horizontal axis corresponds with techniques employed in the early stages of conventional art, as Boas describes:

> The prevalence of horizontal and the rarity of vertical symmetry is presumably due to the absence of vertically symmetrical movements,—except in those rhythmic movements in which the arms are alternately raised and lowered,—and in the rarity of natural forms that are vertically symmetrical.[22]

This bilateral symmetry characterizes many of the monsters and demons found through

---

[20] Franz Boas, *Primitive Art* (New York, NY: Dover Publications, Inc., 1955) p. 84.

[21] Ibid. p. 70.

[22] Ibid. p. 35.

Figure 9

out the games: the ubiquitous *Space Invaders*[23] [*fig. 9*], the demons of *Demon Attack*[24] [*fig. 10*], all manner of birds, frogs, spiders, and bugs.

This technique can also be found in the many horizontally scrolling games, a fine example being U.S. Games' *Commando Raid,* in which delicate bands of blue, purple, and orange at semirhythmic intervals suggest a sky at dusk [*fig. 11*].[25] A similar technique is used in Activision's *Barnstorming*[26] and *Chopper Command.*[27] Bars of color of subtly varying hue may be found in countless games; they are part of the aesthetic conventions that define the singular appearance of 2600 games. Unable to employ fine detail of form or line, the designers relied heavily upon color.

Initially, the games "took place" in a flattened, two-dimensional space, but the game designers, like painters (though of course on a much more accelerated timeline), would come to discover Renaissance perspective, giving the two-dimensional screen an illusion of depth. This was done, in some instances, through the use of parallel bands of color, the distance between which shrank as they approached the horizon (see *Robot Tank*[28] and *Battlezone;*[29] or *Beamrider,*[30] which is enhanced by vertical lines, wide near the viewer but shrinking toward a single point in classic Renaissance perspective). Additionally, first-person maze games would be developed that employed Renaissance perspective, such as *Survival Run*[31] [*fig. 12*] and *Crypts of Chaos.*[32] In the majority of these games, however, the third dimension merely pro-

Figure 10

[23] Atari. *Space Invaders,* 1978.

[24] Imagic, *Demon Attack,* 1982.

[25] U.S. Games. *Commando Raid,* 1982.

[26] Activision. *Barnstorming,* 1982.

[27] Activision. *Chopper Command,* 1982.

[28] Activision. *Robot Tank,* 1983.

[29] Atari, *Battlezone,* 1983.

[30] Activision, *Beamrider,* 1984.

[31] Milton Bradley Co., *Survival Run,* 1983.

[32] 20th Century Fox, *Crypts of Chaos,* 1982.

vides a backdrop, a false sense of perspective: the action takes place along two-dimensional vectors, the protagonist never moving from a fixed plane.

Later games would experiment with three-quarter views, such as *Congo Bongo*[33] and *Crystal Castles*[34] [*fig. 13*], both of which were conversions from the more powerful and graphically sophisticated stand-alone games of the arcade. A few unique approaches to perspective include *Space Chase*,[35] in which a vaguely round planet unfolds below the action, and *Nexar*,[36] a rare instance in which objects grow or shrink in size to suggest three dimensions (due to the 2600's limited memory, all objects appear with uniform distinctness). One rarely encounters atmospheric perspective, alterations of color or hue to suggest distance. This false three-dimensionality is also a trait found in primitive art and addressed by Boas:

Figure 11

> Nevertheless most of the older paintings of large scenes represent all parts with equal distinctness, as they appear to our eyes when they wander about and take in all the different parts one by one.... But the distant figures are distinct in outline, although dark in colors.[37]

Figure 12

These visual formal elements I have discussed are only one set of reagents, however, in the spell that the games cast in order to draw the player into their spectacle. For it is a kind of magic spell which is cast;

---

[33] Sega. *Congo Bongo,* 1983.

[34] Atari. *Crystal Castles,* 1984.

[35] Apollo. *Space Chase,* 1981.

[36] Spectravideo. *Nexar,* 1982.

[37] Boas, *Primitive Art,* p. 73.

Figure 13

the act of interacting with these texts (early hypertexts, if you will) is a kind of ritual whereby the human enters the realm of the machine and operates by its rules. The hardware being too primitive to generate the kind of virtual environments and experiences we find in video games today, the player of these early pieces descends into an altered world, one of little sense, meaning or linear narrative. They provide a kind of ritual in their repetitions, their shifting variety (wave after wave of aliens, of continuously varying forms, patterns). The act of playing them is a kind of ritual whereby the performer enters, shamanistically, the world of their mythology.

The discourse Barthes speaks of is certainly present in the continuum presented by the games—while the formal graphic elements of the games may follow the rules of primitivism, the messages expressed by way of their primitive metonymy are at times distinctly modern. There is a kind of loneliness, the lone spacecraft battles UFOs or monsters with no aid, the skeletal protagonist of *The Mountain King* wanders the darkness of the mountain alone, in search of diamonds, with only the Fire Spirit and its drifting strains of Edvard Grieg's "The Hall of the Mountain King" to keep him company.[38] The objects of *Megamania* [*fig. 14*] rebel, the baker in *Piece O' Cake*[39] is faced with a production line of relentlessly increasing speed and malevolence. In *Reactor*, the player faces a series of subatomic particles that whip around the inside of the cyclotron/reactor.[40] The product itself rises up against the consumer. Through the lens of this new technology, the world runs amok. As Derrida states:

> Far from the machine being a pure absence of spontaneity, its resemblance to the
> psychical apparatus, its existence and its necessity bear witness to the finitude of the

Figure 14

---

[38] CBS Electronics. *The Mountain King,* 1983.

[39] U.S. Games. *Piece O' Cake,* 1982.

[40] Parker Brothers. *Reactor,* 1983.

mnemic spontaneity which is thus supplemented.[41]
These games, insofar as they are an archive, contain traces of the zeit-
geist present during their creation. By interacting with these games,
we gaze into the emotional and intellectual climate of the age that
produced them, in this instance the terrors and hopes of a digital age
in its infancy.

Figure 15

Insofar as the technology created a new and sinister world, the image of technology was
also offered as a kind of salvation (a literal deus ex machina). In countless examples we see
the signifiers of technology: spaceship, car, robot, facing more archetypal foes, such as demons,
monsters, or malevolent animals. In *Condor Attack*[42] and *Phoenix,*[43] a spacecraft must defend
itself against attacking birds [*fig. 15*]; in *Cosmic Corridor,*[44] a craft resembling a hydrofoil is
paired off against an inexplicable series of adversaries: ogres, abstract shapes, and scorpions [*fig.
16*]; in *Cosmic Swarm,*[45] the ubiquitous delta-shaped vehicle attacks angry millipedes; in *Space
Cavern,*[46] a lone astronaut on a field of blue color-bars shoots at fantastically colored insects
[*fig. 17*].

Figure 16

In my personal favorite, Imagic's exquisite *Subterranea,*[47] a beautifully depicted spaceship
faces a series of bizarre adversaries as it horizontally scrolls through a cave decorated with

---

[41] Jacques Derrida, (tr. Gayatri Chakrovorty) *Of Grammatology* (Baltimore: Johns Hopkins University Press, 1997).

[42] Ultravision, *Condor Attack,* 1983.

[43] Atari. *Phoenix,* 1982.

[44] Zimag, *Cosmic Corridor,* 1983.

[45] Comma Vid, *Cosmic Swarm,* 1982.

[46] Apollo, *Space Cavern,* 1981.

[47] Imagic. *Subterranea,* 1983.

Figure 17

Figure 18

human skulls (the skulls, too, could cost the player his spaceship) [*fig. 18*]; for this particular game, Imagic invented its own mythology and printed it on the cartridge label:

The hideous HEXUPLEX guards the dark tunnels. Its evil genius tracks your Ranger, wherever you fly. The creature sends up lethal Aerobots, one after the other. Grab the Treasure Crystal and slide into the underworld. You're in for an unforgettable adventure!

If you survive flocks of flying enemies, escape through the high powered flash pulses of the Electro-Gates. It takes steady nerves to make it! Then, go even deeper to more wild battles. Keep shooting, and never give up![48]

Figure 19

The Hexuplex resembles a hairy spider with a mandibled head that spits (!) flying saucers at the player [*fig. 19*]. Birds and amoebas await the player who conquers the cybernetic arachnid. In the Hexuplex we see a kind of chimera, a symbol of base abjection and fear (the spider, the insect) regurgitating a symbol of contemporary anxiety and fear (the unidentified flying object, the machine).

Technology becomes a means of self-discovery. The early game designers were fascinated with the rendering and exploration of the symbolic properties of the human body. In this limited mimetic space, the body is often reduced to its elements: eyes, hands, mouth. In *Beany Bopper*, a disembodied eye (looking rather like a pimento-stuffed olive) stalks evil (indicated by frowning faces) flying beanie caps [*fig.*

Figure 20

---

[48] Ibid.

[49] 20th Century Fox. *Beany Bopper*, 1982.

[50] Atari. *Haunted House*, 1981.

20]. The vector of this evil eye's gaze represented, like so much else, by a bullet-pixel.[49] In *Haunted House,* a pair of disembodied eyes fly

Figure 21

through a maze, avoiding bats [*fig. 21*].[50] It is significant to note that the topic of disembodiment is never mentioned in these games' manuals; the reader is assumed to be conversant in the symbolic language of the medium. An eyeball or a set of eyes or a face represents a person and not simply a body part. In this world of animated objects and antagonistic radial tires, what else could represent the human presence apart from a series of dismembered parts or skeletal outlines of figures?

In *Jawbreaker* a set of teeth darts through a maze, eating pellets, and is beset by a group of rotating (and presumably toothless) smiley faces; upon clearing a level, the victorious choppers receive—what else?— a brushing [*fig. 22*].[51] The perils of oral hygiene are similarly addressed in *Plaque Attack,* in which a miniature tube of toothpaste protects a group of approximately eight teeth from similarly miniature hamburgers and hot dogs. Struck teeth turn yellow and subsequently disappear.[52] *Fantastic Voyage* also explores the interior of the human body, with a tiny craft swimming through the bloodstream avoiding white blood cells.[53]

Figure 22

Sex in this world is similarly disjointed and mechanistic. None of the supposed erotic titles even approaches the elegance or sophistication or ingenuity of design shown in the more conventional titles. War, it would seem, supercedes love in this world. In the execrable *Bachelor Party,* an abstract object (not nearly phallic enough to be a penis) bounces a garish female silhouette (breasts=female) against

Figure 23

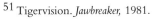

[51] Tigervision. *Jawbreaker,* 1981.

[52] Activision. *Plaque Attack,* 1983.

[53] 20th Century Fox. *Fantastic Voyage,* 1983.

[54] Mystique. *Bachelor Party,* 1982.

other such silhouettes, an endeavor presumably intended to solicit an erotic response from the viewer.[54] In the revoltingly titled *Beat 'Em and Eat 'Em,* a creature consisting of a face, a pair of stick-like arms and an engorged member, engages in activities I will not describe here.[55] In *Custer's Revenge*[56] and *A Knight on the Town,*[57] ithyphallic protagonists avoid various obstacles to unite with female characters oddly reminiscent of mudflap silhouettes [*fig. 23*]. In keeping with primitivism, the characters in this particular genre suggest some kind of infantile fertility cult with their distorted features and the nausea of their appointed task of repeatedly achieving coitus after overcoming ludicrous obstacles. The romantic is advised to turn to *Donkey Kong*[58] or *Krull*[59] for the more traditional, albeit platonic, damsel-in-distress scenario.

Figure 24

The broken-hearted may seek solace in *Journey Escape* where Steve Perry avoids amorous groupies represented by valentine hearts with legs [*fig. 24*].[60]

The charm of these games lies in their innovative use of a limited palette in creating a mood in which conventional reality, while obliquely addressed, is momentarily suspended. In the repetitive motions and straightforward objectives of the games, the mind is drawn into a simplified space where primal tropes are enacted. Here the adult can play with spaceships, or dolls, and run from the hordes of sinister creatures which lurk in every corner of our technological malaise and postmodern longings for suspension in a constantly shifting and glowing menagerie of signs and sounds—we are lulled by "The Hall of the Mountain King," made anxious by a relentless beating heart or the thrum of wings.

The formal elements I address here are perhaps best summarized in the aforementioned

---

[55] Mystique. *Beat 'Em and Eat 'Em,* 1982.

[56] Mystique. *Custer's Revenge,* 1982.

[57] Play Around. *A Knight on the Town,* 1982.

[58] Coleco. *Donkey Kong,* 1981.

[59] Atari. *Krull,* 1983.

[60] Data Age. *Journey Escape,* 1982.

*Demon Attack,* in which the player pilots a spacecraft that hovers above a horizon made of blue color-bars of progressively lightening hue, suggesting space. The bilaterally symmetrical demons hover above, and the player hears the pulsing of their wings as they glow in a myriad of colors and emit shrill chirps, disintegrating into shimmering dust when stuck. As soon as one is dispelled, another materializes out of thin air. If the player progresses far enough, these demons begin to split along their central axis into smaller bird-like entities that descend upon the lone hero, shrieking. Underneath the action can be heard a metallic pulse, a drumbeat which increases in tempo as the action progresses. The hero faces wave after wave of these monsters, with no hope of assistance or anything resembling an objective. When the final craft is blown into glitter the landscape hisses and shimmers and the whole scenario begins again, Marduk and Tiamat eternally feuding in the autonomous two-dimensional space of myth.

# KATIE DEGENTESH
## PLAYING MATERIAL GIRL

I was born in 1974 and grew up in a working-class Maryland suburb.

Around age nine I remember having a euphoric dream. The source of my bliss: I owned a unicorn purse in yellow with rainbow handles, wore a bright yellow outfit with rainbow trim and barrettes to match, and rode my pony around and around the yard whenever I wanted to.

Even more than twenty years later, it's difficult for me to admit in print that I enjoyed such a syrupy, girly-girl dream. But I think it's important to note that at age nine I had been exposed to the idea that if I possessed the right objects, all would be right with the world. In fact, I had internalized it enough to dream about it.

Boiled down to a pony, a rainbow and a purse, the idea that objects can make you happy sounds laughable. But this is what capitalism teaches, and the American brand I was exposed to at the time proselytized the ownership of Strawberry Shortcake and rainbow-colored everything. The New York brand I'm steeped in now teaches me to covet Prada shoes, Bliss spa appointments, and the perfect co-op apartment, but the cravings—always for items to wear and own—have not gone away. Like most people, I suffer from the illusion that possessing this stuff will make me happy and get me where I want to be.

What does this have to do with video games? A lot. In the real world, consumerism, though omnipresent, is often unconscious, veiled, or at the very least considered something to be ashamed of in front of certain people. In the virtual world, particularly that of the third-person adventure or action game, it's the only way to play.

Sometime in 1980, my father bought an Atari 400 computer, hooked it up to a black-and-white television, and started to teach me BASIC.

I remember the thrill of hearing the tape recorder CLOAD or CSAVE a program, the noise a strange alien prehistoric ancestor of today's pinging modem. The best games would take thirty minutes to an hour to CLOAD, with about a two-in-three chance that the load would be successful.

By the time the Atari 400 became an 800 and the black-and-white screen a blue-and-white one, I was writing strange little programs that were designed to do nothing much more than ask my little sister and her friends for a password they wouldn't know and insult them because they didn't.

Although my programming skills never really matured beyond this stage, my interest in video games was just beginning. In the early '80s, my dad, who "knew someone" in the gaming business, brought home a slew of 8-bit games on five-and-a-half-inch floppy disks. Every few weeks or months a new batch appeared. There must have been hundreds of titles, but to give you an idea, I'll list a few here: *Star Raiders. Space Invaders. The Mountain King. Necromancer. Claim Jumper. Qix. Fast Eddie. Genetic Drift. Wizard of Wor. Drelbs. Serpentine. Donkey Kong. Eastern Front 1941. Caverns of Mars. Spelunker. Choplifter! Fort Apocalypse. Pac-Man. Kangaroo. Salmon Run. Centipede. Zaxxon. Defender. Dig Dug. Frogger. Joust. Miner 2049er. Pole Position. Qbert. Shamus.*

My favorites were almost exclusively what gamers today call third-person adventures. Other writers have traced that lineage in detail elsewhere, but in my personal gaming history this genre had its roots in two places: first in text games like *Adventureland, Zork,* and *Hitchhiker's Guide to the Galaxy;* and second in visual games, starting with games like *Shamus* and *Spelunker,* and taking a giant leap forward with *Prince of Persia,* the predecessor of modern-day hits like *Tomb Raider.*

Now as then, I'm most interested in the second category of games, but the basics of the two types are strikingly similar. Your character, be it prince, detective or spelunker, runs around a designated area dodging enemies or obstacles and gathering daggers, keys, money, magic, food. If you have the right objects, you can get to the next level and eventually win the game. If you don't, you can't. It's that simple.

Anyone who has ever played one of these games knows what happens to players who don't have the right stuff. They run against a locked door. Or they go through a door that locks behind them, leaving them to wander a small room endlessly until they literally kill themselves out of boredom. Or they get to the next level and face an enemy that, whoops, can't be faced without the object that they should have picked up (or sometimes, as in the Zelda and Link games, bought) when they had the chance.

The older games, especially, also foster and reward obsession. *Spelunker,* the first of them to capture my undivided attention, was housed on a very buggy floppy disk. Often my sisters and I waited anxiously for several minutes to load the game only to watch it freeze on the third note of its theme music. When this happened, we took the disk out, blew on it, put it back in the drive, and tried again. We did this as many times as was necessary. The inconvenience was nothing compared with the frustration of spending hours getting to the deepest point yet in Spelunker's caverns only to start over from the beginning because our miner jumped at the wrong time, ricocheted against his own elevator, and fell to his death.

Don't get me wrong here: this was exasperating. But we loved it. Why? Were we masochists? No. We were moralists (If at first you don't succeed, try try again). We were capitalists. And, of course, we were kids with an exciting new toy. In other words, we were being raised by conservative, working-class Americans.

All of these action-adventure games follow the American formula for success: work hard, obsessively hard, unbelievably hard, and you'll get the treasure, the girl, the money, the power. In the games, however, the formula actually works.

Today these games tend to be viewed as "unforgiving," "punishing" and "frustrating." In the original *Prince of Persia,* for instance, if you failed to stop walking by pulling the character backward at the right instant, you took one step too far, fell off into a pile of spikes, and died. Start over from the beginning.

Growing up, I was taught that if you failed the test, you didn't get into the right college, didn't know how to get an interview for the right kind of jobs, and became a poet instead. Start over from the beginning.

Obviously, things aren't so two-dimensional in real life. I don't have to tell you that our lives don't have reset buttons. Even if mine did, I don't think I would want to use it.

If I were a highly successful investment banker, or Britney Spears, I might still be able to view my life as a well-played video game. But I'm not. I'm just a poet.

For most people, but especially for writers and artists, life is not a series of well-defined tasks that need to be completed—yet many aspects of American culture are relentless in their efforts to convince us that life is exactly that. This is just one of those little paradoxes that creative people have to deal with now and then.

In part, I deal with it by playing video games. High dork factor aside, they continue to be a consolation at the times when I need to feel that life is systematic, structured and justly rewarding. They answer a yearning for specificity in direction and task—one that I actually would feel dismayed to find more of in my real life. Used in moderation, they can even provide a healthy dose of a false sense of accomplishment by substituting simple tasks for complex ones.

For example, if I don't know where or how to connect with a press that will publish more than 1,000 copies of my next book of poetry, I can spend an hour or so inhabiting the latest *Prince of Persia: The Sands of Time,* moving mirrors around to create a beam of light that lets down the platform to raise me to the next level.

This may not do a thing for my book, but in bolstering my confidence and my sense of agency, and allowing me to act out my consumerist urges relatively inexpensively, video games lend a strange kind of support for my poetry. And I love them for it.

# MARION WRENN
## marking out: consuming inauthenticity

"We're Video Games."—WWE, *Hollywood Reporter*

You sit alone in a darkened room, a TV monitor flickers.

Or maybe you are not alone, maybe you've got a handful of friends with you. Pizza remnants and empty coke cans litter the coffee table, end tables, any flat surface. The humid smell of boys fills the place.

The fighting is intense. You are taken with how real it looks, and how fake. At key moments your otherwise passive crew erupts with shouts of praise or cries of woe: *ooof,* that character just took it in the gut; *whooooaaaa,* he did *not* just beat that guy. Emotions pop. You are on your feet. You reach for another slice.

There are no joysticks: you are watching wrestling. And the only difference between watching professional wrestling and playing video games is that you don't pull on that joystick or beat on that paddle in your lap.

OK, perhaps I exaggerate. Watching professional wrestling and being a gamer are different in important ways, but it's their similarities that are worth investigating, links that show that the kinds of pleasure gamers derive from their play have deeper roots and a much longer history than the techno-hype surrounding video games admits.

Most scholars claim that the advent of the joystick signaled a shift in entertainment forms: it was a technological revolution allowing for immersion in and interaction with the goings-on on screen. But celebrating the joystick as such a crucial innovation misses something important: wrestling fans have been interacting with professional wrestlers and matches long before the joystick. Witness: the frying pan. Or better: BBQ tongs.

Live wrestling matches have long been the site of radical interaction between performers and audiences. You can see traces of this any time you flick on a televised broadcast and see fans wave posters; fans play for the cameras as much as they play for the performers and the live audience. They know the cameras might catch them, so with posters scrawled with "The Rock Sucks," "Austin 3:16," or even simply "Bob" (with an arrow pointing down to the fan holding it), wrestling fans are part of the game, egged on by the industry to "make their debut."[1]

But that's a tame iteration of such interaction.

Extreme Championship Wrestling (ECW), a now-defunct federation out of Philadelphia, made a practice of handing out said BBQ tongs, pots, pans, spoons, you name it, to their patrons at the entrance of their arenas. Fans were encouraged to, ahem, *play.*

Now, granted, walloping a live wrestler with a soup ladle is a different modality of "real," than, say, a first-person shooter game. But they share an important link: inauthentic authenticity.[2]

## From Tongs to Thongs

In a recent *Nation* article called "Strip Till You Drop," authors Alison Pollet and Page Hurwitz decry a budding trend: the recent commodification of the stripper aesthetic, the bethonging of "tweens" across the nation. Thirteen- and fourteen-year-old girls are heading to the mall and scarfing up lip gloss, body glitter, and the mother of all impulse buys:

---

[1] This according to the World Wrestling Entertainment website, <www.wwe.com>, which once invited fans to "make their debut" at the now-defunct WWE restaurant and broadcast facility at Times Square in New York City.

[2] A term I'm borrowing from Lawrence Grossberg in *We Gotta Get Out of This Place: Popular Conservatism and Postmodern Culture.* New York: Routledge, 1992. It's an oft-cited term, and one that gets picked up by John Sloop in "The Emperor's New Makeup: Cool Cynicism and Popular Music Criticism" in the journal *Popular Music and Society,* Spring 1999, Vol. 23. I echo them both.

Abercrombie & Fitch thongs. The authors worry that kids are being exposed to the heightened sexuality of the exotic dancer's aesthetic yet are not fully aware of the irony with which that aesthetic is being offered to them; these kids don't know how to *not* be sincere. While today's tween girls might be simulating stripper sexiness (without the wry irony of the best burlesque peelers), inadvertently authentic in their "Wanna Bone?" thongs, today's tween boys seem caught up in a whole different flavor of confusing experience.

See, I have a secret: professional wrestling is fake. *And it's not.* This is what the industry wants me to believe. I am a smart fan. Or more accurately, I am a smark, a smart mark, someone hip to the inner workings of the industry who at the same time is willing to give myself over to the pleasures of the spectacle, and the possibility that some of it might actually be real. A smart mark.

## WE ARE SMARKS

If you have merely a passing knowledge of professional wrestling, you might recall that the game increased its stakes—becoming excessively violent, excessively crude, adopting a Jerry-Springer-cum-Howard-Stern shock aesthetic called "WWF Attitude"—in the '90s. Gone were the days of babyfaces like the early Hulk Hogan and Brett Hart; in their stead were cursing, beer-spewing antiheroes like Stone Cold Steve Austin and the New World Order.

This turn in the industry occurred simultaneously with a number of factors: the WWE (World Wrestling Entertainment) was competing for ratings (and its survival) with WCW (World Championship Wrestling, Ted Turner's fledgling federation). Turner's organization beat the WWE in the ratings war for eighty-six consecutive weeks. The tide turned with the ascension of Steve Austin, the departure of Bret Hart, and the WWE's masterful—and controversial—move: they broke "kayfabe."[3]

*Kayfabe* is wrestling jargon, some say dating back to carnival days, that means "keep the secret," meaning, particulary, to keep the industry's secrets. According to one of hundreds of online wrestling glossaries, "The word is often said by one in the business to indicate everyone around him should stop talking openly because someone not privy to the inner work-

---

3 I call it controversial because not only did it affect fans and performers, it's been rumored that McMahon received death threats from old-school promoters.

ings of the business just entered the room. ...[T]he term was yelled to signal trouble."[4]

When the WWE announced that it produced "sports entertainment," that its performers were characters engaged in "angles" and "works" (meaning a rationalized lie or a predetermined match), they betrayed the industry-wide policy of disavowing wrestling's fakeness. Some say this kayfabian turn was due to a tax loophole: when McMahon began broadcasting his shows on cable, he would have had to pay a tax on live sporting events; by calling his shows sports entertainment he aligned with narrative fiction and avoided this tax.[5]

Under the reign of Vince McMahon, Jr., the WWE broke the industry-wide code of silence about wrestling's supposed reality, and sanctioned the sharing of its insider language of scripts, characters, and story lines with its audience. Wrestlers no longer observed the practice of remaining always in character, sustaining the illusion of the performance. Instead, the WWE's performers let their audience in on the industry's supposed secrets and in doing so hailed its audience more generally as "smart fans."

Prior to this shift, a "smart" was a fan who was aware of wrestling's contrivances. The term *smart fan,* used by audiences and performers, once referred to those fans who sought insider knowledge despite the industry's code of denying wrestling's contrivances, its disavowal of any fakeness and its assurances of authenticity. Smart fans subverted the industry's code and sought a position of expertise; thus the term came to refer to those fans who were savvy, aware of professional wrestling's angles and were keen to accrue insider information about the industry by turning to "dirt sheets" or "dirt rags," newspapers and magazines anathema to the industry where fans could get the scoop on backstage struggles and intrigues.[6]

The antithesis of the smart fan was the "mark," the naïve viewer (a.k.a. a kayfabian). Also deriving from wrestling's carnival roots, the term *mark* is believed to refer to the practice of putting chalk marks on the chairs of a show's potential dupes. The term is used by perform-

---

[4] *Pro Wrestling Torch Yearbooks, '92-'95;* Wade Keller; <www.pwtorch.com>.

[5] New Jersey Governor Christine Todd Whitman signed professional wrestling's status as entertainment into law. See *Reason Magazine,* June 1997 at <www.reasononline.com/9706/balance.shtml>.

[6] In the early 1990s *smart fan* came to refer to those fans who accessed information about wrestling through new communication technologies, like the web, where they found not only fan-run sites, but websites run by industry giants like WWE.

ers and announcers in the wrestling industry to refer to blinkered fans who wholeheartedly believe in the legitimacy of the performances. Given wrestling's demographics (41% of its audience is between the ages of twelve and thirty-four; 12% are younger than age twelve) it refers to a childlike willingness to believe.[7]

It's also important to note that a *new* term has gained currency in the industry: *smark.* Fusing *smart fan* and *mark,* the term was apparently coined by the industry itself to name the contradiction of being a smart fan who nonetheless relishes the game, someone awed by and engaged in viewing professional wrestling despite being expert in its construction. It has recently appeared on numerous wrestling websites, and has been ascribed to industry professionals who use it to describe *all* wrestling fans. Even though the wrestlers will cop to engaging in "sports entertainment," and know that most fans are hip to the form's choreography, the implicit message is "you might be smart, but we're still gonna trick you."

In the case of professional wrestling we have an example of an industry with a rich language for how it imagines its audience's responses to its products. This seems to be unique in popular entertainment. As McMahon himself said recently on National Public Radio's *Marketplace,* "We are closer to our audience than perhaps any one in entertainment. We touch and literally feel our audience on a nightly basis. We tweak our shows and live events accordingly. [We've got] automatic feedback." As an analysts' report at a recent WWE stockholders meeting claimed: "We are a preeminent global-media provider of entertainment that evokes a uniquely passionate emotion from our fans."

But the roots of this kind of entertainment stem from the mid-late nineteenth century. We can see it in the spectacles/hoaxes/humbugs produced by P.T. Barnum. The author of *The Art of P.T. Barnum*, Neil Harris, makes it clear that Barnum knew his audiences enjoyed being humbugged, and would pay a second time to find out how the hoax was perpetrated upon them. Harris focuses on an "operational aesthetic"—turn-of-the-century audiences delighted in knowing how things operated—and his is a useful analytical category for understanding the smart fans' delight in becoming expert in how the hoax of professional wrestling is perpetrated.

---

[7] These percentages are taken from a WWE investor-relations presentation dated March 10, 2004, citing 2003 research by Nielsen Media research and Doublebase MRI.

But what seems to be different is the simultaneity of the pleasure of being both expert and uncertain at once. And that seems to be the key distinguishing feature, one that actually links professional wrestling to gaming. Today's wrestling fans describe their desire to "mark out," to give themselves over to the pleasures of being engaged and immersed in a choreographed match.

There is an important difference between the so-called expertise constructed by fan magazines, corporate-owned websites with the air of dirt sheets, and *Access Hollywood*-style pre- and postmatch shows, and the bliss of (un)certainty created by something like pro wrestling—when that expertise and knowingness is threatened in moments of "pop."

Wrestlers and fans talk about extreme audience reactions as *pops*. The crowd tends to "oooooo" or "aaaaaahhhh" when 1) a wrestler does something clearly in character, 2) when s/he does something surprisingly out of character, 3) when the wrestler's moves are so well executed as to convey the potential of violence, and 4) when the move is done in such a way as to look like it is out of the wrestler's control, that it *is* violent. (This latter moment is also called "heat," a term regularly used in promotional ads: "Nitro: We've Got Heat." To satisfy their audiences, performers are caught up in creating authentic-seeming violence, a violence that sometimes results in real harm, or heat.)[8]

The fascination with pro-wrestling violence seems to emerge from the sanctioning of a voyeuristic gaze (pro wrestling is fake so it's OK to watch, no one will get hurt); this fascination is stoked by the ways in which hardcore matches challenge the permissibility of active looking (and yelling and shouting): pro wrestling is fake, *but that's blood, a metal chair, thumbtacks in his arm flesh, a tooth up his nose.*[9] What happens to smart fans in moments like these? They believe in the candidly fake, but that fakeness is covered in blood. Thus, in these moments when the boundary between what is staged and what is real seems to blur, the

---

[8] Professional wrestling has a long tradition of performers using razors in matches to self-inflict bloddy forehead wounds. There is also the legendary Martin "Farmer Burns," who had an eighteen-inch neck. He would hang himself by a noose and whistle "Yankee Doodle" to carnival crowds at the turn of the century. He's clearly the forerunner of someone like Mick Foley, famous for matches in which he's lost teeth, parts of his ears, etc.

9 This is a reference to an infamous cage match between Mick Foley and the Undertaker. See *Beyond the Mat,* directed by Barry W. Blaustein, 1999.

status of the smart fan is threatened, rendered paradoxical, *and* maintained. The savvy viewer gets caught in uncertainty...and finds pleasure there.

As smarts, audiences now have the insider language to match their growing sense of experise. Wrestling programs, and pre- and postmatch shows are peppered with this jargon. And, what is more, the smarts' sanctioned expertise is stoked by the promise of authentic violence.

Let me be specific: An "angle" is industry jargon for a story line; a "work" is a predetermined outcome (or a rationalized lie); a "shoot" or "shooter" or "shoot match" is a work that becomes a legitimate wrestling match or contest. "Shooters" are those wrestlers who know how to cause real pain, and are used to police other wrestlers who might double-cross an angle and try to win a match, despite it being predetermined that they fail. Thus, the simple use of the term *work shoot* by performers *and* audiences in the mid-1990s resonates profoundly: it implies that a real-life argument might be fuel for an in-ring or onscreen feud. According to longtime wrestling fan Michael Bryson, "the term acknowledges that it's fake, but that every now and then there's stuff that'll be real, and that's exciting." We are invited to participate as experts, but that expertise is rendered unstable by moments of authentic violence.

Fans report how titillated they were when the WWE took this turn. Breaking kayfabe was verboten, and there, on recurring national TV programs, the industry's secrets were part of the show. Plus, the turn provided loyal fans with the perfect comeback to nonfans who'd sneer, "Wrestling is so fake." Wrestling fans could then say, "Yeah, and? So's that soap opera you watch." Voila: fakeness bodyslammed.

## Wherever They Are, We Are Too

The issue of authenticity remains vitally important. And it's in the concept of inauthentic authenticity that the ghosts of gaming can be found. Don't mistake this for the academic ravings of a scholar busy sucking the joy out of popular entertainment via the jargon of cultural studies. The WWE knows its audience well, and it regularly promises those viewers to potential advertisers, advertisers like Xbox, Nintendo, and more. In a recent episode of *WWE Thursday Night Smackdown* (an hour-long network show), sixteen spots were purchased to advertise video games like *Final Fantasy* and *Drakengard*.

A publicly traded company, the WWE has seen its stock value slide up and down of late.

To bolster its earnings, it has launched a series of trade ad campaigns in the last few months. In March 2004, for instance, the WWE launched its "Think Outside the Ring" campaign, the brainchild of Philadelphia-based ad agency Red Tettemer. Designed to entice potential advertisers to place their ads in WWE magazines, and network and cable broadcasts, the WWE placed ads in *Advertising Age, Ad Week, Multichannel News, Broadcasting and Cable, Brand Week, Media Week,* and the *Hollywood Reporter.*

It's the ad in the *Hollywood Reporter* that caught my attention. The March issue featured a special section dedicated to the WWE's Wrestlemania XX—their ad campaign was capitalizing on the buzz surrounding this event—and a remarkable ad from the "Think Outside the Ring" campaign figured prominently on the inside cover—prime real estate. In a full-color, full-page ad, two teenage boys and one girl sit cross-legged on the couch and on the floor of a nondescript room that looks very much like someone's game room at home, or a spartan college dorm. The three stare at a video screen, just out of frame, as the boys intently make with their thumbs on the game paddles they hold. Standing next to them, indeed looming over their snack tray, is the impossibly muscled Brock Lesnar. Fists clenched he stares menacingly into the camera. "Wherever They Are, We Are Too" reads the headline. The WWE claims to know how to capture "the elusive twelve- to thirty-four-year olds, and quench their insatiable thirst for all things WWE," which at this point includes video games, Pay-Per-View, video on demand, DVDs, music CDs, books, magazines, live performances, the list goes on.

Gaming companies are capitalizing on the WWE's promise. But I think the wrestling industry is mistaken about one key point: the "elusive" twelve- to thirty-four-year olds might be "insatiable," but their desire is not merely "for all things WWE." Rather, that desire is a tendency to relish the inauthentic authenticity of it all, the bliss of (un)certainty: We know it's a game, but we're not a hundred percent sure how it will turn out. Smart as we are, we still want to "mark out."

Clearly gamers don't mistake their play for real life, but they do find themselves deeply immersed, deeply engaged with the narratives and strategies in which they find themselves and their characters. And when those games are violent, when the simulation is specific and excessive, gamers experience a pleasure, I would argue, very much like wrestling's smart fans. Borrowing from Susan Sontag, who writes of an altogether different context for the depiction of suffering, "There is the satisfaction of being able to look at the image without

WHEREVER THEY ARE,
WE ARE TOO.

flinching. There is the pleasure of flinching."[12] Perhaps that's the real link between gaming and watching wrestling: we've learned to love to flinch. Perhaps we always have—and our games have simply caught up.

_____

[12] *Regarding the Pain of Others.* NY: FSG, 2003, page 41.

# LUIS JARAMILLO
## SOME FINE SHOOTIN' "BIG BUCK HUNTER" IL

**1.**

The Beyond War group met in our living room. I listened from my room. My mother and the others talked about guns and the connection between guns and nuclear weapons. What were the links between the two? Wasn't it possible that the use and ownership of personal weapons brought us closer to the brink of nuclear war? I understood this much and I agreed, until it turned personal.

Maybe children shouldn't have the guns that came with action figures. Maybe that was the problem. The thought that I wouldn't be able to keep the *Star Wars* guns made me very worried. What was she talking about?

Next came a demonstration with BBs. One BB represented one nuclear warhead. She dropped the BB into the metal trashcan brought home from her classroom for this purpose. You could barely hear the BB over the noise of the wine drinking. The one BB represented the power of the bomb dropped on Hiroshima. To show the difference between the one warhead and 10,000, the number of warheads that existed in the world, she dumped a whole bag of BBs into the trashcan. The noise was fantastic.

My brother and I got to keep the BBs when the demonstration was over.

**2.**

I spent all of my teenage years saying that I wouldn't do things, and it wasn't until later, after college, that I decided to do everything.

Unlike my brother, in high school I wouldn't ride four-wheel drive trucks up the sides the hills. Didn't my brother know that some kids had just died doing the same thing? I didn't go to keg parties on the dried up riverbed. I only once made it to Arroyo Seco, the river that joined the Salinas Valley to the Carmel Valley and where the thing to do was drink lots of beer from cans and then dive off the cliffs. I waded in the water and didn't drink any alcohol.

So when it came time to try everything I hadn't tried before, I made up rules. I would not seek out a drug or a club, but I would do whatever found me. I would do whatever anybody else suggested. I had other rules that I tried to follow. Be kind. Refrain from violence. Although these rules may just have been a symptom of my willful passivity. It was near the end of this period of my life—when I would try anything that came to me—that I first saw people playing *Big Buck Hunter II.*

I was horrified. Players used the fake gun attached to the machine to shoot deer on the screen. The players had murderous looks in their eyes. Guns were against my rules. Hunting—against the rules.

**3.**

But it wasn't that simple. If I scratched the surface, I found guns everywhere. When my father was in high school, he was the commanding officer of the high school ROTC. He could take apart and put together M1 rifles while blindfolded.

The ROTC commanding officer who graduated two years before my dad had one dream: to go to West Point. He went. His first day in Vietnam he got a bullet through his head.

**4.**

*Big Buck Hunter II* sat at the back of a real bar. You could tell it was a real bar because it had regulars, drunks, who knew the bartenders.

The place smelled of urine and spilled beer and the millions of cigarettes smoked. The video game sat in the room past the pool table. It shared the room with a honky tonk piano missing all of its piano string. The piano had graffiti tags on each of the keys. Somebody tagged every single key, laying claim. Otherwise there wasn't much to claim. Ancient black paint peeled off the ceiling and walls. Underneath some of the paint you could see a peacock blue that looked out of place in the presence of all the grime.

The game looked like a normal arcade game, two black boxes stacked on top of each other, a screen in the top box. An orange shotgun rested on two prongs where the joystick would be.

I got over my squeamishness once I got the my hands on the shotgun. Someone told me the rules: pump the gun. You get two shots per pump. Only shoot the ones with antlers.

I held the gun up next to my right ear. The deer ate the grass in pretty meadows, half hidden by trees. Light rain fell. One of the deer with antlers raised his head. I shot at him.

I missed him and the second who ran right at me and the third who, unfairly I thought, ran at the back of the screen in and out of the trees. You only got three chances per turn and I'd missed them all.

"You're a terrible shot!" The machine said after my turn. Not liking to be insulted by a machine, I swore I'd do better next time. Fortunately, you got five rounds, or stands, for each dollar you put into the machine. I had four more to go and thank goodness.

I waited anxiously while my opponent brought down two deer. His tactic was to shoot as much as he could, hoping that one of the shots would kill the deer. The machine rewarded him with a Double Buck Bonus, but he got very low accuracy points.

The gun safely back in my hand, I aimed right at the buck drinking water on the foreground. He fell down with a thud. My heart leapt. At the end of my turn, I got to see the buck get shot again, in slow motion. He tumbled headfirst, over his antlers, legs flying in the air until his body settled to the ground in a heap. There was no blood.

"You'd better make some room in the freezer," the machine said. Then the machine showed a diagram of the buck, with red dots representing where I'd shot it—in the butt and in its eye. This seemed a little unnecessary, but was deeply satisfying. Unlike my opponent, I was highly accurate and on the final three stands of the trip I got my own Double Buck Bonuses.

**5.**

It was about this time that I was in the middle of writing something big, a novel. I was interested in stories. Not to read, but to write. I pumped everyone I knew for information. I wanted to know about guns. I'd never even touched a real gun. What did everyone think about guns and hunting?

**6.**

One time, I took a trip to the East Coast with my godfather and visited his mother. Before dinner the first night, she told me to get a napkin to put underneath my cocktail. We ate a dinner of fish and potatoes that we made and a fruit salad from a local gourmet food shop.

We all wore clothes but we weren't dressed.

After dinner, my godfather loaded the dishwasher all wrong. His mother had a system. Her system worked. Never mind, she would load the dishwasher herself.

The next day I remembered to put a napkin under my gin and tonic. She beamed.

"*You* can come back to visit," she told me.

My godfather's mother was deaf in her right ear from shooting skeet. She was right eyed, so the barrel of the gun fit against her right shoulder. She practiced at the Vicmead Hunt Club in Wilmington, Delaware.

Her younger sister married a DuPont who got into beagling, as in the gerund of "to beagle." The sport had its own outfit, similar to fox hunting clothes: white shorts, knee high socks, leather shoes, a green jacket and a black cap. Other than the clothes, and keeping the dogs, the only other requirement was that you own thousands of acres of land. The humans ran after the beagles, which chased down the jackrabbits. Once the beagles got the rabbits cornered, the humans watched the dogs tear apart the rabbits.

Except for one other notable exception, this was a very civilized slice of society. Well into the 1960s, everyone dressed for dinner. For a normal weeknight dinner, even if no guests were invited, the men wore tuxedos with a black tie. The women wore long dresses. Everyone drank two cocktails, minimum, before dinner and then wine with each course.

Every year at Christmas, the family rented a room at the hunt club. They paid extra for the room because it would need to be cleaned once they were done with it. It needed to be cleaned because of the massive food fight that my godfather's grandmother started each year, catapulting a spoonful of mashed potatoes at her brother. After the first attack, it was every man for himself. Peas, roast beef, rolls, flew through the air. You ought to be allowed to let loose one time a year, for godssake.

**7.**

My mother wouldn't let my brother and me join the Cub Scouts because she thought they were paramilitary.

**8.**

It got so that I'd pester everyone about the game.

"Can we go shoot the deer?"

I told people who were practically strangers about the game, how fun it was to shoot the deer, the funny things the machine said. "Boy howdy!" or "That's the biggest deer I've ever seen."

The machine had a Southern accent. A nice sort of bluegrassy electronic music played.

I hummed along with the machine. The machine couldn't keep its mouth shut. It had something to say about everything:

He fell like a ton of bricks!

That's some fine shootin'!

That's a big ol' buck!

Look at the rack on him! (in a whisper)

You winged 'em!

That's a bona fide buck!

Go for the big fella!

You'll be eatin' some venison tonight!

**9.**

The bar was is Fort Greene, in Brooklyn. For some confusing reason, Fort Greene Park is the former site of Fort Putnam. The standard history asserts that Fort Putnam and its commander General Nathaniel Greene supported George Washington in his retreat across the East River.

It turns out that the truth isn't so simple, or heroic. The night before the British were set to attack, every last one of the Americans slipped across the river in the middle of the night. There wasn't a fight at all. In the war, the Americans preferred to ambush the British and in this instance they were far outnumbered even though the Americans had something of an advantage because they had rifles. Muskets had to be reloaded after each shot and were notoriously inaccurate. To make up for the inaccuracy, the soldiers had to stand in a line, making targets of themselves.

The American rifles were more accurate because they had grooves carved into the barrels of the guns that made the bullets fly straighter. The Americans could hide and shoot as though hunting game. In one way, the Americans beat the British by changing the rules of war.

The shotgun attached to the machine didn't have to be reloaded at all, just pumped, which made possible my inaccurate opponent's strategy of shooting as much as possible. The downside of this strategy—besides getting fewer points for accuracy—was that he might end up shooting a doe.

The machine said, "We don't shoot doe in these parts."

## 10.

One Sunday, Augustitis brought his American flag into the church. He was a Vietnam vet; he had a long gray beard, and smelled as if he hadn't bathed, ever. He sang the "Star Spangled Banner" at the back of the nave. When it was time for communion, he marched to the altar and saluted the cross before he drank down the rest of the wine.

When Augustitis ran for president, he promised that when he won he'd appoint my dad Attorney General.

## 11.

One winter break before my brother went back to Harvard, he went with his friends Eli and Pierce to Eli's neighbor's house in north Florida. The neighbor lived fifteen miles away. The neighbor, Willie Ray, had a shooting range on his property. He had all sorts of guns, including a black powder buffalo rifle. When he fired the buffalo rifle, flames came out the end. The plan was to shoot balloons and targets at 200 yards away.

Willie Ray checked the scopes on the .22's and then ran to check the targets. He took lots of trips. After coming back from his last trip he panted, "You do that all day, you'll run a mile?

My brother, Eli and Pierce finally got to shoot the guns.

On the way back to Eli's house, Pierce cried.

**12.**

The machine's official name is *Big Buck Hunter II: Sportsman's Paradise,* and it has its own website (<www.itsgames.com/Products/bbhII>). It also seems that there are monthly tournaments. The machines are networked and the winner gets a $1000 cash prize. There is no mention of *Big Buck Hunter I.*

The machine has "operator selectable bloodless and tagging modes." At first I assumed that the tagging mode had something to do with affixing scientific markers to the deer so that their populations could be tracked by satellite. After further research, I learned that tagging is the alarming practice of attaching actual tags to the carcass, writing down where and when the deer was shot. This is done so that the fish and game department can make sure that the deer wasn't poached or hunted out of season.

It wasn't clear from the website which was right—either way it doesn't seem that the machine would be interested in keeping tabs on the deer. The rule about shooting doe is just a rule. After all, the electronic deer can't be hunted to extinction.

Finally, the website brags:

> *For Him Magazine,* one of the nation's most popular men's entertainment journals, named *Big Buck Hunter II* one of the 50 Greatest Games of All Time in a feature published in their January issue.

> The list was not limited to only video games. *Big Buck Hunter II* came in at #44, beating out seemingly immortal rainy-day diversions as *Twister, Battleship,* and *Hungry Hungry Hippos.*

**13.**

My grandmother refused to have anything to do with the dead ducks, or anything else my grandfather hunted. If the birds were shot and killed and cleaned, she might think about cooking them.

Once, she and my grandfather had to eat dinner at a pharmaceutical salesman's house. They were given a treat: fresh game. They spent the evening picking at bloody doves that still had shot in them. They tried not to giggle. They had to laugh into their napkins and pushed the rare meat around on their plates.

My grandfather kept his guns locked in a cabinet in the basement. The cabinet was so flimsy my mother claims she could have broken down the door. By the time I came around the guns were gone but the cabinet wasn't. The door was made of plywood and was locked with a small padlock. But the rule was that the lock wasn't to be messed with. Not even the time my uncle Bob was in high school, and a member of the rescue squad. He wanted to go up Mount Pilchuck with the rest of the squad to bring down some hikers, but my grandfather wouldn't let him. My uncle threatened to get a gun out of the cabinet and to use the gun, violently, even though Bob was normally the gentlest man around. The scene blew over.

Years later, my uncle moved to Alaska because he liked to hunt and fish and he liked living in a place where people minded their own business.

He sold insurance in Anchorage. His friend, also named Bob, was a lawyer. They took expensive trips to remote islands, remote even for Alaska. Once they went to an island at the end of the Aleutians to hunt ptarmigans. It was so windy on the island that the doors of the rental van had to be chained shut.

They paid three hundred dollars a night to share a motel room with dogs. You badmouthed the other person's dogs behind the other person's back.

"Well, that Casey, he is very poorly behaved. He's not much of a hunter."

"You've never seen such a raggedy looking dog until you've seen Butch."

The dogs had a fight in the middle of the ratty carpet. It was decided that one of the dogs had to go sleep in the van.

There was a discussion about which dog should go since it was clear to both Bobs that the dog that did not belong to him was at fault. Casey had to go out and sleep in the van.

When they got back to Anchorage, the wives, who sometimes went downtown to catch a thirty-pound salmon during lunchtime if they felt like it, asked the Bobs if they got anything.

"It's called hunting, not killing."

14.

One time, some friends met the man who held all the high scores on *Big Buck Hunter II*. They watched him shoot squirrel. After shooting the deer you go on to a bonus round to shoot smaller game: wild turkeys, pheasants, doves. In an especially grisly bonus round set in a cornfield, you shoot gophers who jump out of holes. The impact of the shot tosses the gophers back onto the corn stalks. The gophers look surprised.

Like the gophers, the squirrels seemed harmless, and cute.

The guy had the gun right up next to his ear, pointing down at the screen. Bang, bang, bang, bang. He shot four squirrels scampering on the telephone line.

"Wow, you are really good."

The guy was modest. He drank his Coke.

"You can thank the United States Government."

He was AWOL from the Marines, twenty-six, and on disability from his job so he had plenty of time. He didn't even have any booze in the Coke. He just came to shoot the deer.

## 15.

The name of the bar is Alibi.

## 16.

"Wait, I think that might be a bear," I told the girl cousin. Something brown and huge crashed slowly through the bushes toward us. We stood a mere fifty feet away.

My legs wouldn't work, like in a dream. We were in Alaska, where it was possible that a bear might charge through the bushes at us. You are supposed to fight a black bear—scream and make yourself look big—but if a grizzly comes after you, your best bet is to curl up in the fetal position and put your arms over your neck.

A gun doesn't help at all—heavy-duty pepper spray for bears works better— although I thought if I had a shotgun I'd be able to blast the hell out of the bear. I still couldn't move my legs. I decided that I would let the girl cousin run faster, I'd be the one mauled and on the news.

The brown humped shape came right at us.

It was a moose cow, blinking her eyes and chewing the leaves vigorously.

"Were you afraid?" I asked the girl cousin.

She shrugged. "No."

I felt silly walking up the path. Of course it wasn't a bear. Much more likely a moose. We saw moose everywhere. We'd seen a moose in the yard earlier that day, ripping pansies out of the planters. Her mouth moved with a slack-jawed languor, not eating the pansies so much as mashing them, leaving the pulpy flowers on the ground.

A half a year later, the girl cousin came to New York look at graduate schools. I convinced her to go to the bar to shoot deer with me. She was finally old enough to go to a bar legally.

A fire flickered in the fireplace. It didn't have any smell because it was a fake fire, gas, which was unfortunate because the place still smelled like pee and old liquor and cigarettes, even though by then, smoking was banned in New York City.

The cousin was as placid in Brooklyn as she was in Alaska. She had a bad cold and couldn't smell a thing.

"Just try it out," I said, like a pusher. I was the oldest cousin and was famous for being bossy. She took the gun from me and pointed it at the screen.

"I'll probably like it," she said.

"Of course you will." I said.

# K. THOR JENSEN
## FINISH HIM

In 1987 I had one goal in life—make it to the end of *Double Dragon* with my best friend Andron by my side. There was an arcade in Seattle that his parents would take us to on Saturday afternoons after Seventh Day Adventist church, a week's worth of quarters bagging down our pockets. And every Saturday would end the same—with us shambling away from the machine, defeated, to try our luck on some other game.

Every weekday, I'd stop by Arnold's Arcade during the forty-five-minute wait for my bus home from school. And in the mornings, I would loiter in a Chinese deli on 2nd Avenue that had a half-dozen battered video games set up, craning my fingers under the cabinets for quarters lost and feeding them back down for another few minutes of play. I started stopping by every convenience store between my home and my school, pretending to drop change on the ground and then craning my fingers quickly along the grubby, sticky floor under the counter, fishing for loose change abandoned by other customers.

The arcade was my life, my locus. The clamor of digitized noise and epileptic flashing was a talisman to ward off adults, the gateway into a world of the future where the past was no longer relevant. I counted my allowance out in quarters every Friday, and down the rabbit hole they'd chase throughout the week.

> **Ryan O:** *Arcade* Tetris. *One Saturday I went down to this huge arcade near my house in New Jersey with fifty cents in my pocket. I had to shoo off soccer moms who kept trying to play me in two-player. I played until the score display rolled over and the machine froze. It took me about four hours straight.*

Most early arcade games were not designed to tell a linear story. Due to memory and processor limitations, difficulty was increased mathematically while reusing levels over and over again. The only difference between level one and level 254 of *Pac-Man* is the speed at which the ghosts chase you.

The designers never bothered to test the games to their limits—they figured, quite logically, that human beings would reach the end of their endurance faster than the tireless machines would. However, this didn't turn out to be the case. A few years after the initial arcade boom of the early 1980s, reports started to come out about amazingly skilled players who were playing games until they could play no more—until the games themselves gave out. Since games have a finite amount of memory, if that amount is exceeded, unforeseen events happen. The most famous example was level 255 of *Pac-Man.* Upon reaching it, the player notices that the familiar maze is gone, replaced by a jumble of garbled symbols. Some dots can't be eaten, some flicker on and off randomly. The system simply cannot parse numbers that high (because of a limitation in binary encoding), and it instead displays gibberish. Other games broke in different ways—when the display space for the player's score was exceeded, it often would flip back over to zero, or display strange symbols. Some games wouldn't allow the player to reach that point—the difficulty and speed would increase so high that human reflexes were simply insufficient to deal with them, no matter how good the player was.

Players had become so good, so fast, that they had internalized the patterns being executed by the machine. The marathon players were simply predicting correctly what the game's next move would be. It still required an inordinate amount of reflex skill, but the important thing was seeing the patterns, reading the series of logic trees the machine was using to simulate intelligence and then feeding it the correct signals to confuse that logic. They had taken game playing to a meta-level—not interfacing on the surface of the screen, but with the programs underneath.

I wanted to be one of those marathon players. I entertained fantasies about bending a machine to my will so far it broke into a mess of data on the screen, being known as somebody who was so good no arcade game could stand up to him. I sent photographs of my Atari 2600 high scores in to *Electronic Games* magazine. I knew I had the skills. It was just a matter of being able to play enough video games to polish them to a fine luster. But playing a game at home is very different—you already expressed your ownership of it, you can choose to play it any time you like. You're under no obligation to prove yourself. An arcade machine is a foreign body, a public challenge. Each quarter you put in was guaranteed to eventually lead to the public humiliation of you stepping away from the machine in defeat. It's a John Henry story where the Inky-Poo always wins.

> **Mark H:** Space Gun—*I must have pumped forty dollars into this game. There was a period where I got a little nuts about it. My obsessiveness is short lived. I go absofuckinlutely crazed when in the arcade, but once I am out I calm down, until the next time I am within a few miles of the same arcade. It was in a deli next to my first apartment in New York on 93rd street. I would play it two or three times a week, finally getting through it the third week by sheer force of will and a pocket of quarters. I never play games again after I beat them.*

And then, a few things changed that made this marathon mentality not only more feasible, but also more profitable for an arcade owner. After all, there was no money in some idiot savant being able to come to your arcade and tie up your *Gorf* machine for six hours on one quarter, aside from the spectacle itself. There needed to be a way to demand additional financial investment along with extended playtime.

The first major change was the introduction of a Continue feature. Before this, a quarter demarcated the span of a game—a discrete unit, you had twenty-five cents worth of play and no more. Now, the player could extend that span not only with skill, but also with money. Starting with Exidy's *Fantasy* and becoming more and more prevalent through the mid-1980s, the Game Over screen was now joined by a countdown and an appeal to insert additional coins. On doing so, the player was whisked back to where they left off, with nobody the wiser.

Tied into this development was the insertion of finite narrative elements to games. Players needed an additional motivation to keep inserting money—and story was that motivation. If the player had a visible goal and could mark their progress towards it, they would be more inclined to continue paying for that progress. So designers introduced the element of closure into games. Instead of letting the machine run until it memory-glitched out or the score table flipped, programmers were now building a discrete, linear sequence of events that, once the player completed them (whether through skill or purchase), the game would end on its own volition. When you'd beat a game, the other people in the arcade would gather around the screen, briefly bonding over the achievement, before going back to their own tasks.

This was financially smart for arcade owners—no longer could a skilled player occupy a single machine for hours. With a finite narrative, the game could end through no fault of the player's—punishing them for being too skilled instead of not skilled enough. Of course, the punishment was sugarcoated—players who did invest the time and money to beat a game were still impressive, but maybe not as much as the marathon players of the past.

Games became less about skill and more about milking money as quickly as they could. Arcades became dominated by side-scrolling beat-em-ups like *Double Dragon* and *Final Fight,* games that were virtually impossible to finish with one quarter, even for the most skilled player. And yet, these games also boasted denser narratives, better graphics, and more reasons to continue playing. They also introduced a cooperative aspect—most of them could be played with at least one friend, the two of you united against the machine for as long as you could keep paying for it. This, again, played right into the pockets of the arcade owner—twice the earnings from one machine.

This shift happened concomitantly with my early adolescence—the perfect time to develop obsessions. Finishing video games became (one of) mine. The arcade was a brief respite from reality, where I could take control of a loosely rendered fantasy world for as long as my quarters held out.

**Bill W:** *My brother became fiercely competitive towards* Street Fighter 2. *For him, it was all one-player—he had no interest in beating other people. If somebody else put a quarter in,* *he'd silently decimate them, usually in under thirty seconds, and go back to what he was doing—trying to play with only one button, find codes or secrets, basically explore the machine to its limits.*

In 1990 I started playing *Street Fighter 2* with passion. This is the game that has been credited with leading the last major resurgence in arcade culture. There were always crowds around the machine, and getting your turn was an event. The arcade had become a performance arena, where you were facing another human at all times, and your every move was being analyzed and judged by your peers.

The creation of a fiercely competitive two-player mode with a range of choices for players to make brought a new aspect of depth to video games. No longer was it solely a man/machine fight—now, the machine acted as mediator between two competing players, and the winner was the person who communicated best with its controls. The interfacing with the deeper level of anticipating the machine was lost.

This changed the cooperative aspect of the last generation of games to a competitive one. You were on your own against the rest of the arcade. It wasn't uncommon for actual fistfights to break out over perceived lapses in *Street Fighter* etiquette, such as jostling or "scrubbing"— playing with acknowledged cheap tactics. A whole vocabulary grew up around these games. I was what was known as a turtle—somebody who played a primarily defensive game, holding back and waiting for my opponent to make a mistake that I could capitalize on. This didn't make me popular to spectators, who would usually cheer for my more aggressive opponents. But I won matches, slowly and surely.

I played as Guile, a blonde, vaguely militaristic prettyboy who combed his hair a lot. His moves were easy to accomplish compared to the arcane motions of Ken's Sho-Ryu-Ken dragon punch or Zangief's spinning pile driver. I would go to the arcade pretty much every day after school, spend my lunch money, last as long as I could, and go home.

This period was the dawn of hardcore arcade culture, as a generation raised on the marathon exploits of Billy Mitchell came to financial maturity. Arcades became more than a casual hangout—lives revolved around them, new games were discussed in hushed whispers and surrounded by straining semicircles of eager players. There was little discussion about anything but games, and friendships didn't go farther than the change machine. The focus was never on your fellow man, but on the games. The arcade was a place that repulsed your parents, an alien culture so far removed from the days of *Pac-Man* and *Pong* that it might as well be another planet.

Things got very macho at that point. The early games, nonviolent and easy to learn, were fairly gender-neutral, but as controls became more complex and games became more difficult, women gamers tended to filter out of arcades. Most of the female characters in games of this period were huge-breasted fighting vixens, dispensing panty shots and cleavage poses with every quarter spent. So the rarefied air of the video arcade became even more of an arrested-adolescent boy's club.

I started getting out of serious arcade play in my late teens. I began to notice that younger kids had faster reflexes and were more attuned to the rhythms of the games than I was. I was starting to lose my touch, and my infrequent trips to the arcade were usually ended by royal beatdowns laid upon my old-man ass. My old techniques weren't working anymore—the games had evolved so that more aggressive, flashy play was rewarded, and games ended quicker and more decisively, usually not in my favor.

After the wave of fighting games crashed in a slurry of shoddy knock-offs and repetitive sequels, the arcade became more and more marginalized. The macho atmosphere and increased complexity frightened off everybody but the most hardcore, and the rapid evolution of home consoles made arcade games continually less impressive. Inflation also contributed to the decline of the arcades—a quarter a game didn't cover rent, electricity and machine costs, so game prices increased. A handful of change wouldn't get you nearly as far with games more difficult and carrying a higher price tag. So the arcade crowd grew more and more rarified, composed more and more of people solely devoted to the games. What started with a tiny storefront in Ithaca, NY crawled to an ignoble end in the late 1990s. Less than 1% of the number of arcades that were open during the golden age of arcade gaming were open in 2002, and more were closing by the week.[1]

And, of course, one Saturday, Andron and I beat *Double Dragon*. I had twenty dollars in birthday money from my grandparents and threw the whole thing in the change machine.

---

[1] From an interview with Walter Day of Twin Galaxies in *1-UP Zine*, issue no. 2, 2003.

We threw silver down the coin slots of our nemesis for a solid hour that day, bulling through challenges not with skill but with lunkheaded determination. And then, we did it. *Double Dragon's* a short game—four stages, the last of which is impossibly brief and impossibly difficult. The final enemy conquered—some crime boss with a machine gun—we looked at each other in astonishment. We'd done it, finally. The ending animation played—our characters reunited with their stolen girlfriends, impenetrable Japanese programmer credits scrolling by. And yet—no elation. No triumph. Just a weird emptiness. And then, a few leftover quarters rattling in our pockets, we stepped outside. I never played that game again.

# DANIEL NESTER
## Are You Hot Enough to Play With Journey? Todd Rogers Is.

It was the morning of Tuesday, July 15, 2003, and Todd Rogers was passed out.

His 265-pound body was splayed across his bedroom floor, his right hand still wrapped around a joystick.

The Florida sun peaked in the window of his bedroom, where Rogers' face still bathed in the light of the flickering TV screen. The score stopped at $105,779,605.

No one in the small rural town of Brooksville, fifty miles north of Tampa, in the shadow of the Space Shuttle's flight path, could have known that history had been made.

The forty-year-old Rogers had been playing Data Age's *Journey Escape* video game for eighty-five hours and forty-six minutes on his original 1977, six-switch Atari 2600 console. By the time his fourteen-year-old son Chad woke him up, he had set an unofficial world record for playing one game nonstop.

News spread fast of Rogers' achievement throughout the world of gamers. On the message boards of the Twin Galaxies website (<www.twingalaxies.com>), described as the "world-wide authority on player rankings, gaming statistics, and championship statistics," reactions ranged from praise to pessimism. Ron Corcoran, a championship gamer and a member of the Twin Galaxies Board of Directors, pointed out that Rogers' marathon on *Journey Escape* was proof that "an Atari 2600 title ACTUALLY has the provision to track scores past the 100M mark, though not via 9 digits, but instead by the 10's and 1's digits."

He also proclaimed Rogers' feat was "the longest a human being has played a game on the same credit in TG recorded history," as well as the "highest ever recorded score on an Atari 2600 title, ever."

A poster identified as Wntermute was skeptical:

> How is this possible? 85+ hours? According to an instructor of mine at HTI [High-Tech Institute of Phoenix], sleep deprivation-induced psychosis occurs at around 40-60 hours. I realize I myself have entered a state of extreme concentration while gaming that I call "the zone"...but I've never been in "the zone" for longer than 20-some hours.

Wntermute's signature read, "Former TG World Record Holder, *Mines of Minos* for Atari 2600." The official world record holder at the time of his posting, with a score of 9,150, was Todd Rogers. (Ron Corcoran is the current record-score holder, with 11,450.)

Others said it was not an "official" Twin Galaxies-sponsored event. Rogers had not notified officials before starting his marathon match, one poster wrote, and had not abided by "100% verification marathon rules" with referees present for at least part of the time, as well as blood tests for performance-enhancing drugs.

Corcoran defended Rogers, saying that he did in fact clear the attempt, and that since he had not received the "fourteen or so" videotapes, he could not comment yet on verifying the score. He also pointed out that he "was able to survive and function, with a high degree of proficiency," for seven months of U.S. Army training, on "only four hours of sleep and one meal per day." "While I do not recommend this," Corcoran said, "it is possible and doable."

Rogers' response was more direct. "Anyone willing to put up $10,000," he wrote, "and I will replay the entire game to the same point and duration at a moment's notice in front of you at a place of your determination (within reason)."

No one was disputing that Rogers was a great video game player. The holder of more than

2,000 of the approximately 75,000 official high scores on the various gaming platforms, including the long-standing high score for the arcade game *Gorf* (653,990), *Space Invaders* (Atari 2600; 475,800), and *Donkey Kong* (Nintendo; 863,500), Todd Rogers was not unfamiliar to the gaming community. The thread that announced the *Journey Escape* marathon read: "Todd Rogers does it yet again."

Another poster, bigfatleo, offered a vehement defense of Rogers and the record's legitimacy:

> I will tell all of you non belivers this, I have known Todd for over 25 years. I have seen him play for over 2 strait days, closer to three before ending. If he is posting any high score it is because he did it without any help from anyone. He never let no one play on his game when he was into it. It was like either wait a day or two or go and get your own system and play. I will also tell you this is your put your money where your non beliving mouths are i will up the bet even more. Now i heard of this from Todd himself this afternoon, and the only reason you all are talking like this is because you can't beat him!!!!!!!!!!!!!!!!!!!! HOW MANY HIGH SCORES DO ALL OF YOU LOSERS HAVE? I AM SURE IT IS NO WHERE CLOSE TO TODD. TODD IS THE MAN YOU ALL WISH YOU COULD BE!!!!! SO WHEN ANY OF YOU WANT TO BACK THE BET LET ME KNOW I WILL BE THERE

I found out about Todd Rogers while doing research for an essay on the *Journey Escape* video game. It's a subject I had been attracted to for years because it encapsulated a time when a band like Journey could have a video game as part of its merchandise. Most of my friends don't even remember Journey had a video game, let alone played it. I always thought this was a case of selective memory, the reluctance to admit that Journey, far from being a power-ballad punch line, was in fact once the biggest rock band in the country.

While deep-Googling the phrase "*Journey Escape* video game," I found a post from Rogers on Twin Galaxies, in which he said he had played *Journey Escape* for fifty-four hours (score 59,050,059). I sent an email to him, asking why he did it, did he like Journey, and what's his secret to playing the game. He responded immediately and sent me his phone number.

In my first conversation with him on the phone, I was at my desk at my day job at an advertising firm, and was trying to arrange a time for an interview. The first thing he pointed out was that he had since shattered his own previous record on *Journey Escape* by thirty-plus hours.

We talked for a full hour. He changed the subject to other matters, such as how boring living in Florida was ("Flor-i-*duh*"), how he had movie ambitions, and whether I could introduce him to shock rocker Marilyn Manson.

"You live there in New York, you must have some connections," he said, speaking in the thick accent of a native Chicagoan.

"Ask me anything you want," he said, "I don't have no inhibitions." We started talking about women. He prefers thin women— "I go for the Olive Oyl types."

"I got my first piece of hairy pussy when I was nineteen years old playing *Wizard of Wor,*" he said. "She came to my house to visit, and well, so much for that video game. We fucked 330 times in ten months."

Because I work in an open office, I couldn't think of an appropriate response to say out loud, and so began our long email interviews.

**You said you had sex 330 times in 10 months? Did you count all those times?**

Well I dont know if i can really say that i counted all those times but she just reminded me so often so how could you forget if you were the one fucking her. I'm good with numbers and i suck with names. I count cards in the casinos thats why i don't go often for the simple fact of being kicked out. It's just something I do [to] amuse myself and to catch people by suprise. I mean I know all three of your phone numbers already, Shit Dan i can tell you the numbers from the pass code from my friend Franks security alarm on his car back from 1986 do you want it?

I tried to stick to my subject of Journey and their video game, but over the course of several months we turned less and less to Journey and more and more to Rogers' story: his accomplishments, his other gaming records, his life, his personality. During those months, Rogers and I spoke on the phone and emailed several times.

**Did you know there was an arcade game called *Journey Escape* that was completly different?**

Yeah I never played it that much though.

**It was supposed to be the first game with a digital camera. It was supposed to a picture of the player's face and put it in the game. But people started taking pictures of their body parts, and so they just replaced them with digital photos of Journey members' faces.**

LOLLL! sounds like something I would do.

**Tell me about the first time you knew you were good at video games.**

Well the first time that I realized was when I was beating all my family members and then it progressed to the neighborhood kids. Then when Activision came out with their video games and with the chance of gaining notoriety for beating their gaming scores from their manuals. Shit I jumped on that like hotcakes and here we are some 25-plus years later.

The game he was talking about is *Dragster,* a drag-racing game that Rogers, at the age of sixteen, claimed as the first of his 2000-plus high scores. Activision had a computer-simulated perfect run time of 5:54, and encouraged players to submit their own times. So when Rogers sent along a Polaroid of himself with a time of 5:51, he caught the eye of the folks at the company.

"Activision thought this score was impossible," he said. "I told them how I engage the clutch until 0 and then pop the clutch, already in second gear. I max all four gears and let off the gas before the end, so I don't blow my engine." Rogers imitated the sound to me on the phone, mimicking the whirring sound of a popped clutch. It sounded exactly like an old video game.

**Have you ever hustled people for money on video games?**

HaHaHa I like the way you think. All I'm going to say is that there were a LOT of broke people out there back in the day that didn't know who I was when I played against them. Shit I would play a game, high score wins 20 dollars, it would be a game like *Pac-Man,* and kill off my extra men, just die miserably, and then use my last and only man to kick their asses, adding insult to injury especially if my opponent had his girlfriend with him. They'll think they're gonna win, and I'll just keep going and going. I like seeing someone suffer, grovel. I'm a sick bastard.

Those were the days. That and push-ups. I'll do five for every one somebody does.

**Do you trash-talk other players when you play?**

I have no reason to. I let my scores speak for themselves and that alone does the trash-talking to them mentally. I scored a 161 on the Wechsler's IQ test, so why would I degrade myself into making my competition not be their best? If you want to make a name for yourself don't do it on the weak. You are judged and perceived by other gamers by the talent of your best competitors.

**When you marathon a game, is there a training regimen involved? I mean, I imagine you don't eat Mexican food with plenty of jalapeño peppers the night before.**

Well, I'm an insomniac, so that helps. I actually hate Mexican food. It gives me the runs and besides I'd fart flames for a week with that shit. I like pizza and/or seafood, and I can eat anything with curry. Food with an acidic base sometimes give me heart burn. I don't do anything special. I drink liquid that's air temperature, and fruit. I don't feel like making mud in the middle of a game.

**Todd Rogers' top five high scores of all time?**

#1 Atari 2600 *Dragster* 5.51 for beating Activision's computerized perfect dragster run. I am the only person to do so, even after 24yrs since its conception.

#2 Atari 2600 *Journey Escape* for having the longest game play of all time at 86hrs.

#3 Arcade *Gorf* for setting a world record that still stands for over 22yrs.

#4 Atari 2600 *Decathlon* for beating Olympic star Bruce Jenner at the game the first time that I played it.

#5 Pinball Expo 1986 for being a part of the U.S. National Video Game Team and playing the designer of *Gold Wings,* John Trudeau, and having 88 million on my first ball.

To speak with Todd Rogers on the phone as I have is to embark on a roller-coaster ride of subjects and levels of candor. I learned that Rogers, a widower since 2001 from an unhappy marriage, lives with his parents as their caretaker; that he possesses psychic powers he is reluctant to use; that he speaks eight different languages (Greek, Japanese, French, Spanish, Russian, German, Swahili, Polish); that he modeled swimwear, leather briefs and suits for *International Male* and *Mello Male;* that he has accumulated or claimed titles over the years such as "The King of Video Games," "Mr. Activision," as well as the more informal "TODDzilla," and "The Howard Stern of Video Games"; that his wrestling record junior year at Argo High School in South

Rogers posing beside *Gorf,* for which he earned one of his top five high scores of all time (653,990).

Side of Chicago was 38-0, 155-lbs weight class; that in the early 1980s he bedded an up-and-coming porn star whose name he will not let me reveal, except to say that a "certain type of bread house in a children's book sounds like her first name"; that he was once able to bench press 460 pounds, using the unorthodox method of facing his knuckles away from his face; that he was an extra in the Goldie Hawn football vehicle *Wild Cats*; that he had worked as a repo man, bounty hunter, roofer and telemarketer, as well as doing radio voiceovers when he lived in Chicago; that he raises forty-five different species of tarantulas in his home and sells them to wholesalers, private collectors, and public zoos.

**Didn't you also bounce for metal bands?**

I use to bounce with Pantera. I was the HEAVY. If something got out of hand I took care of it in a TODDLY way. I also bounced for Quazimodo, Slauter Xstroyes.

**Did the people in the bands know about your other life as a champion gamer?**

You bet ya, but at that time I was intrigued by the music industry and the HOT chicks that encompassed all those bands that I worked for. But since I was usually the bad guy, the girls were intimidated by me. I mean I've been called EEEEEvil so what the difference between Evil and EEEEEvil? I don't know so I guess in the publics eye I'm Evil Times FIVE. I use to kick box and do martial art along with weight lifting.

So picture this a video gamer with 18 1/2 inch arms that bench presses 460 Lbs runs the mile in 4:08 my school record and still plays with an Atari and raises tarantulas. I bet your thinking that's an Odd combination and it was but that's who I am.

ARE YOU HOT ENOUGH TO PLAY WITH JOURNEY?

Introducing "JOURNEY ESCAPE," the challenging new DATA AGE. Video Game. You're on the road with America's hottest rock group, Journey. And they're counting on you. You're the only player who can help Journey make it to their scarab escape vehicle. Only you can outsmart the promoters, avoid the photographers and fight off the love-crazed groupies. If you can handle it!

It's a tough game. As Journey says, "Some will win, some will lose…"

Are you hot enough to play with Journey? Don't stop believin'. Get your JOURNEY ESCAPE video game today!

DATA AGE

*You're on the road with America's hottest rock group, Journey. And they're counting on you. You're the only player who can help Journey make it to their scarab escape vehicle. Only you can outsmart the promoters, avoid the photographers, and fight off the love-crazed groupies. If you can handle it!*

*It's a tough game. As Journey says, "Some will win, some will lose…"*

*Are you hot enough to play with Journey? Don't stop believin'. Get your JOUR-NEY ESCAPE video game today!*

— Music magazine ad, circa 1983

Journey is the first rock band to cross over to into the video game industry. In the wake of the success of its multiplatinum 1982 *Escape* album, Journey, along with Data Age Inc., released *Journey Escape,* a game for the Atari 2600 system. The object of the vertical, first-person perspective game involves leading all five band members from the concert stage after their gig to the "scarab escape vehicle," that flying saucer-like object familiar from the covers of many Journey albums.

Players must also protect $50,000 in concert cash as they run the gauntlet and avoid from "pesky characters and backstage obstacles," as Data Age's instructions call them: Love-Crazed Groupies (who appear on screen as hearts with legs), Shifty-Eyed Promoters (headless torsos), Sneaky Photographers, and stage barriers.

There are good guys, too: blue Loyal Roadies and the smiling Mighty Manager, also blue, "the only one who can keep you in the game," who grants immunity as well as another $9,900, according to the Data Age instructions. Journey's real-life manager, Herbie Herbert, played a big part in making the deal for the game, and so one can assume that particular role assignment involved his input.

"Basically, I think what's unique about *Escape,* the concept, is that it's nonviolent," Journey bassist Ross Valory said in an interview in *BAM* magazine in 1983. "There's no warfare involved, or monsters. It's not *Berserk* [sic]." (Todd Rogers is ranked #1 in the world for the 2600 version of *Berzerk,* with a score of 811,880.)

Journey keyboardist Jonathan Cain took special delight in the different sizes of the Love-Crazed Groupies. "[W]hen a fat one gets you and it's on you, it's like 'Aaaaaaeeeeeeeeee-eeeeaaaaa!'"

**You said you only peed once during that eighty-six-hour** *Journey Escape* **session. How did you do it?**

Do you want to know the color of my piss too? Kidding. Yes, I pissed once in a Burger King cup—it was during a invincible mode when you pick up the Smiley Guy.

*Journey Escape* is unique in ways other than being the first rock band-themed game. It is the only the Atari 2600 title that has a provision to go over the one-hundred million mark.

Counter systems on video games run the gamut. A game such as *Frostbite* rolls at a million points, meaning it goes back to zero, while another such as *Enduro* flips over to zero at 99,000 miles. This makes verification of high scores, to put it in Rogers' words, "a bitch and a half."

Whereas most 2600 games have a cap at one million with only six digits on the scoreboard, *Journey Escape* identifies the millions in the tens and single digits. It goes up to ninety-nine million and then, as Rogers says, "it starts doing some funky stuff." A score of $512, for instance, really means 12,000,512. A score of $99 is ninety-nine million. When you see a score that looks like this $467$ or $523ss would translate, respectively, as 101,004,670 and 102,005,230 with the initials of one of the band members (drummer Steve Smith) in the score.

In Rogers' case, his final score on the screen was 779,6$5, or 105,779,605.

"It looked really weird with the dollar sign there," he said.

In essence, Rogers played this game for almost ninety hours just to see what would happen when he reached one-hundred million. It's enough of a "because it's there" challenge as any to someone who has mastered 2,000 games. Up popped a dollar sign in the tens column, and, five million points later, he passed out.

I asked him what would happen if he hit 110 million or even a trillion. That question was the only one that was met with silence on the other end of the phone.

I bought an old 2600 system off of eBay, along with an assortment of games. I made sure it came with a copy of *Journey Escape,* of course; other games included were *Yar's Revenge* (Rogers' Twin Galaxies rank #1; high score 3,250,326; flips over at a million), *Space Invaders* (#1; 475,800; rolls over at 9,000), *Defender* (#2; 1,118,000; flips at a million), *Centipede* (#1; 1,110,655; flips at a million), *Venture* (#1; 913,200; was not flipped), and *Missile Command* (unofficial rank #1; 7,232,890; flips at a million).

When I turned on the game, a computerized version of Journey's song "Don't Stop Believin'," the lead-off cut from the *Escape* album, plays in the background.

But it wasn't long until the novelty of playing a Journey-themed game wore off. I was horrible. I couldn't even get past the first wave. I thought I would get a little better and report my progress to the man who had set the human record in gaming endurance, but I was ashamed.

"Push that joystick forward to speed up," he wrote to me. "Avoid everything. Except if it's blue—that will give you temporary invincibility. Hit 'em. With the smiley one, you know you'll be invincible."

By "smiley one," I asked him, do you mean the Roadies and Mighty Manager?

"That's what they're called?" he said. "I just called them the blue smiley guys."

**Is that it? That's the secret?**

There really is NO secret it's just game observation if you look at how the game is played anyone can marathon it. It's really up to the individual gamer and if he wants to spend a duration of his life making a gaming statement to see what the rewards are.

**Tell me about this "gaming statement." It seems like a big concern of yours is whether people are going to remember you. You also seem to be saying, "Fuck you, I know I did it, there's no way you can take away what I did."**

Well, Walter Day, he's the guru of keeping all the high scores. He's a man on a mission and has been actively tracking high scores since 1981. I'm sure he has more from before then BUT publicly since 1981. I have scores that pre-date 1981 and I'm sure he's well aware of that too. As for the "gaming statements" well i wouldn't put it in the terms "Fuck you i know i did it" More like "FUCK you watch the video tape of the game all 14 of them." Yeah some players can be REAL ANAL about the whole score tracking thing but then again most of the aggregators are non Twin Galaxies officials.

Walter Day, president of Twin Galaxies, has the informal title of "Patron Saint of the Video Game Age." It's not an unearned title.

Since February 1982, when he first traveled with a few other championship gamers in a van for what he describes as a "SWAT team score-checking tour" across the nation" to "verify, face-to-face," the claims of gamers' high scores, Day has been developing the rules for gamer high scores and setting up championships. To make sure that scores are official and legitimate in the world of video games is not an easy task. Day describes the gamers' "natural mindset" as hacking games and changing factory settings. "Then there's the collusion with arcade owners who are eager for publicity of having a high score at their location," he said.

Over the years, Twin Galaxies has established rules for games, enforced them, and verified submissions of high scores. When necessary, Day sends out a staff person to crown champions; the day we spoke, he had just sent out a TG staff person to Seattle, where a gamer was attempting a high score on a very "well-known game" that he could not reveal. "If this happens, this will be big," Day said. "The game company will make a big deal out of it. It's going to be worldwide."

"Todd is a winner, not a loser," he said at one point. "He's an unusual, very macho guy." Day tells the story of a recent trip driving across Florida with Rogers on the way for a television interview. "And all of the sudden, Todd pulls over in this place in Hollywood called Strictly Reptiles. And he was all excited—there were crickets swarming everywhere, death-dealing snakes. He wanted to get special food for his spiders." Day, who practices transcendental meditation, had what must have been one of the few moments in his life when he was truly rattled when he asked a store employee if any of the poisonous snakes escape their cages. "He said 'It happens all the time'."

Day's take on Rogers' *Journey Escape* marathon session is at once enthusiastic and standoffish. "I do know of this time you speak of, when Todd played the Journey game for a billion years," Day said. As far as making the score and the record time official, he was reluctant to talk about it. "You see, Todd didn't get blood-tested, so technically we're in a limbo area," he said. In successive editions of *Twin Galaxies' Official Video Game & Pinball Book of World Records,* Rogers' feat would be included as a "score that is verified, but not accepted."

"We'll mention it in the book, for sure," he said. He's "disappointed" it won't be accepted, Day said, "but we have to think of people ninety years from now, people who are alive when we are long since gone, who will demand these standards."

Whether Rogers took any performance-enhancing drugs, Day says, "He says he didn't and I believe him."

I asked Day about Rogers' offer to reenact the feat—provided someone puts up ten grand. Day didn't think that would happen.

"The thing is," Day said, "I think he didn't feel the same since then."

"Do you like the music of Journey?" Day asked before we got off the phone. Very much when I was young, I said. Not so much now.

"I do," Day said. "I like the way they mixed the guitars."

"I did it for personal reasons." Rogers sounds worked up a bit, and although he already knows the Day's take on the TG ruling, he admits he "gets rattled" every time he hears it.

In an earlier email, I had asked him about another verification rule: videotaping the video-taping. He started out diplomatically:

> With all the photo enhancement programs out there its quite easy to manipulate pictures and such so in one way im happy about the video taping and on the other hand when i am marathoning a game of a LONG duration the idea of me video taping my video tape recordings...FUCK that, Why don't i just play in person at a live event and get FUCKEN paid for it. But yet none of these little fuckers will step to the plate and want to pay for such a thing so they sit at home and bitch about it till some one tells them to shut the fuck up

"Day or anybody could actually take a strand of my hair and test me, even now, if he wants to know how the hell I could have done it," he said. Could this be useful even now, a year after playing the game? I ask.

"I have hair down to my ass," he said. "You could get eight years' worth of drug tests from my hair."

"Still," he said, "I don't give a fuck. I have 2000 other records."

"I mean, Walter is so conflict-free. He meditates, and on a professional level he's great. Me, I'm not that way. I say what I mean. If I walked into a psychiatric hospital and started talking, I'd have the shrink in a padded cell."

Rogers wasn't always this way. "I started swearing in 1985," he said. "That was the turning point. It was job at a print shop in Illinois. I worked eighty-hour weeks. Me and my brother worked there. It was 600 bucks a week, simple stuff."

"But we wouldn't get any respect—people just treated us like shit, and I had the realization: why should I be nice to people who don't respect me anyways?"

When I look at pictures of Rogers in the early 1980s, when he was a teenager just starting out as a video game champion, I see a much different person than the one I'm emailing and talking with on the phone. He's a much bigger guy now, sure, much stockier and with a thicker mustache. But there's something else, a much greater difference between the wunderkind in the old news clippings and the grown man today.

"I'm more bitter now," he said to me. "I'm more aggressive. My eyes are a little more wide open to things around me."

The career trajectory of Rogers couldn't be more opposite from that of another record-setting gamer, Billy Mitchell. Mitchell, at 6'4" with long dark hair and a close-trimmed beard, is the golden boy Fabio to Roger's black sheep Ozzy Osbourne. "Women and men alike throw themselves at Billy," Walter Day tells me. He is, to this day, the only championship gamer who is recognized on the street "If it happens six days out of seven," Day says, "then it's a slow week."

Mitchell claims the title of "Player of the Century." His most notable feats would be his being the first person to get a perfect score on *Pac-Man* on July 3, 1999 (3,333,360), along with six world records listed in the 1984-86 editions of the *Guinness Book of World Records*. His scores on *Centipede, Burgertime, Donkey Kong Junior,* and *Donkey Kong* still stand today.

The two championship gamers express mutual respect. "I gotta hand it to Todd," Mitchell says, "when it comes to the variety, no one has the mastery of outside coin-op games."

"There's no place where he and I intersect" with high scores, says Mitchell, who describes himself as a "hardcore coin-op guy." It's a good thing too, he said. "I have a hard enough time keeping my own." If it were the case, "that'd be cool—we'd have some things more to talk about."

The 1990s were dry times for professional gaming. Home game systems took over a chunk of the market, and focused less on high scores and more on one-on-one fighting and sports themes. During this time, Mitchell became president of Rickey's World Famous Sauce, a Hollywood, Florida-based hot sauce brand and restaurant. Mitchell occasionally runs promotions for the retro games, competitions to keep the classic games in the public eye.

"Todd is like a wild theme park—it's nice to visit but you wouldn't want to live there," Mitchell says. "He has so many wild stories it has to be true."

The 1990s were less kind to Todd Rogers, who took an eight-year hiatus from the world of gaming from 1993-2001, a period that almost perfectly overlaps with an unhappy relationship and marriage he is reluctant to discuss.

October 3, 1983

Mr. Todd Rogers
7910 W. 71st Street
Bridgeview, IL 60445

Dear Todd:

Compliments of Activision and Bruce Jenner, enclosed are two photos of you playing The Activision Decathlon with Bruce at our booth at the Chicago CES in June 1983.

Thank you for your support and past assistance, Todd and we hope you enjoy the photos.

Very truly yours,

Denise

Denise L. Steele
Marketing Communications

Enclosures

Activision, Inc. 2350 Bayshore Frontage Road  Mountain View, CA 94043  (415) 960-0410
Mailing Address: Drawer No. 7286  Mountain View, CA 94039

What details that I can cobble together: After his brother Scott drowned in 1990, the Rogers family moved two weeks later from the Bridgeview section on the South side of Chicago to Brooksville, FL. Rogers brought along his one-year-old son Chad from a previous relationship, and both lived with his parents.

In January of 1991, Todd was in a car wreck in which he was on the passenger side, and flat-lined in the hospital for twenty-eight seconds. "I saw no white lights or any shapes," he said, "so I guess my assumptions as a child might be correct—that after you die there's nothing."

Then Rogers met his future wife, whose name he'd rather me not mention, and from the beginning he could tell it was an abusive relationship. "Not from my end, mind you," he said. "I never went in for the wife-beating thing. I would just look at her, and I'd speak slower and slower."

"She was redneck hellion, and I was a city slicker, we had nothing in common," Rogers said later. "Except sex." When he and his wife got their own place, Rogers preferred that his son stay in the grandparents' house. "I didn't want him in the atmosphere with my wife," Rogers says, his voice trailing off.

Rogers in a picture from *Joystick* magazine, 1982. The hands in the upper left belong to his brother Scott, who died in 1990.

Rogers held a series of jobs, the last of which was for the Florida Department of Transportation, working as a traffic supervisor on the Suncoast Parkway from 1998–2000. After work, he would sneak to off to see Chad, reluctant to drive the twelve miles over to his own house, where he would be "walking in a minefield." His wife was on a variety (fifty-four, Rogers remembers) of psychotropic medications, among them Xanax, Paxil, Percocet, Atavan, lithium, and Klonopin.

By March 2000, less than ten months after they were married, they had separated. "A succession of fifteen different people lived in my house over a period of time," he remembers. "Strangers would be eating my pizzas when I ordered them."

Things came to an end when his wife overdosed on what turned out to be handfuls (forty-two pills, as Rogers remembers from the medical examiner's report) of Carisoprodol, a muscle relaxer. "When she took the first four or five pills, I left." They had argued, and Rogers went back to his parents' house, where he was living. "I don't think she wanted to die," he said. "She just wanted the pain to go away."

"The next morning," he said, "the coroner called. And I knew it was for her."

Rogers hadn't told his wife that he was a championship gamer until two weeks before she died. He handed her a printout of a profile just published about him on Twin Galaxies.

"I never found out if she read it or not."

"We're about to get stomped." Todd Rogers is looking out his window as we talk on the phone. Ever since he was three years old and saw a sky that turned green from tornadoes outside his house in Chicago, he's rushed to the windows whenever he hears a severe weather watch on his radio.

> When I was young being in a religious house hold I was saddened that one day I would die and have no place to go when I died. So my parents went out and bought me a plot and a place to be placed when I die as I didn't want to be separated from my family when I died so the thought of that eased my anguish as a child.

"I love weather," he said, thunder in the background. "We're in the lightning capital of the world here. We have tornadoes all year round here, too."

"If they were to strip me of all my records," he said, out of nowhere, "the *Dragster* one is the most important." He's thinking of his first record, the one that has lasted more than twenty years. I hear thunder again. It's almost too dramatic to be true.

"I could do it blind," he said. Thunderbolt. "I got a 5:71 using only my left hand. I got a 5:84 not even looking at the TV." His voice is rising, and there's lightning.

The sixteen-year-old Rogers was taken across the country by Activision's top brass to industry meetings, press junkets, and held up as a clean-cut ambassador of a video game champion. Free video games would come in the mail every day. "I'd make a grand a day just playing video games," he recalls.

Activision sent him an official certificate recording his high score, and a video game star was born. Rogers has played against everyone from Andre the Giant and Sting to Michael Jordan and Mike Tyson, not to mention countless game programmers.

"I've never lost to a celebrity, not even close," he said. "Bruce Jenner showed me how to play his own game, and I still smoked his ass."

One day in 2000, Rogers discovered the Twin Galaxies website. Although he was still gaming at the local arcade several miles from his house, he was, for all intents and purposes, retired. He contacted Walter Day, who knew of his long-standing *Gorf* record, but not any of the others.

Rogers playing *Decathlon* against Bruce Jenner at the Consumer Electronics Show, 1984.

Rogers had noticed a lot of the high scores posted were ones that he had beaten more than twenty years before, and set to the task of submitting old videotapes, photographs, articles, anything that would document and back up his old scores. He also partially reconstructed his old records, replaying games twenty years after they first appeared to make his scores stick. Atari 2600 games such as *Barnstorming* and *Decathlon*. "I've probably added 1000 high scores between 2000 and now," he said. "There are a lot of Commodore 64 high scores that took awhile to be verified. He's also been setting records here and there for the current game systems like Dreamcast (*Crazy Taxi*) and PlayStation (*Skygunner*, PS2).

The return of Todd Rogers to the world of championship gaming is an event not unlike Bobby Fischer arriving at a state chess tournament or J.D. Salinger resurfacing at a creative writing program. People were simply overwhelmed by the submissions of Rogers' scores.

"People just couldn't believe the scores I was submitting," he said. "Most just thought I was either cheating or full of shit."

One person who didn't think Rogers was full of shit is Robert Mruczek (*mroo-sack*), a Twin Galaxies referee and championship gamer. In the case of the *Journey Escape* marathon, Mruczek could tell from the start Rogers was the real thing.

"I've done the marathon thing before," Mruczek said. His most notable marathon high score is *Star Wars* (49.5 hours, intentionally killed game at 300 million; TG rank #1). He's also marathonned *Journey Escape* ($2,054,302; rank #2).

When Rogers marathonned *Journey Escape* in 2003, breaking Mruczek's record, his rival was convinced Rogers was legit.

"I didn't watch the tapes," he said," I didn't have to. When I score and saw the last two digits, I could tell," Mruczek said. "If it was something like two zeroes or something" he would have been suspicious.

"Todd isn't a gamer who brags and boasts about his games. He doesn't go around saying 'I'm the best,' people who like to be in the running but don't have scores to back them up."

By 2002, Walter Day and Twin Galaxies were speaking with Rogers on a regular basis, and soon he came on board as a TG referee himself. "I like being part of the mix again, although I don't like that I can't compete" in the TG-sponsored events.

**Have you ever witnessed anyone beat one of your records? Were you in the crowd or were refereeing when this happened? Did you send flowers, congratulate them?**

That's a good one. I don't know. Always encourage your fellow competitor. I have 2,040 high scores or so out of 75,000 registered ones. Ron Corcoran beat my score on *Ms. Pac-Man* on the Atari 2600, and I said let him have it, I have 2,000 more. I can't have all of them.

But as for someone beating one of my scores in front of me? Naaaah I don't remember such an occasion. Flowers are for pussies—give them more like a kick in the ass. Your fellow gamers know when they are good and also know when you are on your toes.

**What's relationship with other gamers? You said you were like the "Howard Stern of Gamers"?**

I try to be encouraging toward gamers and their achievements but sometimes you get some fucken jagoff out there who thinks that you are shit and they try to have a lynching of me and my scores because one they are jealous and two they don't know how these scores were made. My logic is that because you don't see it done or cannot do it yourself doesn't mean its not possible stick around a while you might learn something. I bet you are thinking that I'm cocky, arrogant, stuck up who knows but the fact of the matter is the minute people see a sign of weakness you're done and it's the same on a video game the minute the game gets the best of you, you hear GAME OVER. Like the "LIL FLIP" song goes maybe that's why he made that song because he heard game over once too many while playing *Pac-Man*.

It's 9:06 A.M., and my phone rings at my desk at work and I forget to look at Caller ID.

"Yes, hello this is Sergeant Warchowski of the Police Department. We're calling about a bar fight you were in a coupla months ago, and we need to follow up on a few things." The voice is so booming that I get a shudder down my neck, even though I can tell by its accent and tenor that it's Todd Rogers again, crank calling me over an incident I told him about recently.

**You got a good voice. You must have been a good telemarketer.**

Yeah, I got tired of it after awhile. I'd put on this voice, like "Hello, this is Todd Rogers here to offer you a special deal," and the people would be saying it was a recording, and I'd say, "Well, I don't know, sir, does a recording talk back to you?" I also made up a list of 200 names in which i said i was that person a name like Oscar Memmelschmemmer or Yates Butternutt a fucked up name so that the people i was calling couldnt repeat to say "oh i got Yates so and so on the phone he's a tele marketer".

The day before I hand the story in, I fire up my 2600 one last time. I want to play *Journey Escape* while I'm talking to him on the phone. The game blurts out the opening theme before I can turn the sound down.

"Ah, that sounds familiar," he says. "The music that haunts my dreams."

Todd Rogers, the man who played this game for 86 hours and has a record score on it unlikely to ever be beaten, asks me if I'm getting any better. "You have a reputation to uphold now, you know."

I'm still losing, I say. I follow his advice as I play. "Push that joystick forward, and never stop."

# MARC NESBITT
## WHY CAN'T YOU CROUCH?

I started out as a tester. Eight to twelve hours a day spent trying to break whatever video game they gave me.

Real game companies, ones with money and whole departments devoted to testing, call it Quality Assurance. But I worked for a shitty little kid's publisher with all the corporate legitimacy of a highway rib shack, so I *was* the entire QA department in this place.

Me and three producers in a small room, each with his corner nest of consoles and controller wires, and I was supposed to split my time equally between the three of them.

Dale was a fifty-two year old redheaded kid with a face folding in on itself. He played late night saxophone gigs during the week in various jazz-fusion rockabilly bands and came in every morning pale and wrinkled, looking like he'd slept beneath a refrigerator that'd fallen on him. He produced a *Sesame Street* extreme sports game that wasn't fit for slow kids. By far the nicest guy, his game was the worst, so I avoided him whenever possible.

Roth was another fifty-year old, a Jew from the Bronx with a moss beard. He had a homemade screensaver of half-naked women he left up even when his ten-year-old daughter came to the office. First day I showed up at work he was looking at *Erotic4U.com,* downloading a video. Didn't even try to hide it as he turned and shook my hand. He supposedly produced all the GameBoy Advance games, but mostly he just IM'ed people, gathered hacked porn site passwords, and sold shit on eBay. He had two games you couldn't tell apart—both looked like tiny pieces of toast absorbing other digital squares.

Then there was Frith, the spastic who'd gotten me the job. He was in his late thirties, but mostly dated eighteen and nineteen-year-old bisexual pseudo goth punks he met online, then whined when things didn't work out. We'd done a lot of e together, but those days were behind both of us, and with no reason left to be friends we were stuck in the same office. He worked on a *Hello Kitty/Tetris* rip-off that was our best game without question.

I'd finish Roth's games in a half hour each at lunch, hand him a stack of notes he'd never read, then spend the rest of the day playing *Hello Kitty*.

You rotated falling shapes to build step formations she'd climb to reach some glowing, spinning reward of whatever was appropriate for that level. On the ice planet it was a multi-colored disco ball snow cone, for example. Badtz Maru was the bad penguin that chased her around the levels with ill intent and his accomplices, Hana Maru the happy seal and Pandaba the angry panda. Hana Maru couldn't harm you, but she made the best face when you dropped bricks on her head.

First I'd play through the game from start to finish. Then I'd play again and start breaking shit: repeatedly mash all the controller buttons at once; yank out the memory card while it was loading; take out the disc while playing; see what happened when I dropped a brick on the seal, grabbed the snow cone, and fell off a ledge all at the same time.

Everything had to be documented, but with no extra computers or plans to acquire one, I got a stack of legal pads, lead pencils, a sharpie and a stapler.

I filled the pads full of glyphs and stick figures describing every game crash, reboot, AI fail-ure, sound glitch, graphical corruption, camera freak out; every coordinate or landmark where a character fell through the map, got stuck between tree and wall, died stepping off a curb. Incorrect error messages, misreferenced controller buttons, false hot reset procedure. But when I started, I didn't know the terminology, so I wrote things like:

*Game broke on Level 10. A couple times.*
*The sound's all fucked up.*

*The menus don't make any sense.*

*She should be able to jump on the brown things. She's high enough.*

*Why can't you crouch?*

Coming in, the only job qualification had been skill with video games. That I had, and a talent for finding malfunctions. But I'd never tried to communicate anything about games to anyone without boring the blank into their face. Now my job consisted of people berating me with questions about everything I'd written:

*The game broke where?*

*What were you doing when it happened?*

*Did it hang?*

*Did it go to black screen?*

*Did it reboot?*

*Is it the sound effects or the music that's fucked up?*

*What brown things? Crates or bushes? Rocks? Where?*

*All of them or just some of them?*

*What would you wanna crouch for?*

I didn't have the vocabulary. Every malfunction had a name, in part to help eliminate vague rambling bug reports like mine. *Bug,* for example. Every video game fuck up is a bug. Any way it happens, they all get reported as bugs. A-C and various classifications beyond that whose names vary depending on who you're dealing with. But the industry standard is A bug: anything that crashes the game or otherwise inhibits you from completing the game; B bug: anything that negatively affects game play as designed or doesn't function properly, but stops short of hindering completion; C bug: any minor malfunction that doesn't adversely affect game play necessarily, yet does not behave according to the specifics of the code. And anything else is generally a D bug, a wish list of corrections the programmers and artists will never have time to change once they're finished fixing the A-Cs.

Once I learned the terminology the job quickly turned into making lists of phrases like *invisible poly, HUD, GUI, V Blank, auto-targeting priority, collision system, polygonal seaming, draw distance, anti-aliasing, volumetric fog, mip-mapping, dynamic lighting.*

Unless I was urinating, I wore headphones. Huge, inelegant, top-of-the-line studio things with ear cushions the size of donuts. Digital sound effects channeled directly to the brain. Taking them off made a sweaty, audible suck.

I'd go out for drinks after work, walk around the city and hear *pong!*s and *kleem!*s underneath everything. Every dive bar had video strip poker or big buck deer hunting or *Golden Tee. Dong! Fleep! Boodleoo!* I was surrounded by sound effects. I started making strange involuntary noises in my free time. More than once I left a bar because I couldn't take it anymore. I'd go home, sit in my quiet apartment with the lights out, eventually turn on my PS2 twenty minutes later.

Any job that doesn't instantly suck the second you punch in on day one tends to follow the same general pattern: uneasy early days, trying to figure out the habits of the tribe; establishment of routine and acquisition of friend(s); salad days and general gratefulness for employment; then, slowly, the ever-increasing awareness of the conveyer-belt of monotony that is your life; the acceptance that these people were never your friends; disillusionment, followed finally by hatred.

Video games are no different. I'd worked for the state highway association of Maryland, weed-whacking rest stops and covering septic explosions with fifty-pound lime sacks in hundred-degree heat. I worked in a tire warehouse and inhaled enough rubber to shit a hose the length of I-95. I'd ladled vomit out of urinals, scraped a deer off the highway with a shovel, and picked soda cans out of trash bags full of bees. So though testing was nowhere near the worst job I ever held, between the people I worked with and the mind-numbing repetition of days, things became unbearable.

It didn't help that around the same time, my girlfriend and I began to secretly hate each other. She grew cold. I drank a lot. I started coming in to work looking like Dale. I'd show up at work hungover and stoned with a hat pulled low and just make Hello Kitty run in circles for eight hours. I stopped caring about pretty much everything. I turned in bug reports that looked like:

*Level 1: Hole in the map, front of the mailbox.*

*Selecting Options from Title Screen = crash.*

*Selma the goat's head is corrupted when she runs around. Standing still she's okay.*

*Missing texture: Right before you get the flame flower, third section of pyramid from the left.*

*When are we getting a debug build with coordinates?*

*The music skips. Every level, everywhere.*

*My score hasn't changed for an hour.*

*Why does this game suck?*

*"I liked falling off the ledges so much I tried to return the game twice!"—adoring fan.*

*This voice acting is beyond redemption. I know the speech is placeholder, but this is fucking ridiculous. Can we get a build with the speech turned off? And did they even play this thing before they sent it? Maybe try to finish a level? Maybe take the time to realize you CAN'T actually finish most of the levels because the goddamn sparkle balloons keep drifting too high for the little bitch to jump and you can't get through the gate without a balloon and here's a bug for you: playing this game fucking hurts. It physically hurts. I give up.*

Before I got fired, I managed to get a job at a different games company as a producer, which was a slight pay cut with a better title for a legitimate company that wasn't worried about making payroll every month. Never has a misspent youth better served me than in that interview. That and my detailed description of an ultraviolent dodge ball game where you blow off limbs got me a call back within the week.

Now any time I tell someone what I do for a living they inevitably say something that equates to, "That's so awesome!" And it is so awesome sometimes, but when you do something every single day you get sick of it, whether it's wine tasting or bashing in cow skulls with a sledgehammer. Though if I could combine my job with those two I'd probably have higher job satisfaction, if the cows were already dead. The point is, working in video games is not the sublimely perfect job you might think it to be, except when it is, which happens often enough nowadays I can keep myself from strangling certain coworkers.

# JIM MUNROE
## PLEASURE CIRCUIT OVERLOAD

I do a video game column for *eye* (a Toronto alt-weekly) called *Pleasure Circuit*. It's a great gig—I have fun playing the games and I get to start discussions about them, and I feel that starting discussions about video games is actually quite important. Not just because it's a burgeoning art form, and benefits from the prod and poke of passionate criticism, but because I believe we're going to be spending a lot of time in virtual worlds in the future. More than any intentional academic or cybervisionary world-modeling, the expansive, detailed and increasingly compelling video game environments are more likely to be where we become accustomed to—and maybe eventually prefer—a nonphysical mode of living.

That said, I don't tend to be that abstract in my column. I talk about imagining punching people out, forgetting things, dancing—the personal stuff that informs how I enjoy particular video games. By speaking honestly about its diverse emotional impacts, creators and consumers alike are better able to cope with the power of this new medium.

## PUNCHY PIXELS

My grandfather was a boxer. Came here from Scotland barely out of his teens as Philip Heron, but his manager figured "Red Munroe" would look better on the fight bill, so he changed it. Either his new name or his right hook worked well, I guess, because he ended up as middleweight champion of Canada back in the '30s. He married a Finnish gal named Esther, and the two of them grew old together, with small framed soft-focus photos reminding them of their glamorous youth.

By the time I knew Grandpa, he was rarely far from his pipe and easy chair. He would, on prompting, show us the tiny golden gloves he'd won, made tinier by his huge battered hands. He'd gently unfold his yellowed newspaper clipping that he kept in the trophy that sat on top of the china cabinet, point at his picture with his pipe.

All of which goes to explain why I was drawn across the arcade as if by strings when I noticed the gloves hanging from *MoCap Boxing* (Konami, 2001). It's an arcade game that uses motion capture (hence the name) to track your gloves and body movements as you fight various digital opponents. You hold the gloves and deliver uppercuts, hooks and jabs, taking care to sidestep or duck away from incoming punches. As I started the game, I thought I could smell pipe smoke in the air.

The left glove on the first machine wasn't responding, so I changed machines after my first game. This machine was working fine and I was able to get to the third round, finishing off one opponent with a twenty-jab combo. I was breathing hard by this point, and noticed that there was a little calorie counter in the corner.

I couldn't quite believe this, so later I checked out the Konami site: "If, like us, you're used to taking your exercise in front of a PlayStation with a bucket of chicken wings, then you'll soon find yourself panting in front of the machine, sweating cobs, and shaking like a jelly.... [T]he game developers have also included a calorie counter which ticks along satisfyingly the longer you stay on your feet."

No, no, no. Wrong. Boxing is not about calorie counting. It is about hitting people in the face until they fall down. Its machismo is about its only appeal, and this is severely compromised by the idea of being concerned about your weight except which division it places you in. Bad idea.

The interface, however, is a great idea. A lot of arcade games with innovative interfaces—guns, driving wheels, snowboards—are dismissed as gimmicky, but in my experience it makes the game more immersive. This is where arcade games have a real edge over the home PC/consoles—designers can custom build the interface to suit the gameplay instead of having to rely on controllers or the keyboard/mouse combo. If I'm going to pay a dollar to play

I don't want to make a guy run by slapping two buttons—I want a goddamn treadmill under my feet.

Konami also put out the arcade game *Police 24/7* (Konami, 2000) which allowed the player to, uh, duck under very slow bullets fired by yakuza—a much poorer use of the motion capture technology. Much more interesting is their *Dance Dance Revolution* (Konami, 1998), which has players tapping panels with their feet as they dance to the beat. These *DDR* set-ups are as ubiquitous as those photo-sticker booths in Asian parts of the city and are as popular with the ladies as with the fellas. Dancing in tandem, side by side in a dark, smoky room—beats the hell out wiggling a joystick. (Sorry.)

Although it's not as good as *Dance Dance Revolution* for getting dates, I enjoyed my time with *MoCap Boxing*. It was about as close to the real thing as I ever want to get. When I was a boy I asked my grandfather to teach me how to fight, but he wouldn't do anything beyond let me throw punches as his listless white palms. When I was a skinheaded teenager roaming the streets I wondered if I inherited his fighting ability, some kind of punchy gene. Even in my twenties a punching bag had a certain appeal. But now that my grandfather's dead, I wonder how useful the skill of knocking people unconscious is; it's dramatic, sure, but doesn't really apply to our lives except in extraordinary action-movie circumstances. The last person my grandpa punched out in an incident on a farm quite justly had him charged. In his sixties he still hadn't learned a better way to resolve a conflict.

I'm happy that my interest in boxing never moved beyond a fantasy. I feel the same way about fighting in a war or driving—although they're often presented to us as being without consequences, the only time they actually are is when they're part of a video game.

I only ever wanted to throw a few punches, bob and sway a bit, and get a little taste of what it was like—I wasn't willing to lose teeth or even hurt someone else for the privilege.

## When Beauty Bleeds

Two ravers are discussing how ridiculous it is that video games are blamed for inciting killing sprees. "Yeah," one says to the other. "We grew up playing *Pac-Man,* and it's not like we're running around in the dark, popping pills, and listening to repetitive electronic music."

This internet joke is funny on one level, but vaguely unsettling on another. Have we been affected by video games in ways we're not even aware of? Obviously our culture has been affected by video games, but do games have a lasting subliminal impact on an individual's intellectual and emotional self?

Of course they do.

In a post on <www.gamegirladvance.com>, "Play=Life in GTA3", the author describes how much playing *Grand Theft Auto 3* (Rockstar Games, 2001) has affected the risks she takes while driving. The scores of "me too!" comments after the article is testament to how common the feeling is.

I was walking down the street and I noticed a store selling silver jewelry. It occurred to me that I needed silver, but I couldn't remember for what. Ah yes, to close the interdimensional rift. I had been playing *Evil Dead: A Fistful of Boomstick* (THQ, 2003), and I'd learned that I needed to find silver to close the vortices to stop the hordes of zombies. If it had been a magic crystal, I probably wouldn't have put it in the same memory slot—but as it was, "silver" was beside bus tickets, bread, and orange juice in my mental shopping list.

Horrified yet?

A lot of gamers downplay the moments when their virtual worlds bleed into their mundane reality. They realize it makes them sound Columbine. And even if they love games, they're often a little freaked out by their own brain processes. That's a shame, because if they looked at it closely they'd realize that there're lots of things that are just as affecting.

When people talk about how affecting a movie is, they mean it as a compliment. "It changed the way I look at baseball," says a sap leaving *Field of Dreams. Fight Club* was very good to boxing gyms. For a long time, I had the opinion that if a movie affected me it was ipso facto a good movie. Then I saw *Bad Lieutenant.*

On my way home after the movie, which features Harvey Keitel as a truly seedy and degenerate police officer, I looked around at my fellow subway patrons through different eyes. Everyone seemed fallen, suspect, nauseating. Certainly the movie affected me powerfully for a while, and I'm not going to argue whether that made it better art—that's another discussion. I just know that I didn't like it.

I had a similar experience when I was playing *Hitman: Codename 47* (Eidos Interactive, 2000). You awake without memory, in a hospital of some sort. A disembodied voice trains you in the way of the knife and the gun, and dispatches you to assassinate a variety of targets.

As a tall bald westerner, you perhaps aren't the best choice to silently murder the heads of two rival triad gangs, but that's your mission. You strangle the limo driver with a garrote when he takes a piss in an alley and dress in his uniform to accomplish this. Your mission also states that you have to make it look like they killed each other—and that's only the beginning of the disembodied voice's Machiavellian plan. After a few levels of being his tool, I felt too greasy to go on.

While these "realistic" depictions of corrupt and venal killers are a justifiable reaction against the squeaky-clean action hero who always kills with moral backing, the question remains: how much grit can you stomach in your media diet? Continuing that metaphor, what appetite you have for a certain type of media is also reflective of you, not just of the media that's taking the heat.

But movies are passive and games are active, you say, there's a big difference.

We're used to the pitfalls of passive entertainment while interactivity still seems deadly and exotic. Everyone who isn't addicted to television craves movies, and so there's a consensus that staring at something for hours on end is normal.

I think this difference between active and passive entertainment is like the difference between talking and listening—just doing one all the time gives you a skewed view of the world. It's also important to note that the excitement around first-person shooters doesn't come from nowhere—it owes a lot to the fact that you get to "be" the action hero from movies, a medium that's nurtured the fascination with gunplay and power for so long that it goes nearly unnoticed nowadays.

The designer of *Pac-Man* (Midway, 1980), when he wasn't secretly plotting the invention of the rave subculture, had pretty lofty ambitions when it came to the future of video games. In the wake of its popularity, Toru Iwatani was asked what he wanted to do next. He said that he'd like to make a game that makes people cry. When a video game does affect mass culture in this subtle way, it will be a profound moment. One that will mirror the undocumented moment when, for the first time, sniffles are heard in the darkness of a movie theatre.

## MY WICKED MOVES, QUANTIFIED

I love to dance. This always seems to come as a surprise to people, me with my big gangly 6'3" frame and all, but I quickly qualify: oh, I'm not good at dancing—I just love to dance.

It all started at a grade-seven school mixer in 1985. Our classroom, once the lights were flicked and a disco ball was plugged in, was transformed. I was surrounded by the few friends I had at the time in a dark room, without even a beer to pose with as we leaned against the desks that had been moved against the side of the wall.

Chris Beharry, a Guyanese kid who'd introduced me to this music his American cousins were listening to the year before—"It's called rap music."—was bopping his head. And eventually, his legs and arms followed suit.

I have no idea why I thought I could do the same, not being a particularly confident kid, but I did. I remember the exhilaration—not from the freedom of the movement itself (that came later), but rather the fact that no one was laughing at me. Despite my rather shaky popularity, the moves I was busting were not singled out for ridicule. After a while I took a break, wandered over to the snack table and enjoyed a potato chip, calmly surveying my boogying classmates from the heights of my new social standing.

Since that triumphant moment, when I find myself in a club or a wedding or anywhere else where the normal rules are suspended in favor of dancing to cheesy breakbeat anthems or hip hop, I'm usually shaking what I got. Once, very drunk in a club in a cruise boat headed for Helsinki, I vowed to dance in every big city of the world—and I was only partially joking. So the idea of a video game named *Dance Dance Revolution* might seem ludicrous to some, but it doesn't seem overly fervent to me.

*DDR,* as it's known to its legions of fans, is a series of games from Konami that uses a foot-pad in the place of a joystick. On the screen are a cascade of arrows (up, down, right, left) that scroll to the top in quick succession. When they get to a specific spot, the player foots the corresponding arrow and is awarded points based on how accurate their timing was—a quantification of rhythm, if not grace. It's all done, of course, to a fabulous dance favorite booming out of the most sophisticated piece of electronics on the game unit: the speakers.

The series has been around since 1998, and I'd seen the game in action plenty of times in Asia itself and in the Asian malls around Toronto. A quick spin on the internet will introduce you to fan sites like <www.ddrfreak.com>, which document the *DDR* competitions held in North American cities. But on a recent trip to a friend's Georgian Bay cottage I happened upon a beachfront arcade—and was delighted to see that the revolution had spread as far as Tiny, Ontario.

It was time for me to stop denying myself. Slipping in a coin, I chose "It's Raining Men" and got to down to it. It took me a few seconds to figure out when I was supposed to foot the pad, so I got a "Miss!" and even a "Boo!" or two before I found my feet. But pretty soon I was nailing the arrows with the right rhythm, and even managed to do a right-left combo arrow—a leg-splitter—without missing a beat.

It was almost as fun to watch my friends dance. In between offering helpful hints, I chatted up the teenaged girls who were waiting their turn. "So what song do you like to play?" They mumbled something, and I said "Eh?" like the grandpa I was. "'Blow My Whistle,'" one of them repeated emotionlessly, staring ahead at the screen. They had on matching white jackets festooned with a logo I believe I've seen in Vice magazine.

When the two teenaged girls took the stage—which they could, since there were two footpads side by side—we shamelessly looked on. They indeed chose the song they said, except that its full name (wisely truncated) was "Blow My Whistle Bitch." Their synchronized dancing would have been more impressive except for the multitudes of "Miss!" and "Boos!" the screen gave them. We floated away, trying not to show the girls how disappointed we were in them, when another young lady took the stage.

She wasn't as pretty or as stylishly dressed as the other two, but you could tell by the way she whipped through the menus that she was a pro. When her song played she hit all the arrows and then some, and the arrows were flying a mite bit faster than they had been with us. Between levels she adjusted her hoodie and gave the audience a whatchulookinat? kind of glare. Then she went back to dancing, staring at the screen, her feet flying, and self-conscious not in the slightest.

Sure, the other girls had the money and the boys. But at the end of the day, who had the fuckin' high score?

## mario's pain

A man is having his first physiotherapy appointment. A woman comes in wearing a white doctor's coat. Their conversation begins on a clinical level, the doctor asking the man about how he sustained his injuries. The man explains that he works in the video game industry, and in fact has come from work. She assumes that he works as a laborer, because of his overalls, but he admits in the tone of a reluctant celebrity that he's Mario from the *Mario Bros.* games.

She isn't that impressed, doesn't seem to know the game, so he describes what he does in glamorous terms, and he shows her pictures: Mario in a racecar, Mario battling monsters, Mario playing sports—shots taken from the infinite supply of Mario spinoffs. She says that his body doesn't have repetitive stress injuries from driving racecars. "Being a game character isn't all fun and games," he says with a grin.

A few seconds later she sits down and fills out a report on him. The questions are about his work-related injuries, of which there are many. He complains (though good-naturedly at this point) about the long hours, having to be everywhere at once, running and jumping at the behest of the players. "Some people have one demanding boss, but I have millions," he says, laughing at his well-worn line.

Immune to his charm, she asks when he started having back trouble. He explained that it was soon after he made the transition into 3-D of *Super Mario 64* in contrast to the 2-D, side-scroller games he was used to. She asked him if he thought it was brought on by the extra demands of the new environment. He wasn't sure—there was a lot wrong at the time. To adjust to the extra dimension, he was on an antinausea drug, and it was a bad combination with the mushrooms he ate to grow big....

The doctor takes him to task for this, erasing something on the clipboard, saying that he was asked if he'd been using drugs and he'd said no. He explains that he has to take the mush-rooms as a part of his job, that they weren't those kind of drugs—but he had noticed that he's begun to crave them when he's off the job. They've always assured him that the variety they used weren't habit-forming, but frankly, he's worried about becoming a 'shroom junkie. He attributes his mushroom use to the job's constant pressure to keep up with the times, stay competitive: the good old days of *Donkey Kong,* where he could really focus on his job and save the princess without performance enhancers, are long past.

"Going 3-D really ruined it for me. First of all, it's like a fifty-percent increase from 2-D, which is a lot....Eeveryone was really happy for me, talking about how realistic it was, but...." He shakes his head. "It's like—I've heard about blind people who get their sight back. But they've spent their whole lives being blind! So they find all this extra stuff confusing, too much. Sometimes they end up going back to being blind."

His complaints become more bitter at this point. He confesses he's been missing jumps on purpose, on-the-job sabotage. The physiotherapist makes an adjustment to his straps and

makes a few other notes. Mario is in a bit of a depressed state, and describes having dreams of falling through fields of gold coins, becoming infinitely richer but never winning the game, never hitting the ground. Just that ching-ching! of the coins echoing in his ears, forever.

The doctor says that it sounds like he needs some time off. He shrugs off his depression, says that he gets put on pause once in a while, and a pause is as good as a rest. "As long as it's not in the middle of a jump!" he says with a bit of his old spark back. The doctor says that she meant a vacation.

"You know what happened the last time I went on vacation?" he says, his big eyebrows furrowing. "I come back and guess who's dressed in red? My brother. Luigi. The second banana, dressed in my overalls." His fists clench. "He jumps over to me like there's nothing wrong, this weird smile on his face. He suggests I dress in the green ones for a while. I punched him in the fucking mouth."

The physiotherapist raises her eyebrows at this.

"You don't understand," he says. "It was their way of showing that they owned me. That week I was away? No one knew the difference. I might be famous and everything but—it's not like I even get any credit. Even the kids. They get a high score? Whatta they put up there—Jack, Jill, Boogerman, I8U—but never MARIO. Just once, I'd like to look up on that board and see the guy who did all the work get some of the credit."

Illustration by Marc Ngui.

# LAUREL SNYDER
## VIRTUAL INTERLUDES

There I was, lying naked on my back, staring at the almost-pink-water-stained ceiling, waiting for it to be over. And there he was, doing what he was usually doing around 10:30, jostling and jousting and shrugging and panting, but mildly. Meekly, dully, and every night like clockwork.

It wasn't too much of a bother, not enough of a bother to complain or move out over, and certainly not enough of a bother to distract me from what I was really doing—which was playing *Tetris.*

My head was squashed against my damp pillow, muffled and buzzing slightly. I could hear the pulsing digital song through the pillow. This had never happened before, this particular brand of entertainment, this imaginary game. And at first I hadn't even realized it was happening, as the pieces began to fall—random geometric shapes descending from the sad ceiling in greytones.

At first I was confused. But once I figured it out, once I realized it wasn't a petit-mal seizure or an acid flashback, once I accepted the distraction my own mind was providing, I welcomed it.

I got excited, held my breath.

He kept on awkwardly, and the music kept on perfectly. Now the game moved a little faster, but my luck was bad. The pillars grew high, and full of gaps. Only the odd-shapes fell, the jagged ones, piling up on both sides of my brain. I was waiting, afraid he'd stop and the game would end. I was waiting, holding my breath, needing the right piece.

I was waiting for a long vertical shape, a thin rectangle to make everything okay. The music grew louder, faster, as one perfect square fell, too wide, and then another. Too square. It blocked so many gaps and time was running out. I was almost done and I wanted to cry. But suddenly, there it was!

My rectangle—my savior. I breathed. My slim shape slid, dropped into place. Then the music stopped, and so did Kevin, finished. He collapsed into me and I paused. I hit pause. We were both spent, though my game wasn't close to over, just saved. Waiting.

He rolled off and the next day I broke up with him. How could I not? But it wasn't all his fault, so I punished myself too. I stopped playing *Tetris*. Forever. I never finished my game, and it was a little agony, but I deserved it.

I'm not a gamer. In fact, I try to avoid games, because I'm highly competitive and I fear habit. When I get sucked into a game, I'm immediately hooked and the routine is absolute. I get passionately absorbed for a short stint. It's terrible.

Instead of perfecting my game slowly, developing a culture around the game, making game-friends, learning the inside jokes and the cheats, I tend to get hooked for short periods of time on something arbitrary, *Dead or Alive 3* or *Pitfall,* whatever my current boyfriend happens to have around. PS2, Xbox, or Atari— it doesn't much matter. Whatever I find— Nintendo or Commodore 64.

I'm no snob. How could I be?

I'm pathetic. I play alone when I play, to beat the machine. I refuse to play with anyone, and I don't much enjoy myself. I lie to people and pretend I've been sick, locked away with a bottle of Nyquil, because somehow that seems better than being locked away with a bowl of Ramen noodles and my sweet *Space Invaders*. It's a brief obsession, a dark journey, a secret.

I drink the same way, in fits and starts. I dry up. I get loaded. There's something I love about breaking up with an obsession. I write like that too, and it isn't dramatic or pensive or lovely or deep, it's awful. But there's something I despise even more about a long-lasting addiction, a lingering cold.

So finally I take a look at myself, sitting in a basement, hunched in the dark with a cramp in my hand and a crick in my neck. I examine the dirty pile of dishes beside me and I become disgusted with myself. I quit. Then about a year later I do it all over again.

Usually when things aren't going so well. Almost always when things are bad.


The worst was *MegaTouch*. I was working in a greasy diner in Iowa, finished with school and unwilling to move home or grow up. My relationship was over. I was living in a pit-of-a-room in a boardinghouse and things were bleak. I didn't have the money for health insurance or groceries. But a girl needs some kind of distraction, right? Even the greasiest diner-girl deserves a little thrill.

So every day after work, I'd count out my one-dollar bills, change them in for twenties, seal the cash in an envelope to keep myself from spending, and dump all of my coins into a paper cup. Then I'd wrap up a stolen tuna sandwich and head next door to Joe's, where I'd order a pint of PBR and pay for my drink with pennies. Because I had to save the quarters for *Boxxi*.

Oh *Boxxi*, my *Boxxi!* My *MegaTouch!*

It was so physical, so slick. It glowed in that dark bar. It was beautiful. I'd stroke the machine a little to begin with, while I waited for my beer. I'd run my greasy fingers along the screen, surfing through the other games, the porno games and the poker. I'd enjoy them briefly, knowing I'd never play any of them.

I just loved to watch my grimy fingers against the light.

It was so perfect. There was a wall of color, a randomized wall of colored squares, and I simply touched a colored box to make it vanish, taking with it any like boxes it touched. In the end, if I was careful, nothing was left, a pure black screen. If I was sloppy, and left behind stray boxes, boxes with no neighbors, then the lonely boxes lingered, sat patiently as my time ran out. They taunted.

Usually when that happened, I ordered another beer.

At the beginning of a session, my fingers would feel like lead, but after a handful of quarters and a few beers, my fingers held lightning.

There was a speed to it, an urgency. There was so much color and so much sense. And no matter how many of the high scores I held, no matter how good I got, there was no way to beat it, I could always get faster, fleeter, better. I was always one step behind the machine.

It would get so I didn't even see the shapes. It would get so the boxes lost their edges, turned into a swirl of color I could translate. There was the beer too, but that wasn't all of it. Everyone said I was good. Everyone said so. All of my new fat friends, my mid-afternoon drinking buddies at Joe's. They said I was the best.

I could stay like that for hours if the quarters held out, and the better I got at the game, the more free turns I'd win, so that by the end, a few dollars could last me into the evening. I'd play game after free game while the bartender stared, and suddenly it would be dark.

Eventually, I'd drag my tired drunk ass home, smelling of stale grill-grease, stale cigarettes and stale beer. But I'd be proud. I'd be a winner. A stale winner.

Then I woke up, on a Sunday morning after a shift that began at 5:30 A.M. and ended at noon. I woke up on my bar stool with a bloody mary in one hand and a cigarette in the other. I woke up and my hair was filthy and my shirt was stained and it was Sunday morning and I was spent.

I knew I needed to quit—not the drinking but the game. It was the game that brought me into this place, not the booze.

So I quit my job and I gathered my savings, which amounted to about three hundred dollars, and I moved away. I left my *MegaTouch,* my diner and my friends behind. I went to New York, where I moved on in the world, up in the world. I moved forward for a while.

# MAUREEN THORSON
## BACK-SEAT DRIVER: LUCE CITY

"Okay. You go past Ammo Nation on your left and take the second right afterwards."

"Just a sec. I wanna steal that chick's Infernus first."

I never played video games so much as watched them. I grew up in a vast, sprawling, arcade-free suburb and my first introduction to video games was when my friend Regan got Nintendo. She was pretty hardcore. She subscribed to all these tips-and-tricks magazines that contained letters to the editor where people complained that Megaman's outfit seemed to be one Pantone shade different in level three than level two. But for Regan, only one thing mattered: *Super Mario.* She spent all her time playing it, but only one person could play at a time. So I spent a lot of time watching it, my thumbs itching to master the classic plus-sign-and-button format of the Nintendo controller.

Soon after Regan sank into Nintendo-mania, I started taking babysitting jobs just so I could put the kids to bed and get my hands on their Nintendos. But my dreams of Nintendo glory turned out all for naught. I sucked. And not just because I hadn't played before. I could see that sucking was going to turn out to be a permanent condition. I realized, sadly, that the same quick-thinking hand-eye coordination one needed to play, say, softball or soccer was also needed to excel at video games. The virtual, pixilated enemies relieved you only of the need for muscles, not reflexes. Hand/eye coordination has never been my strong suit. And to this day, I have never gotten past level one of *Super Mario **One***.

So, the cycle of watching continued. I watched Regan play until she moved away to Tennessee and after that, I was in high school, and dating. High school dating consists largely of watching boys do things. You just sort of come along for the ride. If your boyfriend's a jock, you watch football or hockey, or, if your boyfriend's a Canadian jock, curling. My boyfriends were neither jocks nor Canadians. So I watched a lot of video games, lots of PlayStation, which had eclipsed Nintendo by that time, but I also finally made it to an arcade, where I watched a lot of *Mortal Kombat*. It was after I realized that I had spent five dates with a guy watching him play *Mortal Kombat,* and that I consequently knew nothing about the guy, but a lot about Sub-Zero, that I instituted a no-gamer dating policy.

My no-gamer policy held up pretty well. Fast forward through college (where I knew two guys who hooked their computers up to subwoofers, so that they could sit on them while playing *Quake,* and therefore literally quake), and I found myself in law school. I had relaxed my policy to the point where I had a boyfriend who beta-tested online RPGs, and occasionally relaxed in front of the PS2 with his copy of *Resident Evil*. But, he didn't play games when I was around, and video games had pretty much escaped my purview, despite the fact that I spent most of my time glued to a computer screen. I was too busy trying to understand the nuances of property law to play games. Or watch them.

And then came *Vice City.*

You probably already know this, but *Grand Theft Auto: Vice City* has no redeeming social value. It's evil. You play Tommy Versetti, a low level mob thug (the kind of guy who'd be listed in a Scorsese flick's credits as Goon #1). You come down to the thinly veiled 1980s Miami of Vice City to track down some drug money. With the help of a shady lawyer and some people who may or may not be double-crossing you, you work your way through the local gangs to become crime overlord of Vice City, eventually taking on your old mob bosses to solidify your position.

But *Vice City* isn't a linear game. So while you can do the missions that lead you to becoming a mafia kingpin, you can also just sort of ride around the city. In other people's cars. Rule One: if it moves, you can steal it—cars, motorcycles, city buses, fire engines, police cars, taxis, ice cream trucks. You can kill random people for the fun of it. You can go on "rampages"— miniature, carnage-filled missions tucked throughout the city. You can get a change of clothes at a store, buy a gun at Ammo Nation, bribe cops, buy real estate. You can take drugs. And yeah, you can pick up whores.

My boyfriend still hadn't figured out the part about the whores when I learned about it from the other research assistant in the legal clinic where I worked. I mentioned to him that my boyfriend was playing *Vice City* a lot, and his eyes lit up as though he were in the midst of a religious experience.

"You know about the whores, right?"

"The *what*?"

"The *whores*," my legal clinic friend said, as though talking to a five-year-old. "So, at night, look for scantily-clad women and pull up beside them. If one gets in your car, she's a whore. Drive to a back alley and park. You'll totally see the car start rocking. It gives you life points. But it costs money. But, you know what the best part is?"

"What?"

"If you shoot the whore and kill her, you get your money back."

It's just this sort of attention to detail that led *Vice City* to sell more than eight and a half million copies within four months of its launch.

"Okay, so how many packages do I have?"

"That's 35."

"What do I get at 40?"

"A flame-thrower."

"Cool. Anything else good?

"Um...at 90, you get a tank."

"Rock!"

Another element of *Vice City*, the element that brought me, as the girlfriend, out of my position as cheerleader and turned me into a valued member of the Tommy Versetti Team, is secret packages. A hundred packages are hidden throughout Vice City. For every ten you find, you get some prize. The prizes are increasingly better…find all hundred and you get an attack helicopter and $100,000. But the tank's my favorite: you can really see the destruction you're causing. Plus, you yourself are pretty close to unstoppable. You can just run over anything in your way, you have armor plating, so the police can't stop you, and even the troops from the Vice City Army Base are sort of at a loss when faced with your artillery cannon. Unless you manage to flip the tank over (which can be done), you can wander around the city at your ease, blowing things to smithereens. The tank rather reminded me of a happy time when I nullified the effects of my bad coordination by figuring out how to play *Wolfenstein* in god mode, resulting in many carefree hours of blasting away Nazis. Yeah, I know. There's no sport in that. But sometimes it isn't about sport. It's about blowing things up.

Armed with a printed cheat sheet, I sat on the couch, directing my boyfriend, a.k.a. Tommy Versetti, all over Vice City. Without such a cheat sheet, and a cheating companion, it would be totally impossible to find all the packages. They're hidden in alleys, on rooftops, inside airplane hangars—those packages are everywhere.

Rockstar Games, creators of *Vice City*, had done the impossible. They had turned a first-person shooter into an interminable buddy-buddy roadtrip. Driver. Navigator. "No. Your other left." And you could argue over which of Vice City's fine 80s-rock radio stations to listen to. Being a *Vice City* gun moll wasn't that different from regular passenger-side existence, except that instead of clicking my tongue over run-through red lights, I clicked it over run-over cops. "Was that really necessary?"

Eventually, though, the thrill of *Vice City* faded. The drugs had all been taken. The whores, procured and well, disposed of. The packages were found. My boyfriend started beta-testing some new online games, and life returned to normal.

Looking back on it, *Vice City* didn't really empower me all that much. I went from watching to giving helpful advice from the sidelines. I still wasn't there in the driver's seat. But neither was my boyfriend. He was in a leather La-Z-Boy, madly pushing buttons.

But the experience made us both happy. It let us work together to accomplish our virtual task. In the real world, we have totally separate jobs and lives. We even live three hundred miles apart. But hanging out in front of his TV on a weekend, we could bond over our race to get to the next package. In the midst of gun-slinging, sexist, foul-mouthed, violent chaos, we found the one thing *Vice City* wasn't supposed to offer—redeeming social value.

# THOMAS KELLY
## Stroke This

I never liked golf. When I was young it was a class thing. Nobody we knew played it except for the miniature kind, slapping little balls around windmills while we sipped beer down the Jersey shore. The real game was the province of rich men with beefeater faces and bad slacks and as foreign to us as cricket or bridge. The only association we had with those people was stealing their Cadillacs in the dead of night. We'd joy ride with force and élan, cracking all that Detroit steel off of trees and into light poles, flattening their shrubbery and picket fences and even occasionally plunging into the deep blue sea of some country clubber's backyard pool. What fun.

We knew golf was out there. On certain afternoons I might walk into the joint where my Uncle Artie was the bartender and resident degenerate gambler. Stranded in a downtime between Belmont and baseball, he'd be betting the rent money on golf. He'd flare his Lucky Strike and yell horrible things at Nordic men in Ban-Lon whose missed putts sank him deeper into debt. What pissed him off even more was the whole golf clap hush and aren't we nifty politeness of the gallery. Artie had seen some combat and worked as a topnotch butcher before the shakes made that trade untenable. He knew grace under pressure. "What?" he'd say,

"You telling me it's harder to whack that little thing off a tee than to hit a ninety-mile-an-hour fastball? My white ass it is." I agreed. How can you even call it a sport when you can't heckle the players?

Uncle Artie is long gone, dead from cancer of the jaw. It's just as well. It's not that he was adverse to change; he was the first guy in the neighborhood to switch from Old Spice to Hi Karate after all. I just don't think he'd appreciate the democratization of golf. In the last few years it is suddenly the sport of the everyman, taken up and spewed about by garage mechanics, cops, laundresses, and fry cooks, and it reportedly competes with NASCAR for the title of fastest growing sport in America. I have lots of friends who play it. One, a carpenter named Boston Bob, moved all the way to the Central Coast of California so he might play the game more often and at better courses, Pebble Beach, even. Like so many blue-collar duffers, he sings the game's praises with the zeal of a convert. One constant refrain from Boston Bob is the game's Zen-like properties.

I drive a cart for Bob once in a while when I go to see him, refusing to play but drinking cold bottles of beer while Bob relaxes. Sure, every outing seems to start always with verve and a bouncy step, a go-getter air. His optimism is catchy. He strives for excellence, perfection even. Soon though, balls go astray prompting the odd curse, grave mutterings, then grimaces that flare up into the mother-of-fucking gods, until he is snapping clubs over his knee, crazy eyed, throwing the broken halves like tomahawks down impossibly green fairways, the blue veins throbbing as his face turns the color of tropical sunsets. Golfers gape, alarmed. For some reason Boston Bob rarely gets through a round without chasing blood pressure pills with Maalox. Still he's back three, four times a week, relaxing.

There are lots of reasons I don't like golf. For one, I am too much like Boston Bob and can easily envision my own Rumpelstiltskin tantrums spoiling the day. Then there are the awful clothes, all the crap you have to buy to get started, and the fact that it is pretty much a game you have to drive a far way just to play. Then there is the obnoxious bonhomie and pervasive bullshitting and cheating that goes on. You ever get stuck at a bar next to six golfers fresh from their triumphs? Finally, it's just not rigorous enough for me. My Uncle Jimmy who survived hand-to-hand combat at ten below zero during the Battle of the Bulge sums it up nicely, claiming at seventy-eight that he is still too young for golf.

Video games never held much attraction for me either. Sure, I cut school and spent lots of hours making little ones out of big ones playing *Asteroids,* but after that I lost interest. They always seemed to be too much about doing nothing and if I was going to sit still that long it was going to be with a book in my hands. I had a roommate once who lost his job at a squid-packing plant and for months sat in front of the TV day and night gaining his revenge on this cruel world by smiting electronic goblins. Still, it wasn't until he started having long, hollering conversations on his disconnected phone that we convinced his family to come and take him and his Atari away.

So my recent addiction to video golf came as a shock. It started in the very same bar where Uncle Artie had plied his trade, drolly referred to by my mother as Cuckoo Flats. It's a bitty place, a small windowless room with maybe fifteen stools stuck in the backroom of a liquor store. I was waiting for my brother and bored to near weeping by the fellow next to me whose rants focused mainly on alimony and immigrants. I wandered over and slipped some dollars into the jukebox and played songs that I had liked in high school. I looked over at the bar, at the same faces my uncle had served back in the day, fatter and sadder now, as they gazed up through the smoke at a Jimmy Stewart western drowned out by Lynyrd Skynyrd. Across from the jukebox was a boxy video game called *Golden Tee.* Seeking only momentary distraction, I slipped a dollar in.

That dollar bought me three holes of video golf and about a year of obsession. It was simple enough. You chose a club and then used a three-inch diameter tracking ball to power your shot forward. Ignorance of the game was no barrier since the proper club was suggested by the machine. You just rolled that ball and hacked away until you got yourself up on the green and putted. After the first shot the screen prompted me to fill in my initials. TPK. I was now an official *Golden Tee* player. I parred the three holes and the game asked me for more money. I obliged. By the time my brother showed I was wrapping up on eighteen and had fallen to twenty strokes over par after a disastrous sixteenth hole where I found myself repeatedly putting off the green into the ocean. I'd show this fucking game. My brother soon realized the only way to interact with me that night was to put his own lifelong aversion aside and join me. By the time our Uncle Artie's successor closed the bar and pushed us out the door we were as hooked on that game as crackheads on the glass pipe.

The game was fun. It took some skill and strategy and had enough variations that you never got bored. Like all entertainment it started out as a bit of escapism. We played courses like Tropical Falls and Anchor Cove, Heartland Creek and Scorpions Bend, Blue Horizon, Swords Point, and Shadow Swamp. We developed our own style, mine more of a finesse game, using thumbs to drive, laying up when it was wise to do so, his more a John Daly game, beer-driven and brute. We learned tricks, how to curve that ball around a desert bluff or ricochet it off a redwood. We figured out the best clubs; the woods are for thumping and irons give you more lift, that backspin can be your best friend. There was wind to factor in, sand traps, ponds and tree line, roughs and deep rough. An electronic voice heckled you after a poor shot, the gallery cheered when you lofted that little ball with majestic grace onto a distant green. There was a greatest-shots club that provided instant replays, recognition for longest drive, or putt sank. It was good, clean fun.

But soon we went only to bars that had the game, preferably to ones where it was a novelty and we would not have to wait because if we did we would stand and twitch hitting whoever was playing with bad golf juju. It was a drinking game for sure, but at first we drank less when we played it because we did not like to stray too far from the game. Even virtual golfers don't trust the other guy as far as he can kick him. We got other friends hooked and would meet to play but never more than the foursome the game allowed. But then we drank more because we went out more just to play. That thing sucked dollars.

My sister-in-law took to calling it "that goddamned game." We laughed her off. She just didn't get it. We huddled grim-faced over the glow of that machine's light like ancient hunters over a kill. It became an antisocial experience. Competition grew in intensity until we stopped sharing tips. We shunned better players and pounced on new converts. The only thing that kept us from full-throated Boston Bob-like meltdowns were the closed spaces of the venues. For to scream like a deranged hyena in a bar was to risk banishment. Like all junkies our denial skills grew sharp. Hey we never play it alone, hey it's only a game, hey we still hate golf. But we did not back off. There was crazed talk about creating a diversion so we might roll the game out the door and stash it in my brother's basement.

Finally, it was a fever, and all fevers either beak or kill. Lucky for us, this one broke. One day I strolled into Cuckoo Flats anxious to play and there was a line to get on the game. I walked out and just stopped playing. I'm not sure why, but not long after so did my brother. We don't talk about it much any more and when we do it's just to look back on a little foolishness, like enjoying Foghat when you were younger. That's as close as I'll ever get to playing golf for real. And at least I did not have to wear plaid slacks to do it.

# SHANNON HOLMAN
## Delicious Absence

By day I'm a mild-mannered, reasonably well-integrated lesbian New York poet, but a couple of times a week, I become an American. I go over to my friend J's apartment, where we eat pizza with meats on it, drink full-sugar, full-caffeine beverages, and play video games until our eyes bleed. It's fun to shoot things, and when we make conversation, our eyes never leave the screen.

It's slightly creepy when grownups play kids' games, but less so for queers because our culture is profoundly adolescent anyway. Maybe because all that early repression stunted our emotional growth, being gay means never leaving high school behind. It's all about cliques, gossip, drama, and spending lots of time in the bathroom, a world where tastes in fashion and music dictate social groupings. I once got branded as a poser and booted from a lesbian chat room for failing to come up with the names of three "wimmin" musicians (I prefer Gershwin), and any bear can tell you that a stroll down 8th Avenue can be a long walk indeed if you don't fit the Chelsea-boy uniform. Being gay is a haven—an often dangerous haven, true—from the crushing banalities of the straight world, but video games offer an escape from gay life, a refreshing dip in the mainstream. A PlayStation is pehaps the only place in the world where two lesbians can spend an entire evening together and not process a single feeling.

I started sleeping with girls in 1984, the summer of Mary Lou Retton's Olympic thighs, but my first vid was back in 1982. Packing a roll of quarters, I'd be dropped off at the mall and head directly for the arcade, which was—except for the Cineplex, and sometimes not even there—the one place outside the home where I could be safe in the dark. I had a brief thing with *Ms. Pac-Man,* from whom I learned that the way to escape my pursuers was to consume everything. Having thus digested the rudiments of capitalism, I moved on to *Moon Patrol,* my gateway game.

*Moon Patrol* is a linear game: you move your cute pink dune buggy across the screen from left to right, "reading" the surface of the moon. (Each level is even broken into 26 sections, A–Z.) It's kind of a lightweight game: lots of jumping over craters, some shooting. The thing I liked best about it was the Continue button. When the game ended, you could just put another quarter in and pick right up where you left off, no backtracking, no recriminations, just a coin in the slot and you're good to go. Another plus was the fact that—perhaps because of the whole pink dune buggy thing—*Moon Patrol* wasn't a popular game with the pimply boys sublimating their aggression in my local arcade, which meant that nobody ever came up behind me to watch my progress or claim next game by placing their quarter on the plexiglass. I'd just continue and continue and continue. It was like a bar: I was allowed to just be there, for hours, minding my own moonscape for as long as my money lasted, with others, alone. Emerging cottonmouthed, blinking, dazed, with the peculiar brand of hangover known as video head, was a small price to pay for the privilege of renting such a manageable world.

When I was a young child, before Mary Lou, before *Moon Patrol,* the loveliest thing I knew was falling asleep—under the dining-room table, or on a bed of overcoats—while grownups had a party around me. I heard the collision of glasses and the shouting and laughter and it made me feel safe, not least because I didn't have to participate in any of it. I was there, but not there. I wonder if maybe I still play vids not because I'm an emotionally immature homosexual, but because I don't drink anymore. Now that my getaway isn't in a bottle, where else but vids can I go for that feeling, that delicious absence? Plus, I know how to do this thing with my joystick that makes Lara Croft's perfect conical tits fill the entire screen.

# AARON McCOLLOUGH
## Fake Football, Real Manly

My wife Suzanne and Matthew's wife Kelly agree. As nerdy as Matthew and I were when they first met us, they could never have predicted what we would become. Which means: they didn't know we liked sports or video games. Once, we were purely boho nerds or indie boys. Now, we are something else—something wearing real team paraphernalia and talking about imaginary rushing stats. We are threatening to turn into men.

But normal men come home from a hard day of breaking rocks with their fists, open a beer, and watch television. Matthew and I aren't normal men. We spend our days fretting over writing, students, and student writing. We are supposed to blow off steam by listening to Schubert and practicing Tai Chi. Instead, when we want to relax, we turn on *Madden NFL Football,* and all of the day's tiny agonies pass gently from us. This may be bad form.

The first thing we learn about relationships is not to try to change the ones we love. We all—Suzanne, Kelly, Matthew, and I—agree. You can't change the ones you love.

The first thing worth knowing about football video games is how much they *have* changed. The first truly great football video game has to be *Tecmo Bowl,* which came out for Nintendo in 1988. *Tecmo Bowl,* and its immediate successor *Tecmo Super Bowl,* inaugurated a new style of fake football competition. Previous to 1988, the closest thing to a football video game for me was a handheld LED game (a glorified calculator) called *Mattel Football.* The game had three basic buttons. The players were represented by a few red diodes. You could only play offense, but you had to play offense for both teams. The sounds were unsettling. Nonetheless, I played *Mattel Football* incessantly, using my imagination to fill in the game's gaps. I supplied my own color commentary, for example. On family road trips, the network bosses in the front seat often put the kibosh on the play-by-play announcing in the back.

Tecmo was light years ahead of *Mattel Football.* It wasn't portable, but it had players that looked vaguely like human beings (with actual NFL players' names), and it had defense. *Tecmo Super Bowl* added all the actual NFL teams and a full-season mode. It had a memory chip (rare for Nintendo) built into the cartridge, so you could return to your team day after day. These enhancements were the moveable type of fake football.

*John Madden NFL Football* is the most successful football video game of all time. They now call it a franchise. It is the number-one selling pro football franchise (I'm reading this off of the box). The word *franchise* (I'm not reading this off of the box) comes from Old French and originally meant freedom. Obviously, the timbre of the word has changed somewhat in its shift to the marketplace. Although the unveiling of another Starbucks in the college town where I live does offer a sixth location to obtain that company's products, I don't feel more free for the addition. That said, I have to admit that I *do* feel more free every fall when the new edition of *Madden* appears. What comes on that one silver disc is more than just a game. That disc offers TOTAL CONTROL, albeit fake control, of a world I have loved and dreamt of controlling for twenty-five years. So, this is about more than violence or winning. It's about those things, but it's also about inserting myself into the fairly complicated world of rosters, statistics, trades, scouting, drafting, salary management, uniform design, league expansions, and the like.

When *Madden NFL Football* first appeared in 1989, for the Apple II home computer, it had nothing on *Tecmo Super Bowl* except the "realism" of thirteen-on-thirteen play. *Tecmo* only had eleven players on each side of the ball. Many people still credit this initial difference between the two games as the signal difference that explains the distinctiveness and longevity of

Madden's game. When originally approached by the EA Sports people about endorsing a product, John Madden allegedly gave them a tentative yes, telling them to come back when they could make it "realistic." As the years have passed, Madden's game has put a premium on making the simulation faithful to the real game. Since I can't claim much empirical knowledge of the real game, I can't say I care much about the many tweaks and fine-tunings from year to year. Someone can always be found to endorse the enhancements in the game's fake physics, but fake physics do not a great game make. No matter how cool the graphics get, the game doesn't *look* like anything real to me.

Unlike his eponymous game, John Madden will not be changed. He does things his way. Madden was born in 1936. He was a real NFL coach. Madden now jokes that the kids who love his video games probably don't even know he was ever in the real game. Is it only a gratifying coincidence that Madden's game was the one with which EA Sports began its now famous koan/slogan: "if it's in the game, it's in the game"?

I remember Madden as he was in the game. He coached the Oakland Raiders at their scroungiest, scraggliest, and most severe heights. In the 1970s, before the Raiders' logo was a ganster-rap staple and before members of the Raider nation were brutalizing people in the stands, the team itself was busy perfecting the art of on-field thuggery. I respected this, but it also made me queasy. Madden was headman of this strange crew—from rednecks (Kenny "the Snake" Stabler) to roughnecks (Jack "the Assassin" Tatum). Madden was famous for his emotional coaching style. He seemed like a chubby, dipsomaniacal id on the sidelines. This perception was only intensified by the Miller beer ads he made, which featured him breaking shit with his head. Ironically, Madden is also afraid of flying. He covers 80,000 miles a year in a bus called "The Madden Cruiser." In a further irony, the Latin and Greek roots for our word fear, *fuga* and *phobos,* both mean flight. So, Madden's ceaseless peregrinating is a flight from flight. He lives in a van that embodies a fear of fear. Masculinity is complicated.

My father was born in 1941. He is five years younger than John Madden—a younger contemporary, you might say. I remember watching Madden when I was a kid. I also have a particular memory of watching my father scream until he cried at a small black and white television screen in Knoxville, Tennessee. This had nothing directly to do with Madden. The

Pittsburgh Steelers were losing to the St. Louis Cardinals. My dad was yelling and weeping. It wasn't scary. I have been a die-hard Steelers fan ever since.

In the late-seventies, my best friend Nate was an Oakland Raiders fan. He loved Madden. His dad did, too. Whenever I was at Nate's house, his dad would give me a hard time about the Steelers. Did I know why they only had an emblem on one side of their helmets? *Too cheap to put them on both sides.* And did I know what the team name meant? *They didn't win games, they stole them.* I remember this dialog, in its many instantiations, as my first real experience of impotent rage.

No doubt, one of the roots for all the hostility in this case was one play—one play that predated Nate's or my own fandom. The "immaculate reception" is the name given to a touchdown play involving Steelers' running back Franco Harris during a 1972 playoff game against the Raiders. The catch and the touchdown following it saved the game for the Steelers. It marked the end of a horrible era for the team and the beginning of their best years, but the play has been disputed since the moment it happened. I saw Madden talking about it a year or so ago on television, still claiming the ball bounced off Frenchy Fuqua, which should have ended the play as an incomplete pass. Madden's still pissed after thirty years.

My dad and I would recreate this play and others out in the yard almost every weekend. We loved Franco. He embodied everything right with the world. Nate and his dad thought Franco was a thief.

In the interim between the great football years of the late seventies and the great video game years of the late eighties, I had discovered that I would not be capable physically or emotionally of playing real football at any level. For fake football, however, I've always had a gift.

In 1979, Nate and I converted a Star Trek play set into a NFL hall of fame, which we adorned with images from *Sports Illustrated* and various books. We held hall-of-fame games there between our "football guys" (Super Friends figures whose nylon bodysuits we cut off just above the knees and whose heads we protected with helmets bought from gumball machines at Hills Department Store). Admittedly, the level of competition was less than intense. One might be inclined to say we were playing with dolls. This was a bit of a sore subject at the time.

My friendship with Nate didn't survive to the Nintendo era, which is too bad. From the very beginning, *Tecmo* and *Madden* felt like the realization of multiple, complex football fantasies Nate and I had shared. Perhaps we were fated to be enemies. Perhaps John Madden and his grudge against the Steelers loomed too large. Made our friendship star-crossed.

In high school, my best friend was Andrew. He and I spent countless hours alternating between hating the boys on our school's football team and hating ourselves for not being more like them. We also spent countless hours playing *Tecmo*. We taunted one another. We cursed the game. We cursed one another. Both of us had a tendency to throw the controller. Once in a while, Andrew or I would rack up an insurmountable lead (78 to 3, for example). The satisfaction of being on the right side of this kind of drubbing is difficult to express. Likewise, the frustration of the loser is hard to put into words. Generally, the ascendant player remained quiet as he calmly, calculatedly enhanced his advantage. The victim, however, tended to question the allegiances of the CPU, claimed that the whole thing was bullshit, became an existentialist, then a nihilist, and finally began begging for mercy. Mercy was never granted. I distinctly remember occasions where either Andrew or I lurched for the power button on the Nintendo (sometimes in tears), turned away from the static-filled screen, and left the other's house without another word.

These days, I tend to play my fake football alone. Every once in a while, my buddy Dan and I do a little damage to our friendship playing head-to-head. The old methods of ungentlemanly play surface even now, and they seem to have a universal allure as we two grown men from different backgrounds like nothing more than the chance to denigrate our opponent. Dan likes to verbalize what he imagines is going through my head whenever I'm playing well (e.g., "I'm Ron [he calls me Ron]; I'm just gonna keep throwing this dinky button-hook to David Boston all day"). I suspect he practices for weeks before asking me if I want to play.

Generally, however, the game has become something of a personal project for me. It has—that is, it feels like it has—about the same ontological weight as the other major, ongoing endeavors in my life: my dissertation, my marriage, my poetry-writing career. Occasionally, I have made the mistake of telling people how well a certain player on my team has been doing or how good I feel about a trade I made with one of the CPU-managed teams. More often, playing is just something that I have to do. It's just part of the work of being me.

I like the game to be only slightly challenging. I play season after season with the Steelers in "franchise mode" (which allows you to manage your team for up to thirty fake years). At this point, I am far more interested in the way my players' individual performances are ranked by the game than I am in the overall performance of the team. Every fake week, offensive and defensive players are lauded for their superior performance. Pro Bowl voting begins after fake week eight, as does the race for league MVP, best running back, etc. My style of play revolves around generating outrageously good statistics with players that are generally mediocre in real-life. This seldom gets old for me. Again and again, I am deeply satisfied to see the Cinderella story unfold and to feel like a part of it. My friend Matthew takes this method a step farther by creating a character with his name, tuning the game to its easiest setting, and breaking all the league records with a rough, animated facsimile of himself—a facsimile who happens to be a fake five inches taller and a fake hundred pounds of muscle heavier.

For many years, I did not play any video games at all. In college and for several years follow-ing, I felt my taste for video games (and sports, for that matter) were an embarrassing piece of evidence confirming the fraudulence of my literary and intellectual pretensions. When I attended the Iowa Writers' Workshop, playing *Madden* was one of the few things that helped me briefly forget about being a fraud. There is nothing literary or pretentious about *Madden*. His gratingly repetitive voice-overs range in tone from the vaugery of claims like "when you talk about fourth-down situations, this is what you talk about" to the double inanity of mis-quoting Yogi Berra, "they say ninety percent of the game is half mental." What can I say, it's in the game, so it's in the game.

Matthew has a friend who started playing *Madden* about three years ago and subsequent-ly became obsessed with the NFL, having never had any previous interest. To converse with him, you'd think he'd followed football his entire life. My experience has not been so extreme, perhaps, but the fake sport has rekindled my love of the real sport, and my love of the real sport has led to rekindlings of love for other real sports. My second year in Iowa, I had season tickets to football, basketball, and wrestling. The workshop was great for me and for my writing, but I think the wrestling was even better. When I was back in Iowa City recently, I went to the barber. In my previous life, I had put off haircuts for months just to avoid the social agony of the barbershop. This time, however, we talked about the Hawkeyes, and I was only marginally uncomfortable. At moments, I was genuinely enthusiastic.

Once again, sports are as strong a medium for my relationships with other men as any other category of experience. How strange this would have seemed to the college me. How strange this seems to my wife. Even with fellow writers, like Matthew, it is often easier and more gratifying to talk sports than craft. Sometimes this is true because we are flying from something infelicitous (competition, aesthetic differences of opinion, etc.), and sometimes we're just tired of thinking like writers.

The game I love does keep changing. Players come and go. Announcers move around the country and shift from network to network. It's in the nature of the game to change, and thus it's in the game. As I was writing this piece, I read a rumor on the internet claiming the 2005 edition (that's this years' game) will be Madden's last. The rumor is probably false, but presumably Madden, and also therefore his game, must come to an end someday. What will the next fake football milestone be?

My suspicion is that fetishizing realism is the wrong way for software developers to go. Ultimately, very few people care about the different effects produced by throwing the ball with a firmly planted back foot versus those produced by throwing the ball on the run. People care about themselves, and finally fake football is about wish fulfillment. If the game could ever get better, it would have to do so by finding new ways to show us what we want and are afraid to want from real life.

I still feel a little guilty firing up the Xbox at midnight, when I should be resting for another day of intellectual labor. I console myself with another fantasy, though. I picture Madden hurtling through the North Dakota badlands in his tricked-out R.V., decompressing from a hard day by playing a flight simulator.

# BILL SPRATCH
## Cheating Our Way to the Top
## in _America: The Game_

## Walkthroughs & Cheat Codes

David Callahan, the author of *The Cheating Culture: Why More Americans Are Doing Wrong to Get Ahead* (Harcourt, 2004), argues that "[s]ocieties [that place] the greatest emphasis on getting rich while having the fewest avenues to get rich in a legitimate fashion tend to be societies with the greatest amount of cheating." (I didn't actually read this book; I just cribbed the quote from some interview I found online.)[1] We cheat to improve our station or to maintain it, to climb higher and to attain greater wealth, to become invincible. We do it because everyone else does. Just look at the political scandals that have rocked the country in the last few years, and the corporate scandals, too many to name here. Those are cheaters in the decidedly upper classes. But everyone wants to get to the next level. In fact the more powerful you are, the easier the cheating becomes.

Everyone's cheating so damn much that we don't know whether to feel pity or pride for the straitlaced players of *America: The Game.* Of recent-generation immigrants and poor

---

[1] "What Makes People Cheat," R. Morgan Griffin, *WebMD,* August 4, 2004.

Americans in the inner cities and rural areas, many have bought into the descriptive copy on the back of the *America: The Game* package: work hard, solve the problems, evade the pitfalls, and wealth and comfort will be won for you and your family! I love the idea of the big bad guy at the end of a level, the supervillain the video game player has to defeat in order to move being called a Boss. But when I buy a pack of smokes in NYC and the guy says, "You need matches, boss?" I cringe. I am not a Boss. You do not have to destroy me to get to the next level. Skip me. Cheat. Read the walkthrough.

```
====================================================
```
## LEVEL 2. VIETNAM
```
====================================================
```

```
*********************************************************
```
**Items:** Cocaine power-ups
**Weapons/Armor:** DAD
**Enemies/Bosses:** Ho Chi Minh / War Protesters / Liberals / Texas Air National Guard Admissions Board
```
*********************************************************
```

If you've been following this walkthrough closely you should have just waltzed through the Yale level. Your score won't be very high because of the shortcuts I've provided in this walkthrough, but that's not the point here. The point of the Yale level is to gain exp. points and contacts that will be useful later in the game on some of the higher levels. especially if you complete the Skull and Bones side-quest. Truthfully, you could skip the Yale level altogether and still win quite easily.

You should save your game at this point.

This next part gets tricky. Because of all the shortcuts, your character is not very well developed. Your money levels are still acceptable, and will remain so throughout the game, despite setbacks that might spell disaster for other players. (That's thanks to the cheats that I've mapped out for you in this walkthrough.) Now the draft is in effect and the VietNam War is raging, and during the Yale level you never experienced an opinion on this war one way or another. In fact you seemed oblivious. That's fine. You were busy collecting beer power-ups. And cheerleading. You're not a good pilot. Never will be. Now you're gonna get just about the lowest score possible to even be considered for flight school. Plus there are 100,000 other players ahead of you with higher scores. This is one of the toughest levels in the game. But relax. Check your inventory. You're going to have to use some of your DAD. Using DAD is distasteful to you but it works every time. There's an outfit with the Texas Air National Guard called the Champagne Unit. This is where you need to get, so once you use enough DAD....

## you always Remember the first time

My cool world-traveling uncle had a *Pong* console when it first came out. Along with his zebra skin rug and Hi-Fi stereo with reel-to-reel tape player and, of course his fondue set. And definitely *Pong* amazed. But in the end it was two bright bars of light slapping a small blip back and forth. Plus it required a partner, someone else to man the paddle. Same thing with the *Combat* cartridge, of course, the game that came bundled with the console. And despite its name, *Combat* participated little in the kill-or-be-killed mentality that became so prevalent in later games, survival in a world of tooth and claw. You simply maneuvered your awkward block with its rectangle cannon around obstacles to fire upon your adversary. One direct hit sent your opponent's tank spinning and you scored a point. No life or death situation.

Then I got *Space Invaders*—*Space Invaders* in which a direct hit would explode your shuttling gun turret; *Space Invaders* in which the invading ranks marched ever faster, descending patiently, blasting your defensive barriers to pixel rubbish. I was fighting for my life, dodging and firing, practically tearing the rubber casing from the joystick as I pulled it hard this way and that, leaning my body in the direction I was moving, as if that would help hasten my escape. But *Space Invaders* had a trick, a trick that to me serves as a sort of unifying example of and a starting point for two common dynamics in contemporary video gaming. If I held the reset lever down on the Atari 2600, after inserting the *Space Invaders* cartridge, then flipped the power switch, I was suddenly capable of much more rapid firepower. Rather than waiting for a shot to hit a target, or disappear beyond the border at the top of the screen to fire again, I was now capable of a nearly fully automatic mode.

This was self-improvement, but it was also sort of cheating.

## Healthiness is Next to Godliness

In Don DeLillo's novel *White Noise,* Jack Gladney, Professor of Hitler Studies states: "All plots tend deathward." I would argue that the action in most video games, and the history of video games itself, tends godward. (One might explain this by making the connection between the blossoming of video game culture and the roughly coincident high-gear shift into a culture of self-help, the self-improvement promises of fad diets, religions, and methods of proper breathing.)

Death is everywhere in the game worlds we visit, but we work hard to avoid it, and even when we can't it's usually only a minor setback. We overcome it by acquiring wealth, new weapons, and skills. We ascend past level after level, gaining experience with each action that further improves our health and increases our strength, and prepares us for the next level after that, and the next. We're cheating death all the way, seeking immortality. After all, that's the ultimate self-improvement; that's the final level to achieve. And wherever we find opportunities for advancement, for climbing to the next level or earning that extra man, we'll find opportunities for cheating. Healthiness is next to godliness. And the urge to cheat along the way is impossible to deny.

## From Extra Men to Inventories

Before long we were past the stage of just earning extra men through high skill and cunning. Extra men gave way to health indicators. Rather than a little row of asteroid-blasting starships or Pac-Men, soon some bar or other icon began to represent our over all well-being. In *Zelda* it was a sequence of throbbing hearts. Heart containers, they were called, and they drained from red to white after injury. First a quarter, then half, three quarters, and finally an empty white heart on the screen as the red began to leach from the next icon in line. Of course we could increase our number of hearts by accumulating items, solving puzzles, fulfilling quests. In games like *Zelda*, our nearness to immortality became less and less a measure of our deeds and skills, and more about accumulation. In addition to the health indicators we started seeing inventory menus. We were required to collect items, to accumulate money in order to buy the tools or abilities we required to grow, to improve our characters, and progress.

## Character Growth: An Aside

This idea of character growth really started with the old pen-and-paper games like Dungeons & Dragons. But let's ignore that for two reasons. 1.) Those games were played in groups with everyone attentive, knowing exactly how the twenty-sided die fell. Cheating proved difficult in a situation like that. Also, video games like the *Final Fantasy* series have taken this role-playing aspect and run with it, making it very much a part of the video gaming world and then some. In many of today's games the player spends more time juggling statistics, swapping a +3 helmet for a +2 leather cap just to increase his speed, that it seems to take up the majority of the game time. That's exactly the point of all the hustling, the bartering, and so forth—to extend the gameplay and provide filler between lush cut-scenes.

In my all-time favorite games there are no health meters; immortality has either already been achieved or else death is just a nonissue. These are the *Myst* games and the *Oddworld* games. As anyone who's played any of the games in either or both of these franchises can tell you, they are absolutely gorgeous with compelling story lines. These are the games that have cemented the notion that video games can be artful, that they can be effective story-telling vehicles (though I first had an inkling playing *Zelda* for Nintendo many moons ago). Those classic Infocom text games like *Zork* don't count. Although I love them dearly, and I as I said, they are classics, for me they just don't fit the rubric of video games qua video games, but are closer to hypertext fiction, which requires direct reader involvement. 2.) In case you've forgotten by now there was a second reason for not discussing pen-and-paper Dungeons & Dragons-type games any further while pursuing this theme of cheating, self-improvement and the drive toward god, here it is: All of us must have a nerdly Maginot Line, a point where we declaim *no mas!* For me, it is Dungeons & Dragons or any such game that requires me to sit in a group of fellow wizards and elves and roll weird dice. You don't even want to know how many sci-fi/fantasy references I've already weeded out of this essay. I will watch some of the *Star Trek* marathon, sure. I loved the *X-Files.* I think *Farscape* was hands down the best sci-fi television series *ever.* Growing up I read my fair share of novels with gilded, embossed scripty titles that featured magic swords and cunning plant people whose green sappy blood could heal wounds. But I have not, will not, sit still and fill out a character sheet, agonize over whether my character's alignment is chaotic good or just plain old-fashioned good. I will not come up with a name requiring gratuitous apostrophes like D'Ushe-B'Ag Paladin Warrior. I chuckle quietly every time I'm on the downtown 6 train in Manhattan and pass through the Bleeker Street station with its signs announcing the stop have been abbreviated like this: BL'KER. And I think, Bl'Ker, that's the name of a Klingon. But referring to anyone as my Dungeon Master crosses a line. And we must all have our limits.

## Cheating Ourselves

We want the easy path to self-improvement. And buying it does seem pretty easy. We want a pill that will make us beautiful and in tip-top shape, allowing us to eat everything we please without exercise. Such a pill would be the ultimate blockbuster drug. But for a drug like that to hit the marketplace, the formula for the compound must first be pilfered from the work of some academic researcher by a large pharmaceutical company. Then of course other pharmaceutical companies would come out with their own versions by altering the original molecule slightly. Cheating! The easy way to get ahead!

Yeah, we cheat. We're incorrigible cheaters. And by we I mean you people. You cheat on everything. On your essays, your jobs, you tax forms, your significant others, your diets. You cheat at cards. You cheat even when there is nothing ostensible to be gained. You cheat at croquet—even at fucking croquet. That's right: I had an acquaintance who actually, honest-to-god cheated while playing fucking candy-ass croquet.

The whole thing happened during one of those yuppyish vacations when several couples rent a house together in the mountains or near the beach. Awkwardness ensues, a situation rife for sexual hjinks, a romantic comedy featuring Hugh Grant. There we were, four young men who had discovered an old croquet set in the storage shed, clotted with cobwebs, cottony cocoons, and egg sacs. None of us really even knew the rules. (The last time I had "played" was back in college, after ingesting a not-insignificant quantity of psilocybin, playing only for the colors.) So we had memory scraps that we threw together until we'd sketched out a rough approximation of what to do. This wasn't about competing. The game was an excuse for friends to drink alcohol in the sun, to make fun of uptight WASPs, to affect that Thurston Howell mode of speech—tight lips and jutting jaw as we said things like, "Well played, old boy. Bully for you. Simply smashing." We weren't playing viciously, opting to take an extra shot toward the wickets when our ball clacked against another's. I mean, I was bare-foot and my feet are big, so even if I wanted to whack an opponent's ball into the weeds, my foot, when I stepped on the ball, completely wrapped around it, and I would end up mash-ing the shit out of my toe with the mallet. So most of our time was spent trying to screw our drinks down into the long grass so they would stand upright while we took our turns.

That was when the cheater struck, toeing his ball this way or that while we were preoccu-pied, since sloshing gin onto the lawn was a greater loss than a ball hit too far. We played shirt-less, we played with Iron Maiden concert tees shorn of their sleeves, and congratulated one another on good shots. "Well I daresay, that was most cleverly played. Top notch! Huzzah! Summon the servants for another round of G&Ts."

A quick search online yields no results for any sort of video croquet. Why is that? Certainly there are plenty of billiards and golf games. Maybe because these games have found enthusi-asts outside of the genteel parlors and private clubs? Maybe because, like those absurd games Aldous Huxley invented in *Brave New World,* they are expensive to play and require expen-sive equipment. Oh sure, every saloon in America has a pool table, but the serious players always arrive with their own cue in a fancy leather case from which they remove the parts for assembly with much bravado. And you can get a serviceable croquet set at Wal-Mart for next to nothing. Who knows? The closest I will ever get to video croquet was undoubtedly that spring afternoon in Austin when the colors were impossible, the grass green green green, the balls ablur in their courses, and the clacking like a sound effect produced in a studio.

So why? Why cheat at croquet, when nothing is at stake, when it's all entertainment, just as it is in a video game that we're playing only against ourselves? Are we just hard-wired to climb, to achieve glory and reach the next level no matter the cost? What glory could our cheating friend have imagined he'd find in that croquet game? Impressing his girlfriend with his victory? If I had to guess, I suspect his girlfriend was more impressed by our clever jokes on the grass, our clownish antics, than the actual outcome of the game: he didn't win. On the other hand, I doubt any aspect of the croquet enterprise impressed her at all. Her eyes prob-ably never even wandered from the pages of her book to our bright balls on the lawn.

## NO CONSEQUENCES

The rabid religious right types I grew up with had the quick, easy way to the top figured out. The briefest of walkthroughs, the minimum of effort. Just ask Jesus into your heart, submit to being dunked in some water like a carnival clown, and once he is firmly ensconced in your right ventricle, you're good to go. Your security in the afterlife is sealed now, it's a kind of Get-out-of-Hell-Free card, requiring not a life of good deeds but that singular act. This is closer to Aleister Crowley's urging to "Do What Thou Wilt" than perhaps most folks would like to admit. It's the ultimate cheat code and once it's entered there are few consequences for your moral failings.

Most video games of the shoot-em-up variety allow you to commit morally suspect actions without consequence. You may, for instance, blast away civilians or allies at will. In the *Grand Theft Auto* games it's pretty much mandatory as you make your way to the top.

When I played *Marathon* (a precursor to *Halo* and developed by the same company), one of the few such games available on the Mac at the time, some of the levels featured interstellar marines, allies who would teleport in and help you secure an area overrun by aliens. After the firefight ended some would hang around, tagging along with you as you progressed down corridors, explored this room or that. And sometimes one of them would goofily stop for no apparent reason right in a doorway it was necessary to get through, blocking all progress. Well, at this point there were few options, I'm sad to say. When it happened the first time I tried just running into the guy, throwing a shoulder into him and achieving nothing more than an electronic grunt. Frustrated, I reached for the one thing not explicitly listed on-screen in my inventory—a can of whup-ass. I punched him repeatedly and squarely on the chin. After each blow he responded in one of the following ways: "Yow!" "Hey!" "Watch out!" "I'm on your side!" But he wouldn't get the hint. So, with some remorse, I shot him dead where he stood. And got off scot free. In fact, I wouldn't even have been able to finish the game if I hadn't shot him.

A friend described a similar experience he had playing *SOCOM: U.S. Navy SEALs*. This game for PlayStation 2 was much ballyhooed because it was the first online game for that console and because of the nifty little headset bundled with it. With the headset you could issue commands to NPCs (nonplayer characters) or even communicate with friends if you were playing online, as they also played with you, miles away. Gameplay required you to complete missions with a four-man team of covert SEALs (yourself and three NPCs). Sometimes you split into two-man teams to achieve particular objectives. The NPC that accompanied you in these forays was called Boomer. And, according to my friend, Boomer was no team player. *SOCOM* is a game that requires stealth and guile over firepower. But Boomer missed that day of training. He wouldn't listen to simple commands like "wait" or "stand down" or "hold your fire." While you tried to creep up on an enemy and quietly slit his throat, Boomer rushed in guns blazing, giving away your position, no matter what commands you issued. When you crouched and slithered through the tall reeds, Boomer trotted along like a bumbling simpleton, head held high, lost in his own AI-generated thoughts, again giving away your position. So, according to my friend and the many reviews and walkthroughs of this game, step one to successfully completing certain missions was a quick and merciful shot to Boomer's head. You had to put him down like a sick dog. Sure, you got a slightly lower mission score for not bringing in all your men, but that was a slap on the wrist. The point was that the mission was completed. At all costs. New kinds of conflict called for new rules, fog of war and all that.

Allow me for a moment to wrap you and me in dense layers of tinfoil so that "their" signals can't get through, because I'm about to go a little apeshit, conspiracy-wise. It *was* just a glitch that Boomer couldn't comprehend simple commands (and apparently this has been rectified in later versions of the game). But the name Boomer still bothers me, suggesting an ailing family dog out on the ranch, who just has to be put down for his own good. I'm stretching, sure. But consider this. *SOCOM: U.S. Navy SEALs* comes complete with a U.S Navy recruitment video. Recent operations in Iraq, secret detentions, torture, and the atrocities at Abu Ghraib were sanctioned under a "Special Access Program" (SAP), which is a fancy way of saying "black ops." The official name of the operation was "Copper Green."

Here's investigative journalist Seymour M. Hersh on Donald Rumsfeld and Copper Green from an interview with Lateline (May 19, 2004): "[Rumsfeld] took that process and made it an operational process, got people from our commando units, the Delta Force, the Green Berets and the SEALS, navy SEALS, people that work with your very competent special force people—and these people were given new names, new identities, completely in the black. […] They simply had the right to go anywhere in the world they had information—no visas, no passports, they had their own aircraft, all covert—and grab somebody and do what they want." I think you see where I'm headed with this.

Ah, the fog of war, the lack of accountability. The old saw goes, "the first casualty of war is the truth." For some, the second seems to be consequences for moral failings.

From that little trick with the reset lever in *Space Invaders* we've progressed to fancier cheat codes and devices for inputting them (such as the GameShark SP, a gaming accessory that allows you to upload cheat codes into your home console for things like infinite health, ammo, time). Hundreds of books and websites have been published devoted to the "Ultimate Cheat Codes." And these codes allow for almost anything, including introducing characters from one game into another, or introducing non-game characters. For instance, you can create a hack code that allows you to play *Doom* as Donald Duck, carrying around a bazooka and blasting monsters while you chomp a cigar.

So the rules of the gameworld have become rewritable, and have been rewritten. The most interesting type of rewrite is the suspension of all laws and the logics of cause and effect—those cheats that allow for you to play in so-called "god mode." In god mode you have unlimited abilities, unlimited health and ammo, as you traipse through the levels of the game blasting and killing with impunity.

## God Games

The godward trend has culminated in strategy games in which the player has finally achieved the role of a godlike controller. Your view is from up on high, you are omniscient as you marshal your people here and there, either to scrub a toilet or conquer a continent. My personal favorite in this category is *StarCraft*, in which you rape this planet or that for natural resources. Place your refinery here on this gassy vent on the planet's surface to produce fuel; use robots here to harvest minerals that allow you to build more harvester robots to gather more fuel and minerals; this in turn allows you to build factories and other installations necessary for you to arrive at your final product. And what is your final product? The machinery of war: tanks, starfighters, and cannons, which you'll use to repel and defeat a nefarious alien horde. Within the genre of god games there is a designer, an auteur if you will, who is considered the god of the god games: Peter Molyneux, whose game *Populous* came out roughly the same time *SimCity*, the first of *The Sims* games.

In *Populous* you are a deity charged with helping your followers develop their lands while protecting them from other deities. So while many of the strategy games with their aerial views and omniscience are merely "godlike," with *Populous,* Molyneux allowed the player to play the role of a actual god. Then he took things a step further. He surveyed what he had wrought and it was good, and then he said: Let there be consequences.

Molyneux next created the blockbuster game *Black & White,* which redefined the genre he arguably invented. As in *Populous,* in *Black & White* you play a god overseeing your followers. As the name implies, you can choose to be wrathful, hateful god or a more pleasant one, depending on how often you send floods and pestilence to your people, as opposed to, say helping their community flourish, healing them when sick, and so forth. All of your actions are carried out by a creature avatar sent down from on high to interact with the people. (It's also interesting to note here that though "avatar" is often used to refer to the player's character in a video game, in this game, the word can be taken in its original meaning, "the incarnation of a deity, in human or animal form.") Your actions begin to determine the appearance and temperament of your avatar creature—it may take on the aspects of a devilish avenger or benevolent protector.

As of this writing, *Fable,* Molyneux's much-anticipated follow-up to *Black & White,* is poised to hit the shelves. I've not played it yet, but the descriptions and reviews make it sound breathtaking. Starting as a young boy, your character literally grows and develops according to your every action. Perform certain tasks, say lots of heavy lifting, and muscles will develop that determine your eventual appearance. Injuries that you sustain become scars. As in *Black & White,* your moral choices certainly have their consequences, too. When NPCs approach and ask for your help in some side-quest you can agree and progress further on your way to becoming a hero, or you can ignore them, or kill them where they stand, and be well on your way to developing into a truly vile character indeed. Early reports claim that in the world of *Fable* you can do just about anything. In interviews Molyneux has admitted to being a little surprised at reports of some of the viciousness and amoral actions players have performed. In fact, certain of the more unsavory opportunities were edited out for the game's final version. Such a propensity further suggests that it's in our troubling nature to do what it takes to achieve our goals.

## Attaining godhood

Sometimes it's because everyone else is doing it—and that's a sad justification. Sometimes it's because you have to; there seems to be no other way. And sometimes there *is* no other way, so then maybe it's not cheating, right? Sometimes there are glitches—definite glitches in the gameworld as well as in life, when you *must* act at the expense of another, or ask for a hint, because even though you seem to be doing everything right, further progress has become impossible. Seeking help when you need it, when the chips are down, is human. Providing that help is divine.

# SHELLEY JACKSON
## Robber, Sailboat, Atom, Book

The world is full of other worlds. There are stopped worlds where the air seems as solid as ice or glass: dollhouses, dioramas, the tableaux in the Museum of Natural History. There are worlds on the other side of a page, through the looking glass, as well as, purportedly, through wardrobes, closets, and wells. I wonder how many other kids spent their childhoods walking through anything shaped like a door, in hopes of finding themselves *somewhere else?*

A book is shaped like a door, but it's too small to walk through, though I sometimes imagined, in wishful moments, that if I laid my cheek against the book and peered along the lines of type into the gutter or the margins, I might see something that lay outside the purview of the paragraph. Asking if it persists when we're not looking seems like a pretty good way to tell reality from illusion, so when I first saw a Sim walk into view from somewhere off the side of my computer screen, I thought I'd found, if not a door, at least a window into Wonderland.

The Sims are little virtual people. They walk, and talk, and pee, and play computer games, and they do all this with or without your interference, though you can make it easier for them, or harder (though it is strangely difficult to bring yourself to hurt your little charges).

You create a family for them, move them into a house, try to give them a life. It's a strangely mundane one: they're constantly putting their dirty dishes on the floor, and you have to make them pick them up, or they'll draw flies. If there's time after dinner, they might watch TV. There is no story, just the daily business of getting by, and no way to win. Presumably, you want to give your Sims better and better jobs, more and more friends, the "biggest pimpest house" (to quote one online player). But nobody says you have to replicate the American dream—though when I knocked off playing I did often find myself strangely compelled to do my own laundry or sweep the kitchen floor.

*The Sims* is addictive. I have heard of people who played without stopping for a month, trading in one boring life for another. Because *The Sims* **is** boring. Something is missing.

Or maybe not enough is. What do you need to make an imaginary world? The answer is: not much. Every little girl knows that when you get a new doll, the first thing you do is take off her clothes. At a pinch, she can also do without head and hands. I used to enlist sticks or shampoo bottles as actors in my doll games, turn a crumpled bedspread into a mountainous island. Imagination is the essential organ, the ability to conjure on cue. Props are secondary. Same with books, which give us, in some ways more, in some ways less to work with: words, just ink on a page. But out of a handful of instructions we can construct a world from our own stock of images. These images are necessarily blurry; if all experience were specific to its originating context, we could not imagine anything at all. There'd be no houses, only a particular house: my parents' stucco bungalow in Berkeley. This is the conclusion of Borges's "Funes the Memorious": forgetfulness is as necessary to thought as remembrance. Brevity is the soul of wit, because omissions give us room to move. We know that language, like the atom, is mostly empty space. But so are our most vivid experiences, and this is not a problem, this is good news, this is the essential gift.

So what does an imaginary world need? One thing it needs, evidently, is to fail. It needs to be incomplete. Those toiling away on CGI dinosaurs and VR helmets might give this some thought: when the illusion is perfect, it will no longer amaze. Lifelike is impressive because it's *like* life, meaning slightly but deliciously wrong. The pleasure happens in the translation, the match that is also a mismatch between two worlds: we love reflections. To compare one thing to another is our profoundest joy. Our Mirror Phase goes on a lifetime.

Mirror Phase? Lacan says that in early childhood we see ourselves in a mirror and find *that* self way more beautiful and whole than the mess of tingles, aches, smells, and partial and per-spective-skewed glimpses by which we previously knew ourselves. We admire that resplen-dant individual, we aspire to be her. Subsequently, we form ourselves in our own image. This firms us up; all those fragmentary perceptions and sensations find their center, which oddly enough is outside them, a visual unity that can only be achieved via this detour through the mirror. So we are our own wannabes, copies from the get-go. The sense of being something at all, an original which is capable of reproduction, is actually created by reflection, redupli-cation. We make the real real by imitating it.

The Sims like mirrors too. They can practise their charisma in front of them, making speeches and posturing. A little test tube floats in the air nearby, filling up with blue. When the tube is full, *ding!* They're one degree more charming! This helps them advance in their careers. (Lacan would probably agree.) Sims also like to read. They select a book, sit down on a nearby couch. While they turn the pages, the little test tube appears. When the tube is full, ding! If the book was a cookbook, they are now less likely to burn down the house with a

stovetop fire. They can also read for pleas-ure, in which case no blue. (And frankly, not much pleasure, either—compared to pin-ball, practically none. The books from the more expensive bookcase give a little more satisfaction. Not much.)

What do they read for pleasure? Nobody knows. Their books have no titles, and though you can look down at your absorbed charge from many angles, you can't actually see any words on the page. Even if you could get close enough, it's unlikely you could read them. The Sims have their own language, Simlish. After a while, you might learn some of the key phrases. You might even learn how to use them, since they recur in particular situa-

tions: Sims say one thing when leaving the house for work, another thing when initiating a polite conversation. You might, as I did, find yourself wanting to make those noises to your boyfriend in the same situations, which are more about attitude than information, and therefore don't really require words. It's a bird-song approach to language. But the Sims, though they are certainly simple-minded, are not actually quite like animals, who can convey their feelings and intentions toward the world around them, but can't hold the simplest conversation about the price of milk. The Sims really are talking about something. You can tell that from the pictures that flash above the heads of the speakers: masked robbers, the atom, bags of money, and sailboats are common topics among Sims.

So now I'm God. I've just created Adam and Eve (actually I named them Claudia and Apollinaire, but never mind), and moved them into a small suburban house. It turns out that they don't need to be taught to speak; they come knowing. Certain theorists of language, believers in an original, Edenic tongue, asked what language a baby would speak who had been brought up in silence, outside culture. Hebrew, was one suggestion. All my evidence suggests she would speak Simlish. The Sims language, as a synthesis of vaguely familiar sounds, bears some resemblance to the corrupt language of Dante's demons—a little bit Hebrew, a little bit Semitic—since the demons were consigned to a hodge-podge of tongues after Babel, same as humans. But whereas humans were cast into confusion by their sudden inability to make themselves understood to their neighbors, demons, like angels, as Umberto Eco points out, could communicate without words. In this too the Sims resemble them, because only someone who could read minds could understand Sim conversation. This is because their mind-pictures have no fixed relationship to the words they speak. In Eden, we hear, there was

a necessary relationship between words and things. But that was a long time ago. Since Saussure, at least, we know that that relationship is arbitrary. In *The Sims,* not only is the relationship arbitrary, but it changes from moment to moment. Sims say the same things over and over—or rather, they make the same noises—but different pictures flash above their heads. Without reading minds, how would anyone know that this time "fwada statch nah," means airplane, when last time it meant tennis racket?

These same signs flicker above the Sims' heads when they're asleep and dreaming, confirming that what we're seeing is not a hieroglyphic closed captioning, noting what they say, but a representation of what they're thinking about—a difference, however, that in Sims world makes no sense, because to think something while you're talking *is* to say it. There is no subterfuge among Sims. There is also no Freudian slip, no speech impediment, no lying. Sometimes the person you're talking to doesn't like sailboats, and then she'll shake her head and you'll see a sailboat with an x through it.

Will Wright, *The Sims*' creator, originally wanted to use Navajo for the spoken language, inspired by the Navajo code speakers in WWII. Navajo—a language spoken by so few people that it is harder to crack than a secret code—is, apparently, the paradigmatic language spoken in order *not* to communicate. If there was something decidedly strange about using the language of a conquered people to wage war on behalf of their conquerors, there is something even stranger about using it for the coffee klatch of a sort of virtual reservation, suburban-American-style. I wish it had happened, because the idea of a Navajo kid playing with Navajo-speaking Sims, and possibly building them a Wikiup out of virtual clapboard, makes

my head spin at the weirdness of history. But there were not enough Navajo voice actors, Wright explains in an interview, so he went with a fake incomprehensible language.

The Navajo code-speakers had to synthesize words for weapons and military maneuvers from the vocabulary of a peaceful hunter-gatherer culture—bomb was egg, tank was turtle. To plot war in Simlish, presumably, you'd have a related problem: deploy sailboat, launch bags of money, please debouch from the bathroom so I can pee. If the Sims produced a philosopher of language (though this is not one of the jobs advertised in their local paper), he would have the same problem. We have already ascertained that fine points of meaning are not conveyed vocally, in the Sims world. So how would a philosopher philosophize? With his thought balloons, presumably. So what would we see there?

I think I know the answer: we'd see other thought balloons. The capacity to think about thinking is the beginning of philosophy, surely. Then, if our Plato has a taste for infinite regress, he might imagine thought balloons containing throught balloons, containing smaller thought balloons, at infinitum. He'd also imagine the Sims world, not as we see it (from above, the God's eye view), but from within. We all construct the world we live in: this is our first imaginary world, but also all we know of the real. If the Sims philosopher has imagination, however, he won't stop there. He'll start imagining other worlds. Some of these worlds will seem simpler than Sims. Some will seem richer, stranger, more stirring. If he's really good, maybe he'll imagine ours. After all, they know we're watching. It's an amazing moment when a neglected Sim turns to face you, looks up and waves, an fire-engine-red thought-icon floating above her head to let you know what you have forgotten. "My God, my God, why hast Thou forsaken me?" she cries. (She expresses this, however, with a scarlet hamburger, bed, or toilet.)

Elaine Scarry, in her brilliant *Dreaming by the Book,* demonstrates that a fictional wall seems more solid when a fictional shadow or beam of light slides across it. The magic lantern scenes that glide over the panels and drapes of Proust's room confirm their permanence. Comparing the fleeting to the durable, we take our eyes off the magician's hands, forgetting that both light show and wall are illusions here, projections of the magic lantern of language.

In a related way, enclosing a book within a book, or a play within a play, makes the enclosing world seem more real; if it is not the same as reality, it is at least one degree closer to it than the fiction it contains.

There were three talismanic props my sister and I made for the doll games we used to play: a distorting mirror, a camera, and a collection of miniature manuscripts authored by various dolls. We had invented the desire for the dolls to reflect on themselves. This happened very late in the games and I think in some ways represented the end of their trajectory. Beyond this point, the dolls did not need us anymore. By replicating themselves, they'd become real.

I said that enclosing a fiction within a fiction makes the latter seem more real. This is true only up to a point. There is a backlash (exploited most delightfully by Nabokov in his *Pale Fire*). Reveal what the fictional world and the fictional world it contains have in common—perhaps by the *mise en abyme* of the mirror game, or thought bubbles within bubbles—and the second-order illusion will not beef up the first illusion, but make it and all other illusions seem equally fake. And that includes the so-called real world from which we're looking on. Benjamin (in "The Work of Art in the Age of Mechanical Reproduction") and Baudrillard (*Simulacra and Simulation*) have alerted us to the infectious nature of the copy: a compulsive multiplication of the reproduction undermines the original. Neither of those thinkers are very happy about this. But perhaps there is no original and this is not a problem. Perhaps it is the likening operation that created the sense of an original; perhaps it's the imaginary world that brings the real world to life. Cave artists painted deer so that real deer would come. Mechanical canaries can teach real canaries to sing. Books can show us how to live.

There was a lot of talk, seven or eight years ago, about the dangers of a simulated reality. I don't hear this talk today. The virtual has become part of our real experience; our vivid mental landscape has incorporated the rather depleted landscapes of computer games and thrown them into the mix out of which we synthesize our lives. *The Sims* has not replaced life, but it has altered it. Likening is reversible, like some overcoats. Certain strangely proportioned, prefabricated houses are Sims houses now. Certain abandoned bits of machinery, with foul water lapping at their underpinnings, belong to *Myst*. Even *Tetris,* so abstract that one might think it scarcely posits a world at all, has permanently changed the way I look at a skyline.

So when I ask what an imaginary world needs in order to become vivid for us, maybe I should also ask the question: what does the real world need?

I think it needs a mirror. The world seems brighter in its reflection, and, I would submit, brighter in a dirty mirror than a clean one. The world is too much with us; we do not need more "there there" but less; night is the time our imaginations have room to breathe. Night, and books, and games, and pictures. We need the gap, the blur, the schema, the astigmatism to awaken the real world within us, bring it to life. The world we live in is one we have made for ourselves in our minds, out of what our senses bring home to us. The real world is already an imaginary world. For every tree there is an imaginary tree inside us, either schematic or richly complicated. So those live most vividly who have the best imaginations.

Now, I'm picturing a thirteen-year-old girl sitting at her computer, watching a sort of doll read a book. The girl sits quietly. The Sim

sits quietly. Pages turn with a rustle. The plates on the kitchen floor acquires flies and begin to buzz. The newspaper turns a dirty grey. The need to pee is getting urgent, on both sides of the screen. What is happening? Nothing and everything. When my Sim reads a book, sunk in an illusory inwardness, a bit of code flipping the pages of another bit of code, I imagine for her an imaginary life, and imagining this, my world brightens, and I think I can feel what it is like to be real.

But hang on. In spite of *Myst's* magic linking books, the imaginary world is no longer most frequently attained through the printed word. As I said, the Sims also play computer games. If one of these games were *The Sims,* would my Sim learn to play? Would a little test tube appear and start to fill with blue experience juice, and if it did, what new attainment would it represent? Would my Sim learn that she is made of code, that someone's watching, that real breasts have nipples, and real books have words in them? Would she start writing her own (books, code)? Would she figure out a way to win the game?

*Ding!*

## ROLAND KELTS
### I AM A FREAK

I met my first hero 250 meters above Tokyo when I was six years old.

His name was Ultraman Taro, which in English is closest to "Superman Steve"—an everyman with abilities beyond the pale, and with all the problems that accompany them. Unlike civilian Clark Kents or Peter Parkers, however, Ultraman Taro never looked like an everyman. He looked like a freak.

When I met UT, Japan was transforming into a burnished nation of post-cataclysmic everymen called "salary men." This was the early 70s, and the nation's young men left behind their student protests (mostly against the US-dominated constitution, the military provisions and dependencies) determined to make money en masse—as a nation, to avenge the losses of the last World War with gains in the market, and to, as the novelist Haruki Murakami bitterly told me: "join the company and forget what anybody stood for."

They wore blue suits, but UT wore a leathery red suit that clung to his lean, long-torsoed body, and a silver halter over his shoulders, punctuated by a gem-like orb at the center of his chest. The orb turned red, yellow, green—depending on UT's mood at the time. The red suit grew dusty and creased at the joints after one of his fights with the various foreign space monsters terrorizing Japan. He seemed to grow depressed after long battles, going down on one knee and lowering his head, his orb flashing slowly, achingly violet.

My Japanese mother had returned me to her homeland, ostensibly to introduce me to her family and acquaint me with my Japanese heritage. But I think she was running away, too, however briefly, from a new life in America that must have seemed exhaustingly unreal.

Living abroad will disorient you. The dumb-luck freedom from long-internalized rules and expectations can also induce vertigo, or a panic that somehow accrues. I have lived in London (briefly), Osaka and Tokyo. I fly back to New York whenever the panic spikes.

For my mother, living abroad with a new national identity and family must have been destabilizing in certain hours of reflection. My mother did not speak Japanese at our home in upstate New York, or later, in New Hampshire. We ate rice sometimes, but not a lot of fish, and no sushi.

The classic immigrant narrative posits flight as a necessity, or at the very least, a perceived necessity in order to better one's lot. My mother's family were in fine shape—her father, a poet and educator with ties to the government, was the son of a storied Samurai clan, her mother the daughter of farming gentry. She went to a top university, where she studied languages. She didn't need to better her lot anywhere else.

Tokyo is the only city in the world where being outside—in the streets, the parks, stepping out of a taxi—feels just like being inside. Its air is that humid, whatever the season, that limpid. It's also that enveloping as a city, sprawling and shapeless. And its streets and alleyways are circuitous and claustrophobic. Tokyo can make Manhattan, with its airy avenues and breezy rivers, seem like a national park.

And Tokyo was reconstructed only fifty years ago, which means that the war made it skip a stage. There's almost nothing industrial-age here, nothing iron-rooted, stone-arched and oppressively past tense. The architecture itself is like a game, incongruent, yes, but also free for you to navigate and invent—the way lower Manhattan must've felt to European immigrants in the nineteenth century.

For these and other reasons, and for a long time after I moved to Tokyo, I stayed away from Akihabara—the grungy, neon-grilled neighborhood on the older east side of Tokyo where

Japan's very latest gadgets, hucksters, pornographic animators, and games greet the streets—and where armies of the obsessive, young and old, course those streets for salvation from the known world.

I had lived in Osaka for a year, a smaller, more prideful, down-to-earth industrial city in Kansai, the western region that includes Kyoto and Kobe and serves as Japan's breadbasket. For the same reasons that a friend in Chicago told me she didn't need New York—"Big is enough; bigger is too much."—Akihabara seemed too much.

Akihabara, which translates as "place of fallen leaves," is legendary in and out of Japan. My navigator through the dead leaves has been the forty-something Iso-san, part-owner of a hostess club (where pretty girls ply male customers with drink and flattering overtures, though not, generally, sex itself) who triples as an amateur boxer, a video-catfight producer (he records videos of half-naked women posed erotically as though they were truly fighting) and businessman. Another salary man. But though I have asked him what his actual business is several times, I receive the same smiling nod—a polite gesture of feigned incomprehension in Japan, proffered when the question should not be asked.

Iso greets me at Akihabara station and takes me through coursing back streets of absurdly tall neon signs, many of which advertise an admixture of electronic and sexual delights. But sex is not what Iso shows me; he shows me games.

You can sample them on the street, grab the joysticks and enter digitized urban alleyways with fighting monsters whose heads jostle and bleed in vibrant color, manipulate high-kicking porn queens with pert noses and breasts, and ever-wide eyes. I have played many of these under the watchful gaze of clean-cut proprietors who cut me off as the action heats up: Akihabara may be the truest "blue balls" capital of the world.

Iso takes me upstairs in the Character Entertainment Shop, up six narrow flights to preview a game that posits the player on a planet besieged by swarthy-skinned…"terrorists."

"Japanese games are better than American ones, but only through character," says Sho Matsuhashi, Japanese General Manager of TOKYOPOP, the dominant importer of Japanese manga to the US. TOKYOPOP has offices in Tokyo and LA, and Matsuhashi left cozy positions with Disney and Universal to engage the startup. He speaks to me over a cup of cold tea surrounded by cartoon-filled walls blazing with color. "But character means a lot."

Akihabara is the home of character—characters with no home to claim.

Self-described "super geek" Tetsuto Fujiyama categorizes the seekers: "There are five different kinds of geeks in Akihabara. The oldest are the electric appliance geeks, who come to purchase electronic parts and other equipment. Next are the PC geeks, who like to build their own original computers that run as fast as possible. Third are TV animation geeks, whose brains can't distinguish between reality and animation. The fourth group is the magazine geeks, who have made original animation fantasy stories influenced by TV, Hollywood movies and game animation, and publish them in small magazines circulated among themselves. The last group is those geeks who love to play video games in which erotic animation is used."

In Japan it's called Hikikomori, or "socially withdrawn," a term that is usually applied to maladjusted teenagers, kids who willingly disappear into the cells of technology: mobile phones, the internet and video games. It's applied primarily to kids, I suspect, because they are being monitored most closely—especially in school-uniformed Japan—for signs of straying from the norm.

They are said to be irritable when distracted from their pursuits.

They are said to be disproportionately responsible for acts of violence against their teachers.

Sometimes they drop out of school for weeks at a time—or for the remainder of the year.

They withdraw into a zone of near-pure obsession, crazed eyes and dysfunctional eating patterns, disturbed sleep.

Complete absorption in an artificial world is preferable to encounters in the real one.

I first learned of the term denoting the pathology in 2000, when I began inquiring about the young people I'd been interviewing late at night, the clubbers, the kids on skateboards in convenience-store parking lots well past midnight, the small clutch of teens who drank beer and occasionally break danced beneath the streetlamps below my apartment.

Mikio Nakadoi, my pal and the guitarist in my band in Osaka, had taught those kids in elementary school fifteen years ago. He'd seen the signs then, he told me one night over a beer in Alaska, where I was holed up writing and detoxifying, and he'd come to stay with me and my sister during a summer tourist trek.

"Those kids arrived at school without their books. They had snacks and phones and computer games. They were completely isolated then—and they're even worse off now."

But couldn't that also reveal a lack of faith on their part in the school itself, in the teacher, and the books, and the alleged truths being conveyed? Weren't those kids finding a truer truth elsewhere?

Mikio looked at me at an angle. "The schools sucked," he said.

Hikikomori. Can there be a more acute description of the novelist in all of us?

I would spend several months living with my mother's parents in Morioka, a small city in northern Japan, attending the local kindergarten and coming home to watch lots of TV. I loved Japanese television—partly because I was so miserable in Japan.

My memories: the heat, the buzz of cicadas growing so loud they made my mother raise her voice in the tiny yard, capturing insects—huge black stag beetles and the cicadas themselves, with bulbous unreadable eyes and translucent wings beating violently—gifts for all occasions, toys from my grandparents who said yes when my mother said no, thick slabs of toast for breakfast and the ever-present fried pork cutlets placed before me each time I refused to eat the all-too colorful, misshapen Japanese foods.

Japan forces an American to focus on the small.

These were visions of a boyhood Shangri-la that I sustained for years. Then my mother visited me in Tokyo a few months ago, and over a lunch of pale raw blowfish meat at the New Otani hotel with my great uncle Kanesaka and my uncle Iwane, someone mentioned my disposition as a child.

"He was polite and very cute," my eighty-six-year-old great uncle said.

My mother sighed. "He was very unhappy, wasn't he?"

On the walk back to her hotel room, I asked her about her comment. "You were so unhappy in Japan," she said. "You cried every day at the school, and the teachers were really worried about you. You couldn't understand the language, I guess. You were only happy when you came home."

With my grandfather after school, I watched sumo wrestling fights broadcast in the early evening. I loved the oversized Michelin men. I loved laughing at them, and I also loved the grin on my grandfather's long and angular face as he laughed with me. And I was also drawn to their rituals—the rice showered over the dohyo when everyone grew silent, the priest's claps, the sobriety and intense concentration at the huge men's brows and eyes. Because you must focus on the small in Japan, the oversized have more impact.

In our underwear, my grandfather, slowly getting high on sake (which he would let me surreptitiously sip from a leather pouch), and I reenacted those fights on the tatami mats of their small wood-beamed home. We would get on our haunches and stomp as the big men did. Then he would recite something in Japanese that I couldn't understand, muttering a few English words to help me, and pretend to cast rice over the tatami.

We rolled together in embraces, old man and child, in our white, baggy briefs—he lean and bony with age, me a skinny rubbery boy, our underwear sagging beneath our balls.

After the fights, *Ultraman Taro* would come on. My grandfather had sweated out his last drop of sake and needed a bath, which my grandmother had prepared in a deep silver tub past the tiny slatted wooden door adjacent to the kitchen. But I would lean into the TV, hungry for a fellow freak.

He had a silver-helmeted head with protruding Viking horns that I thought intensely important. (I would later become infatuated with the Minnesota Vikings, despite being a kid in Patriot-crazed New England, just for those helmet-headed horns.) But more compelling to me were his insect-like eyes—bulbous, elongated, and yellow, with the tiniest black points as pupils.

And he didn't just zap his monstrous opponents like so many American superheroes did at the time—Spiderman with his laser web, Superman and his overwhelming powers. He could cross his arms and emit laser beams, true, and he had extraterrestrial strengths. But most often, Ultraman Taro grappled with his foes.

They wrestled. They got close and intimate and fought it out mano-a-monster. I was six and watched men heave their naked skin against each other to win in sumo. Then Ultraman Taro wrapped his skinny arm around a monster's neck and subdued its razor teeth with a headlock.

UT's emotions may have pulsed in the orb at the center of his chest, but you could never read those eyes. Think Clint Eastwood in his Dirty Harry heyday. I became a collector of praying mantises with my scientist father after returning home from Japan. I liked catching them and looking at their triangular heads in the terrarium as their mandibles twitched, their eyes above tear-shaped and numb.

The mystery of masculinity, I thought, was in the eyes.

But also, as I later understood, they were eyes I despised—like the ones I saw and often derided as my own genetic legacy: thinly veiled eyes, distant and soft and slanted—not blue and bracing like the New England kids I grew up with. I hated my eyes when I realized no one could ever trust them.

I stood at the mirror for years into my adolescence trying to widen my eyes, using my fingers to stretch the membranes at top and bottom, to make them more round.

My gaming days hit during the most inspired period of my life—adolescence. The dream of travel, of motion, was critical, and the creators then, like sci-fit writers of the less mobile 1950s, must have known they were in good hands in outer space.

I played consecrated games on the field and ice, as a soccer and hockey player. But I was always lonely on teams—albeit a closet loner who spoke little but played hard and grinned knowingly at inane scatological jokes in the shower. When the pot-smoking guitarist in my rock band introduced me to *Space Invaders* in a pizza parlor near my family's house in New Hampshire, I started buying slices and cokes just to play the game.

*Space Invaders* was beautifully simple. You could shift up and down and fire away at your opponents. I didn't like the graphics much, but I liked the simplicity of the form, the sheer kinetic energy—for an athlete, it was movement without pain. There was motion there, and a faith in the scoring, and seemingly objective approbation. I got better. The tattooed boys around me, smacking their cigarettes into plastic ashtrays, approved. This was more rock 'n' roll than sport, which was very cool at the time. (The roles have since reversed: rock stars now sport basketball uniforms.)

The problem that gaming ultimately circumvents is the problem of other people. It's like the best pornography, which provides an artifice far superior to the reality of life.

I was captain of my soccer team by virtue of my aloofness. The same blue-eyed boys who played with me had hated and resented the me I was as a child, partly for racial reasons. But as the years shifted, they admired me for my adroitness on *Space Invaders*. (It's worth noting that the only physical fight I'd ever been in off the rink was with a white kid who called me "chink" on a playground in New Hampshire.)

"Dwelling in a fantastical, fictional universe for pleasure and entertainment," gaming journalist and editor Max Everingham tells me from London, "that's what matters. Gaming, to me at least, is about wish fulfillment, empowering gamers to do things virtually that they otherwise wouldn't really have the opportunity to do in real life, be that driving a Ferrari, abseiling down a building as a secret agent, or playing a game of *NFL*."

But I didn't really need this substitution. If you play a sport, you have all the challenges laid out before you, each time you step on the grass or the ice. And pornography is also less and more than sex. The artificial doesn't substitute for the real; at its best, it exceeds the real.

Max agrees that games are bigger than that.

"I think the parallel is more between game developers (the guys who write the code for the game) and fiction writers—not gamers, who basically live out the experiences created by the game creators," he says.

I thought about creating these games on a boat trip to Nova Scotia from Boston. I was a member of the soccer team from New Hampshire, slated to play the best of the world in Canada. The ship was well appointed, and boring. But in the hull they had a *Space Invaders* machine, a lone console carefully isolated from the slot machines and pool tables.

I was headed to Nova Scotia while my father's family met for a reunion in the face of his brother's sudden death. I felt guilty and liberated at once—I was a "soccer player." But I hated most of the other guys on the team, disliked the food, and knew, even then, that Nova Scotia was far from sexy.

All I could do was play the game, shoot down evil. There was always another level.

But most important: I never died.

The characters began to appear when I was an adolescent. *All-Star Racers* introduced American kids to Japanese heroes—not as freakish as Ultraman, but smart and stylish. I watched those shows with Jay Burmeister, my reedy and contentious pal in New Hampshire. They were heroes with good haircuts, and since I'd been to Japan, I could tell Jay a few erroneous things about what they meant.

We fought one another on story lines. He thought my interpretations were pretentious, though he didn't use the word. I thought he was stupid. Yet every afternoon, we convened in his single-mother's living room to watch the latest episode.

My first girlfriend, Elyssa, told me I couldn't know who I was without a story of who I was.

*Pac-Man, Asteroids,* others followed. I got lost. I played games and then thought they threatened me. I became afraid of that level of obsession, the way each game led ineluctably to the next, and so I retreated into books and music, both of which allowed for more reflection, and less pizza.

Leo Lewis, my good friend and Tokyo partner in crime from the *Times of London,* a vetran gamer, offers this analysis: "There was a heyday of games in the '80s. Lonely boys played them and became heroes. Then the games got too complicated. They returned to form around early 2000. Now they are being descended upon for Hollywood, which is not ever a good thing."

Literary cool hunter and longtime talent scout Seiichiro Shimono, or Shimo as I call him, agrees. After fifteen years working with Japan's biggest publishers, Shimo is now president of the Owl's Agency, his own attempt to bridge literary East and West. "You had these brilliant kids designing games instead of writing novels or scripts five or ten years ago," he says in his company's condo in central Tokyo. "But the new generation of talent thinks games are played out, and sold out. They're so fast. They're now making their own manga (called doujinshi, or fan-made manga), and they parody older manga. They're in their teens or twenties, and they self-publish this stuff with pocket change. But they're the talent we want. Fortunately, some of them are actually starting to write novels."

How do we tell stories now that story is a commodity?

"Japanese people love fighting as an art form," says Iso-San, citing the massive crowds at Mixed Martial Arts events in Japan, the proliferation of graphically violent comic books that would raise eyebrows, at the least, in today's closeted America. What Americans disdainfully call "Ulitimate Fighting," for example, and see as brutes bashing each other in the ring, is honored here as a contemporary blending of ancient sports.

We're in a cosplay (costume play) café called Café & Kitchen Cos-Cha, where the twenty-something waitresses wear the very short skirts and low-cut blouses of their cartoon counterparts and speak in high-pitched chimera-like voices. Beautiful androids.

"Maybe it's because we are not supposed to fight in reality. We can't have wars, so we make imaginary wars. It's your constitution, isn't it?"

He's right. McArthur decreed that no Japanese army could be levied for acts of aggression. Japan is supposed to be rich and strong—with no teeth.

But sharp teeth are what they do well here—in graphic violence amid a sterile society. I loved UT because he fought. Don't we all love a fighter?

I am half-Japanese, half-American. I find it hard to feel allegiance to either country, the rising sun or the stars and stripes. But I feel comforted by the Hikikomori, the individual isolationists.

Is it wrong to be a gamer? No.

Is it wrong to be obsessive and withdrawn, deovted to a single-minded pursuit of otherness—on your own? Surely not.

But if an artificial world is preferable to this one, why try to fix what we live in?

Games are so good now they can replicate your household life. You can be a Sim. Or you can be yourself. I'm not sure which is best.

I do know this:

When I met Ultraman Taro, 250 meters above Tokyo, in the tower that is itself a simulacrum of Paris's Eiffel Tower—I was very unhappy. My mother took me there. She thought I'd be thrilled.

What we are seeking in games, pornography, and wrestling is not reality.

It's beyond that.

Ultraman Taro held my hand. He was too skinny, too short. The poor guy was trying to make money on the side of his acting career, no doubt.

But what was it about him that made me cry?

He was too real.

# JIM ANDREWS
## Language Explosion
### Poetry & Entertainment in _Arteroids_ 2.50

## The Battle of Poetry against itself & the Forces of Dullness

_Arteroids_ (<www.vispo.com/arteroids>) is an online literary shoot-em-up related to the classic arcade game _Asteroids._ The player pilots a short text (called the id-entity) and shoots other words or phrases, exploding them into sprays of letters. In Game Mode, the id-entity is the word _poetry._ In Play Mode, the default id-entity is the word _desire,_ or the player can write her own. The feel of the game beneath the player's fingers is adjustable by changing the Fictive Friction applied to the id-entity as she drives. _Arteroids_ is the battle of poetry against itself and the forces of dullness. Language is driven into confrontation with itself and the shoot-em-up computer game.

_Arteroids_ is about driving and cracking language and poetry open. William S. Burroughs said about audio tape that when you cut it, the future spills out. When writers and artists use cut-up techniques of all kinds on all types of media, when sound is an inscribable, editable object just as language is—and the same goes for video and other digitizable material information—then language is indeed cracked open in the sense that the fundamental symbols of writing are no longer simply the letters in the alphabet and other typographical marks.

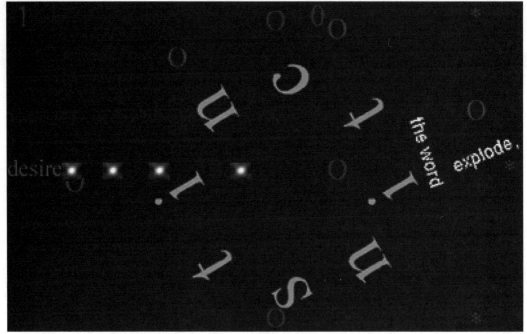

*Figure 1.* The destruction of instinct.

Writing is now a larger thing.

Part of what Burroughs may have meant is that when you cut audio tape, you discover that sound is now object, and very strange object at that, but the analog razorblade and the digitally precise, desktop studios of digital audio deal with sound like the word-processing application Microsoft Word deals with words, in many ways: as fundamental symbol and combinatorially concatenated string of units and signification, pattern, design, extended composition in space and time.

We edit the properties of such objects in much the same way, whether they are images, texts, sounds, videos, applications, etc.; all but sounds can be visible or invisible, for instance but, more importantly, they are all material objects of information that have editable properties and perhaps even methods or handlers at their disposal. And if they have their methods, they are also animistic and slightly marauding entities that have spilled from the future of cutting audio tape and other such acts of media object creation.

The future and the present are involved in the emergence of new media language that multiplies the symbols of writing, and changes writing from dealing with solely typographical material to multimedia composition and cognizing.

## The Audio

The sounds in *Arteroids* are all my voice. Sound poetry is a part of poetry, of course. I saw the audio in *Arteroids* as a way to explore both sound poetry in an unusual context and also some sort of generative music/audio score—generative in the sense that it's generated by the player's actions, but it has a distinct sound. The sounds range from cartoonish to adult, sound poetry to computer game, Kurt Schwitters to Mel Blanc and Gregory Whitehead in their associations.

When the player executes a text, one of twenty-one sounds is selected. A random pitch-change is then made to the sound anywhere between ten semitones above the original pitch and twenty semitones below the original pitch. It is the pitch-change that gives *Arteroids* its sonic range into the animal and semihuman, the female, and the childish. Work that is playable online cannot take forever to download, so it's good to make extensive use of the resources you require the player to download.

Other sounds happen when the player drives her text, and when she shoots. I wanted to make the experience of driving the text satisfying and, sonically, the default sounds are vowels with some grace; the experience of going to and fro and up and down in it should be, in some sense, commensurate with poetry.

## Mutanism & Violence in Video Games

Before the sound went into *Arteroids* (version 1.0 has no sound), it felt destructive to shoot up the texts. Now that the sound is in, it motivates a different attitude toward the shooting aspect of *Arteroids*. I don't like guns, and I do not want to advocate violence or thoughtless destruction. There's too much of it in the world and in computer games, which revel in being as gratuitous as can be.

When the player executes a text, she triggers one of the more pleasurable experiences of the piece. So that the shooting becomes, hopefully, an act of curiosity and composition. Part of what I am trying to do over several versions of the piece is move from shoot-em-up to something every bit as interesting, but different from, shooting a gun.

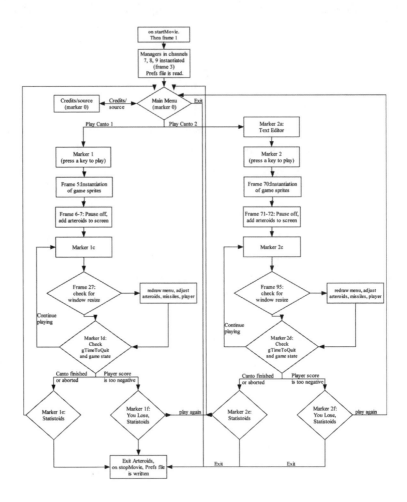

*Figure 2.* Old and distressed *Arteroids* flowchart.

Militarism in computer games is different from violence in computer games. Militarism in computer games trains boys to be good little war pigs (i.e., shoot first, ask questions later), or good little consumers. The games may not be made by war pigs, but by apathetic war pigs who would rather make computer games. Couch-potato war pigs.

Violence in computer games is sometimes a dramatic representation, as it is in books, films, plays (quite a bit of gore in *King Lear,* for example), of meaningful conflict in which the forces of good and evil—and maybe even some shades of gray—engage in a process of realization and resolution. Mostly, however, what we encounter are situations where there is no such meaning to the conflict but, instead, the player is in a constant act-or-die state of concentration on survival.

The player shoots words or texts in *Arteroids.* The focus is, hopefully, on the energy of destruction/creation of poetry and language. It is a bit cheeky toward poetry of course, but I suspect poetry will suffer it without tragic consequences. That poetry should suffer, in *Arteroids,* as never before is—let us be frank—intended.

## Opening a Feeling-Stream

Several people have said to me that computer games should be capable of scaring people. It isn't so much that you want to scare people as in a horror movie. You want, however, to get their blood going, startle them and challenge them, make them ever so slightly afraid for their virtual lives. And that life should, in part, be involved or immersed in the game world, immersed so that the game does indeed get the blood pumping.

It helps for the player to be in kinesthetic touch with the game: to have a feeling-stream open through which the game can pump adrenaline and delight through the fingertips via the dance of the hand across the keys.

There are enough guns in enough real hands, and enough virtual guns in computer games, that the making of guns in games must rise to the next level of message-passing as the real structural nexus of programming in first- or second-person shooter games. That is, it isn't really the gun that is the most strong-

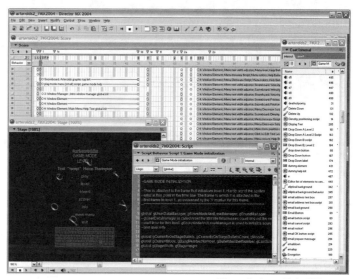

Figure 3. *Arteroids* in Director.

ly dynamic and appealing element (though guns are primal and the game is an imaginary life-and-death power struggle). The real dynamic is the real-time/game-time control over the activity of interaction with objects that the player passes messages to kinesthetically via the keyboard, plus primal drama. If a player doesn't have kinaesthetic control over a game in which he is supposed to have kinesthetic control, does she play it? How about if it doesn't have sound? Would she play it still? Perhaps. But if the kinaesthetics are off, it's time to reboot or call it quits.

Even in computer games we are faced with the problem of guns. One desires primality in art, and excitement. Guns are primally dramatic. They aren't going away. Yet while they have a legitimate role in art, guns in computer games are becoming minor variations of one another, in other words, boring.

The games that will emerge that are the web's own games (not tired retreads) will take advantage of message-passing figuratively and literally, for more playful communications between people, and between people and media objects.

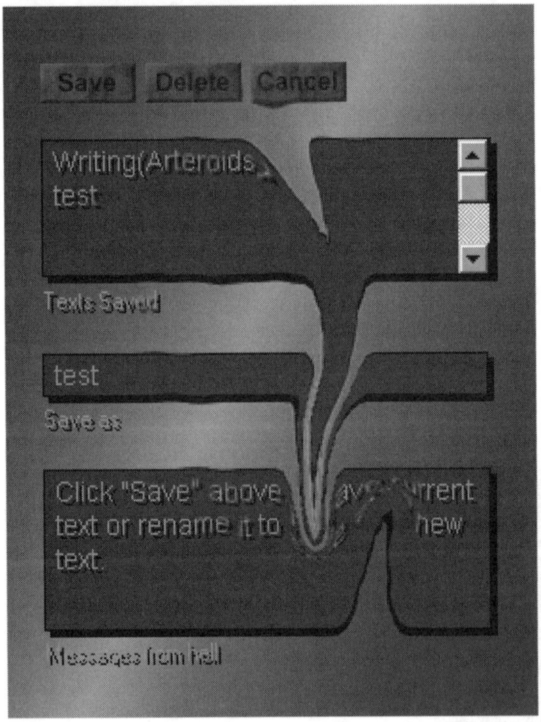

*Figure 4.* Saving poetry from yourself.

### Game Mode & Play Mode

*Arteroids* contains a Play Mode and a Game Mode. In Play Mode, the player or wreader (a combintion writer/reader) has more control over the situation. She can be deathless, in which case the texts cannot hurt them; she can compose/save/retrieve the opposing texts (and her own id-entity text) in Word for Weirdos; she can change the velocity and density of the opposing texts; and she can adjust the amount of fictive friction she experiences while driving the id-entity.

In Game Mode, however, the player has but one life to live and is necessarily mortal. She plays with what she's dealt in Game Mode and cannot advance among the game's 216 levels without successfully maxing out the Meanometer, which is done by polishing off a sufficient number of the opposing texts. Scores are saved in Game Mode, but not in Play Mode. Scores in Game Mode are based on the speed and accuracy of the player's performance. In Game Mode the velocity of the texts gradually increases over 216 levels.

Initially, I wrote two "cantos" for *Arteroids,* experienced separately, but as the development of the game progressed, I saw that, instead, the game needed a Play Mode and a Game Mode. Some of the features I wanted to implement involved a competitive situation; other features required a situation in which the player was not primarily concerned about survival and could explore with impunity. Many computer games have something like Play Mode and Game Mode as when the player can create "skins" or become deathless, for instance. People don't simply want to experience the action of the game; they want to compose aspects of the narrative and creatively explore the range and form of the game's structure. Films about the making of games are another aspect of a type of Play Mode in which the game is examined as a collaborative process. Multiple perspectives permit people to find/create its relevance to their own lives and aspirations. The process of playing a game is only one of many processes we engage in that are related to the game. There are critical and creative activities/processes we engage in that situate the game in the world and in our lives. This essay is a kind of third mode.

To some extent, *Arteroids* came to be about the differences and similarities between game and art, which find their intersection in the notion of play. When we play, we are creatively engaged in guiding processes. The processes themselves guide our activity, but we are also guiding the processes, perhaps adjusting them or departing from them in ways that make the play more meaningful to us and, if we are trying to make art, meaningful to independent observers.

When the velocity of the texts in *Arteroids* is relatively high and the player can be bested by the opposing texts, there is little time to read; the player is challenged to "stay alive," to keep the process going by skillful eye-hand coordination and strategy. She is challenged to play to win/live. When the velocity of the texts is low or when the player is deathless in Play Mode, she is free to read the texts and/or play with the *Arteroids* program as a kind of visual/kinetic poetry display/composition device.

*Arteroids* situates itself between entertainment and art, between popular culture and art. Games are largely associated with entertainment rather than art. What is the difference between entertainment and art? Both often involve the fictitious, the pretend, simulation, and play. Both often involve story or narrative. Both are often deeply involved in matters of art and/or design etc. The difference would seem to balance on the degree to which the work confronts the problematical issues it raises; the degree to which it questions the assumptions of the world it creates or simulates; the intensity of its engagement with that world, and with language, and the shades of gray it is capable of distinguishing; the intensity and consequence of the human drama it reveals; and the vision of the social and individual it draws. These are all factors that we consider in the distinction between art and entertainment. Art can be fun too; but the nature of the fun opens the wreader into the world and their own drama, into confrontation, not isolating fantasy.

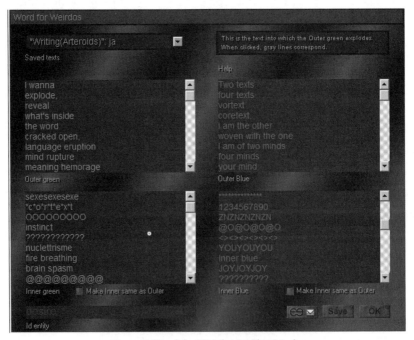

*Figure 5*. Word for Weirdos in Play Mode.

## Word for Weirdos

In Play Mode, players can use Word for Weirdos to create and save texts. The id-entity (the text that represents the wreader and does the shooting) is also editable. Word for Weirdos encapsulates an odd literary form. The wreader creates five texts—1) outer green text, 2) inner green text, 3) an outer blue text, 4) an inner blue text, and 5) an id-entity text—then names the created set (or uses the default text) in Play Mode. The outer green text is the green text you see on screen when playing. The inner green text is the text into which the elements of the outer green text explode. These can be the same as the outer green or not, as the player pleases. Same for the blue texts. *Arteroids* saves these texts to disk for future recall.

Part of the idea of *Arteroids* is to explore the dynamics of this odd literary form. It's the id-entity against the blue and green texts. What should the id-entity be? What should the green text be, and the blue text? Various conflicts come to mind.

The question arises, though: does it matter? In Game Mode and Play Mode at high velocity, the texts are not consciously readable. But they are readable in both Game Mode and Play Mode at low velocity and low density, which the player can set in Play Mode. And they are readable and editable in Word for Weirdos.

That the texts be readable matters to those interested in poetry and digital art, because, really, the question of readibility concerns the degree to which *Arteroids* is involved in poetry, not simply kinetic language (if that is a valid distinction—certainly it's one that a lot of wired poets make).

Some writers must experience the evaporation of readability attendant upon velocity increase as a negation of readable language and of poetry itself. To me, however, it is as though there were also sliders for Readability, Game, and Play. When you change the velocity, you change these conceptual sliders, as it were.

Part of the idea of *Arteroids* is to investigate the slide of game, play, and art into one another. When is a game art? When does a game impose a competitive emphasis that rules out certain types of play? If the text becomes unreadable, it rules out certain types of play that are simply a part of reading. But also, when the text becomes unreadable, it makes for a better game, if you like playing the game.

*Arteroids* shifts the focus between game and play, between text as readable literary object that gets its primary meaning from the meaning of the words, to text as meaning via sound, motion, and destructive intent. When does *poetry* mean poetry, and when does it mean arteroid? It is a question of velocity, density, and other such concerns of visual (even multi-media) rhetoric, of emphasis and intent, which slide around in *Arteroids*.

What are the possible roles of language in dynamic multimedia work for the web? Can poetry go there and live? Judge for yourself.

My own feeling is that a synthesis of media and arts, including text, along with things like programming and its domain of art such as computer games, changes them all in certain ways, limits them and expands them in ways that are challenging and generative of new media language.

## Publishing Arteroids

Part of the, um, challenge of *Arteroids,* for me, is to publish it appropriately. Given that it borders entertainment and art, it's appropriate to publish it on both types of sites so, for instance, it is published on <www.turbulence.org> from New York, an internet art site run by Helen Thorington, and on <www.quadgames.com>, a games site from the Netherlands run by Eric van Riet Paap. It was initially published on <www.theremediproject.com> (curated by Josh Ulm in San Francisco), and has been published on <www.poemsthatgo.com> (edited by Ingrid Ankerson in Baltimore) in a special issue on literary games. It was translated into Portuguese by Regina Celia Pinto and published in Rio, Brazil, at <www.arteonline.arq.br>. It is also published in Montreal at <www.chairetmetal.com> by Olivier Dyens, in Toronto at <www.centennialcollege.ca> by Nancy Paterson when I was Artist in Residence in Toronto, and was a featured work in two talks I was invited to give at the Rochester Institute of Technology by the poet Linda Reinfeld. It has been shown in New York at the August Arts festival on film and new media curated by Hooshla Fox and, more recently, in Los Angeles in the Machine Gallery (<www.machineproject.com>) and the page_space project organized by Braxton Soderman (<www.superbunker.com/machinepoetics>), which focuses on col-laboration among literary digital artists. In the version of *Arteroids* for the Machine Gallery and page_space, there are texts in *Arteroids* by Helen Thorington of <www.turbulence.org> and Christina McPhee of <www.naxsmash.net>. This essay is also published in a book issue of *Anomalie* (in French and English) entitled *Computer Games and Art: Intersections and Interactions,* edited by Grethe Mitchell and Andy Clarke, founders of COSIGN

(Computational Semiotics in Games and New Media). And the first year of development of *Arteroids* was funded by a senior grant from the Canada Council's since-expired Electronic and Spoken Word program managed by Paul Seesequasis.

So *Arteroids* gets around in its own sloppy fashion, and its gigs have been fun. It has had more impact and publication exposure in literary and internet-art contexts than as a piece of entertainment because it is more significant as a literary/digital art statement than as a piece of entertainment. I am happy, though, that it is published on the games site <www.quadgames.com> and won Bernie DeKoven's "Major Fun Award" from <www.deepfun.com>. The context of its publication may grow over time or halt; which it will be isn't clear at this point. If I want it in more entertainment sites, I'm going to have to add several features that currently aren't part of *Arteroids* (toward making it the world's first addictive poem). Whether I will actually add those will depend on several things but, for now, I am not working on it, and have moved on to other projects.

It is oft remarked that no one can build a game on their own, that it is a necessarily collaborative type of project. Yes and no. There are commercial successes and there are artistic successes. Sometimes they are the same thing, sometimes not; sometimes you get what you need to proceed with it; sometimes you don't and proceed anyway. In any case, my experience of online games suggests that original, relevant, fun game concepts are not particularly numerous. Individuals and small groups are best advised to put a great deal of energy there, where it counts. The games that end up becoming best known of those on the web will capitalize on the fun and the possibilities of networked environments, will really have that nailed, and will have a minimal and efficient message-passing logic between players on the net, because bandwidth may widen but it is the main constraint now. In the days of *Asteroids,* I imagine the key obstacle was physical memory and CPU speed. The constraints in which we work have more than a little

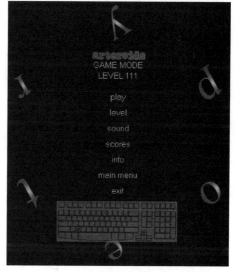

*Figure 6.* The *Arteroids* menu.

influence on what is fluidly, immersively possible. It is said that a story follows from its premises; games are shaped by their environment even when they are fantastical, and exploit the strengths of the message-passing capabilities of the media/um as a body with its own shape and strengths/weaknesses.

## The Conflict of Art & Entertainment

Poetry is not a game somebody wins. Also, I do not wish to glorify the gun and killing things. The pen is mightier than the sword, though it's much slower in its assignations, like justice itself. Justice is slow but we don't have anything else, and it requires wise words. I'm hoping my continuing ambivalence about the piece indicates that *Arteroids* does have an unresolvable dynamic that is a source of continuing energy: the conflict between game and art, entertainment and art, popular culture and art. I attempted to explore these conflicts by making a real computer game, not a faux art game, so that the conflicts would be experienced dramatically. I tried to take the notion of the game and the notion of the work of art seriously and take poetry where it hasn't been before, to make poor old loved poetry suffer as never before.

Whatever we do in making art, it never seems enough, never goes as far as we would like it to go, and our art always remains a deeply flawed artifact. At best, our art is deeply flawed, like ourselves. But human.

# NIC KELMAN
## YES, BUT IS IT A GAME?

Like most American males, I've been playing video games since *Pong*, since the days when the category name made sense. *Pong*. The game of ping-pong played on a video screen. A video game. But as I watched the genre develop—through more and more detailed sprites and on to texture-mapped, object-oriented master works, from simple games of skill to complex, multimillion dollar narratives involving problem-solving and strategy as well as fast fingers— as I watched this development, the question that kept coming to mind was: when does this medium make the leap from entertainment to art?

Yes, it's true that elements of various established art forms have been included in games since almost the very earliest days, the most obvious being music and graphic design. Color palates, bit grids, and musical notes limited to a range of only eight to thirty-two choices forced early game designers and composers to push the limits of their creativity, resulting in some masterpieces of minimalism. *Pac-Man* alone has provided us with unforgettable cultural icons not just in Pac-Man himself, but in the ghosts that chased him, Ms. Pac-Man, and even in the opening theme which I still remember as clearly as any Wham! song. And this tradition has, of course, continued into the present day—games like *Jet Grind Radio*[1] or *XIII*[2] have converted entire artistic traditions into the game format (graffiti and bande dessinée respectively). Likewise, one of the best-selling import CDs in the last few years was the soundtrack for *Final Fantasy VII*.[3] In addition, the games of the last decade have begun to call on the talents of new kinds of artists. When large enough storage capacities were made available in a small enough space and it became possible to save a game's progress, it suddenly also became desirable to incorporate writing into what became a whole new genre of games. With the necessity of beginning a game anew at every sitting eliminated, complex dialogue and exposition could be added, superimposing a stronger narrative element on games then had been present in the past. Similarly, the leap to three dimensions in games has created a demand for game designers who are also talented directors as games now involve camera angles, cut-scenes, and CG movies that, in the best cases today, are far more dramatic than anything Hollywood has produced in a long time.

It is also true that there has been great success with games that serve as prompts for player-generated creativity, creativity which then fits neatly into an already established artistic category. The most successful of these has probably been *Dance Dance Revolution*. Visit any large arcade anywhere in the world at its busiest time and you will see players competing on this game's "stage." In this case, it would be perfectly possible to play the game simply by using your feet to hit the right button combinations on the correct beats and satisfy its Simon Says format. Instead, however, players actually invent their own dances, moving their whole bod-

---

[1] A Sega Dreamcast game in which the player rollerblades around town with a spraypaint can attempting to "tag" as many places as possible without getting caught by the police. The look of the game's environment mirrored the game's goal.

[2] A cross-platform, first-person shooter released recently and based on a French comic book.

[3] One of a series of games that has been one of the most popular in history, this number being perhaps the best selling of them all.

[4] A recent PS2 game that allows players to compete online and asks that they execute button combos that correspond to different chords on precisely the right beats.

[5] An N64 game that takes players on a virtual safari in the world of Pokemon. Players may then take their memory cards to printers in select locations and print out their safari photos as stickers.

ies to execute the correct button combinations and creating their own original choreographies for any given song. Other games such as *Frequency*[4] or *Pokemon Snap*[5] have required players to generate their own music or photography which the game then judges to be good or bad, using that judgment as the basis for competition.

But, as stated already, these examples are of established art forms either being incorporated into games or being used as the basis for games. The real question is: when will games become an art form in their own right?

There are hints, I think, that this leap is occurring right now, today—that we are in the midst of it. One of these indicators, to me, is the comparative historical development of games and film. I believe using this comparative history as an indicator is valid because these two mediums are so closely related in so many ways. Most obviously, we experience them in the same way—as multimedia combining sight, sound, and music. In addition, and equally simplistically, the creation process for both mediums involves the collaboration of a wide range of artists working in their own distinct fields. But, perhaps more interestingly, of all artistic mediums, they are the most closely linked to technology. Yes, it's true that the development of oil paints or the synthesizer caused major ripples in their respective forms, but developments like these are few and far between (and writing and dance have arguably been working with the same toolsets since their conceptions). But for film and video games, technological revolutions with deep-seated executional implications are the norm. For example, when the telephoto lens was invented, suddenly every new film began frequently employing the highly compressed longshots this innovation allowed. These shots are now a recognizable hallmark of the films of the early 1970s, but since that time, while the technique continues to be employed, it is now just one piece of vocabulary in the language of cinema. A nice example of a similar situation in video games is the current use of time control in action games. One side effect of the most recent generation of processors is the ability for the speed at which a game is played to be altered instantaneously. This time control feature is now present in dozens of action games, from *Max Payne* that employed a *Matrix*-like bullet-time effect, to the recent hit *Prince of Persia,* which instead of using a traditional number-of-lives system gave players the ability to reverse time to the moment before their death.[6] Just like the

---

[6] Both games are enormously successful cross-platform third-person action games released within the last few years.

zoomed-in telephoto longshot, however, this result of recent technological innovation will eventually just become part of the language of games and be used only where it has the most impact. These examples are just two small illustrations of how technological advancement has an immediate and recognizable impact on film and games in a manner it does not have on other media. Finally, games have borrowed from film quite explicitly in many ways (and not simply in their employment of directing techniques). One excellent example of this that continually amuses me is the inclusion of lens flare in first-person point of view games. In theory, in these games, the player is seeing through the eyes of a real person. But the game engines almost always include lens flare, an artifact of a camera lens, as a way of making the vision more realistic. That we consider the film image more real than our own eyesight possibly says more about American culture than the medium, but it does nonetheless demonstrate quite well that games consider *themselves* to be linked to cinema—it is not simply a framework I am imposing arbitrarily.

Accepting that film and video games are analogous, the comparative history of the two mediums would suggest that we're on the verge of the first video game art renaissance. Film began as a spectacle—a new technology that was little more than a sideshow. Likewise, the earliest games were also little more than novelties—something to show and amuse your friends, little more than a parlor trick. *Pong* was great, but I don't remember anyone playing it for eight hours at a time. Film then entered its imitative era, becoming little more than a device for recording theatrical performances by the great stars of the stage. Games too had their imitative era—duck hunting, gunfighting, football—all the basis of games from the first five years of the mass-market game era. Then, in film, Edwin Porter, created the first original film narrative, *The Great Train Robbery*, including many film firsts—camera movement, parallel editing, etc. I would argue that the equivalent in the history of games was *Space Invaders*. This game introduced the rudiments of narrative, was the first to display a high score, was the first mass-market game to depart from reality for its theme, and so on. *The Great Train Robbery* ushered in the silent era. *Space Invaders* ushered in the era of 2-D games. And just as the silent era had its masterpieces and its visionary auteurs, so to did the 2-D gaming era. D. W. Griffith and Shigeru Miyamoto. Fritz Lang and Akira Yasuda. Then, a massive revolution came in film with the introduction of the additional dimension of sound. This completely changed the film form in much the same way as the leap from 2-D to 3-D changed the video game form. Old companies that had been very successful in the 2-D format went bankrupt and new giants emerged that understood what this change meant. Interestingly enough, however, and perhaps because the emergence of 3-D gaming was anticipated from the earliest days of 2-D, many of the older companies and designers did manage to make a successful leap to the new format—many more than managed to move from silent to sound film. Most recently, similar to the revolution in filmmaking that took place when equipment became compact enough and low power enough to facilitate easy location filming, bringing the world of reality into the fantasy world of film, we have the introduction of Massively Multiplayer Environments in video games. Many games today allow players to interact with thousands of other real people as they play in much the same way that actors began to interact with real environments after the location revolution in film.

All of which clearly, then, begs the question asked earlier: if video games and film are so closely analogous, isn't the leap from entertainment to art long overdue for video games? If we accept the history of film as reliably analogous because of the mediums' close relationship, games are long past the point in their history where this leap should have been made. What is more, this should be especially true since games have clearly had their own visionary geniuses who understood the medium in ways no one else did, the same kind of geniuses that, for film, were responsible for the medium becoming a new art form. So why hasn't this leap been made?

I think the answer to this question is two-fold. First of all, these changes in the game industry have taken place in a mere twenty years—all of them. From the birth of the genre to a point where there have already been enough technological changes to mirror the entire century-long history of film has taken so little time that I remember each and every one of those changes personally. In film, the single leap from spectacle to original narrative alone took twenty years. And it is the rapidity of these changes that explains to me why we have yet to see the game designers capable of taking the medium and turning it into an art form, but that also suggests we should see them very, very soon. The video game artists of tomorrow are most likely in high school or college today and have not only grown up with games, but have grown up with games advanced enough for them to envision their artistic potential. By not having been exposed to the medium's purely entertainment, game-based origins, I think they will be more capable of thinking outside the box than those of us that have grown up with games (and consequently have a hard time gaining perspective on them as anything other than games). A good analogy here would be the way someone you've known all your life may change quite considerably over time, but it is hard for you to see them as a new person. Someone who meets them for the first time in their current state, however, perceives only the new person and thinks of them in that way alone. I think this is the situation with games. The tools are now there for them to become art, and the similarity of game history to film history suggests that game art is long overdue, but these tools have emerged so quickly, the current designers—even the best of them—have a hard time seeing their potential to be used for anything except gameplay.

Secondly, and perhaps more importantly, film is a passive medium. Like all other art forms to date (except perhaps improv comedy), film, in imitating theater and then in becoming a form in its own right, stayed with the tradition that art is a passive experience. It is a communication between the artist and the observer that flows in only one direction. The artist is active, the medium and the experiencer of the medium, are passive in the process. The viewer or reader may experience the work in different ways, but has no input into the work itself. Video games, on the other hand, are interactive in nature. The central difference—perhaps the only difference today—between film and games is this element of interactivity. And what is interactive art? What happens when the art itself (and not just its interpretation) becomes a collaborative experience between artist and observer? We don't know. When (and not if) video games make the leap to a new art form, they will also be the world's first (inter)active art form. But it is precisely because we don't know what interactive art looks like, and because we are so used to interactivity indicating something other than art, usually entertainment, that we have so far failed to produce games that are truly art. But it is this same interactivity that provides such incredible potential for an art form unlike any we have ever seen. Because it is this interactivity that is responsible for the degree of character transference the player experiences, a degree of transference that eclipses that of any other medium.

In the less abstract art forms (IE not music or dance), what gives them such impact is our ability to empathize with what is being depicted. Can we feel what that woman is feeling in that favorite painting? Can we understand what that character is thinking and do we feel angry (or happy or sad) for them in that favorite book? What is the appeal of action movies to men and romantic comedies to women (a stereotype, yes, perhaps, but the statistics overwhelmingly back the statement) if not our mental mapping onto the characters? What eight-year-old boy has not played let's-pretend *Star Wars* in the last thirty years? It is in their ability to make us feel transference to a character, in their ability to transport us heart and soul and mind into a fictional, imagined environment, that video games excel.

The most obvious example of this effect is the excitement a player feels in a first-person shooter (head-to-head games are exciting, too, obviously, but there the competition with your friends provides most of the stimulation).[7] In these games, you are seeing the world as the main character sees the world, experiencing it as they experience it, and every surprise, every success, is felt significantly more intensely than when watching even the best action film.

But perhaps more interestingly (because excitement has always been the hallmark of entertainment, of pulp fiction and pornography, not art) is the terror a player feels when moving through a survival horror game. Anyone who has played any of the masterpieces of the survival horror genre, such as *Silent Hill 2* or *Resident Evil 2*,[8] is acutely aware of the power of video games to connect player and protagonist with an intensity found no where else. This sympathetic and empathetic link reaches far beyond the link between reader and protagonist or even viewer and protagonist. Only once do you need to see a room full of body builders turn off one of these games for being "too freaky" to recognize the potential for exploiting this acute transference for artistic purposes. (Yes, I witnessed this two years ago, the game was *Silent Hill 2* and I have yet to meet anyone brave enough to get through it). Would these same men have walked out of *The Ring* or stopped reading *The Woman in White*? I don't think so.

I've often wondered why this link is so much closer than that I've experienced in other art forms. Why is the link between player and character so much closer than the link between reader and protagonist or even viewer and protagonist? What is it about "playing" a character instead of simply observing one that makes the narrative experience so much scarier or

---

[7] First-person shooters are games in which the player sees the environment from a first-person perspective and the themes of the games are combat and mission based. *Head-to-head* refers to games in which two or more players compete directly against each other as characters in the game, either in sports, fighting, or other competitions.

[8] Survival horror refers to games in which the player usually takes the role of a normal human being in an environment overrun by demons, zombies, ghosts, etc. These games, interestingly enough, are often third-person, allowing for the use of camera angles and more integrated cut-scenes, both of which add to the drama.

more exciting? Why is it that I have, quite literally, never been scared by a film, but actually had to stop playing not just *Silent Hill 2* but most survival horror games? Why is it that I can find *T2* so relaxing that, on TBS at 2 A.M., it becomes the cinematic equivalent of warm milk, but if I play *SOCOM*[9] after 8 P.M., I can't go to sleep for hours? Is it simply that the threshold for distinguishing the difference between real and simulated input is much lower than we might intuitively assume? Why is it that if we simply watch a character in a low-budget horror film approach the door behind which the monster lurks, it has little to no effect, but if we are the ones controlling the precise moment the character in a game opens that same door, our hearts pound away? Maybe it simply takes much less to convince us something is real than we might otherwise assume. Perhaps walking using two little joysticks to control our speed and direction is not as disconnected—in a neural pathways sense—from using our legs as we might think. Perhaps pressing a button to open a door is not all that different for our brains than turning a knob. But whatever the reason for this phenomenon, I am anxiously awaiting the day when the power of this connection is put to use in the evocation of emotions in addition to terror. Because if the terror survival horror games invoke can be taken as an example, then the potential of this medium to make us feel emotions could exceed film, books, dance—perhaps even music. Imagine, for example, the possibilities for understanding the experience of the other.

I've recently glimpsed the extraordinary ability of video games to help us understand a completely different life experience by playing my first Massively Multiplayer Online Environment game: *Final Fantasy XI*. In this game, I have been playing a female character and am online at any given moment in a complete 3-D world populated by tens of thousands of other players. In addition, as a veteran amateur actor, I have been doing a pretty good job of pretending to be a woman "in real life" (i.e. in chats with other players, etc). And what I have found really fascinating is the insight this has given me into the female experience of the world. As ridiculous as it sounds, I urge you to try it. It has certainly allowed me to understand what it might be like to be a woman better than *Middlemarch* or *The Bell Jar* or *Bridget Jones's Diary*. Again, it is quite different merely observing a male character assume a woman is

---

[9] A Navy Seal online multiplayer third-person shooter in which teams of up to eight people can compete against each other in very realistic environments.

being flirtatious when she is just being nice than actually experiencing it firsthand (never mind the furious helplessness you feel when someone says something suggestive to you...or the number of times a man calls you "bossy" when you make any kind of suggestion as to what might be the best course of action).

Regardless of the cognitive science behind this effect, the effect is there. It is real. And it is precisely this unique effect generated by games' unique attribute of interactivity (the same quality that makes them so addictive) that gives games the potential to become one of the world's most important art forms. If the purpose of art is to make someone feel something intensely, video games, because of the degree of transference they can make us experience through interactivity, have the potential to eclipse all but the most brilliant executions of other art forms as the world's most significant medium.

What this medium might look like is anyone's guess. Last year a game called *Rez* was released for the PS2. It was essentially a 3-D form of *Space Invaders* but graphically resembled the most cutting-edge German packing design and also played specific chords and notes as the player fired their various weapons. With a driving backbeat behind every level, as the game was played, it became a quite spectacular integration of music and design. If Oscar Wilde was right about beauty being the sole justification for art, then *Rez* would qualify as perhaps the first video game that was designed purely as a work of art (the gameplay was certainly several years out of date...but that was not the point of the game, which is precisely the point here). But this nod towards abstract beauty, even if carried further, would not fulfill the kind of potential discussed above. There was no character to transfer to, there was no emotion experienced (except, perhaps, the wonder of beauty which is, I recognize, to many, all that is required for a work to qualify as art). There is a game due to be released soon called *Shellshock*, which promises "a graphically harrowing depiction of the terror of war." "Prepare to experience the fear, chaos, and atrocities of the Vietnam War," reads their advertising. Now, giving the company the benefit of the doubt that they are not being exploitive, a game that attempted to do this seriously would be breaking new ground in the medium and could perhaps fulfill some of the potential discussed above. It seems likely, after all, that a war game would be the first to attain some level of artistic achievement because of the combination of the opportunity for game related tasks in a potentially serious and moving environment. Whether this game lives up to its claims or simply exploits an even lower common denominator than the *Vice City*[10] series is another question. (Whether or not the game lives up to the marketing, what's most interesting is that the company has chosen to market a game in this fashion—as a serious experience rather than entertainment. This is perhaps the first step in the direction of games as art—the acknowledgement that the demand could be out there). Of course, the possibilities are endless and all that is really required is that the medium begin to be taken seriously by people with talent and skill. It has the potential, it simply needs to be fulfilled and the time for that fulfillment has clearly arrived.

To conclude, I would like to propose what could be a manifesto of a Video Game Arts Movement in the hopes that this might be taken as a jumping off point for this moment that is already long overdue. The points below would, I believe, go a long way toward jump-starting the usage of the medium for artistic purposes.

---

[10] A mature-rated, third-person action game series in which the player takes the role of a criminal in various cities.

11 Opposite is the first 15-20 minutes of *Silent Hill 2* described fairly accurately. The interactive part of this essay is for you to play through the above yourself to compare the passive experience with the active one. Good luck.

My girlfriend passed away last year, a driving accident, yet here, in my hand, is a letter I received from her only yesterday. Her handwriting, her scent, the date on the letter and the postmark, both last week. She asks to meet me in "our special place," and I know she means down by the lake in Silent Hill, a town a few miles up the coast. That is where I am right now, except I can't get into the town itself. The tunnel through the mountains has been blocked and a strange fog lies heavily on the road. But I won't turn back, I must find out more about this letter and suspect I may be able to get into the town on foot if I climb down to the lakeshore. It is strangely quiet, I hear nothing except perhaps the waves of the lake lapping against the shoreline. From the car, I take a transistor radio and switch it on, attempting to find some news about the road blockage. It receives nothing but static. Nervous about the lack of visibility and the silence, I take the radio with me, as well as the tirejack and flashlight from the car, and head into the fog, down the hill.

As I climb down, slowly, off-balance, I hear strange breathing, panting, coming from the fog around me. Then it is gone. Somewhat further down, something moves suddenly through the bushes nearby, but when I move closer, it too disappears. Eventually, I reach the lakeshore and find the entrance to the tunnel's ventilation system, a metal door in the rock that hangs slightly open. Again the panting, this time behind me, but when I turn, there is nothing, only a shuffling sound that moves momentarily across the face of the fog from left to right. As I approach the entrance, the static on the radio blares louder and louder as I move closer. I stand before the door, wondering what might be behind it in the darkness, but if I want to solve the mystery of the letter, this seems to be the only way. I ready the tirejack in one hand, the flashlight in the other, take a deep breath, and open the door. Nothing. I shine the flashlight into the corridor and see its rusty, humid, concrete walls are also splashed with what seems to be blood. There are no bodies to be seen anywhere, just a dark, abandoned stairwell, a cracked mirror, and sparking fuse box.

I take a step inside, the static growing louder, and shine the light up the stairs. As I do so, I hear the shuffling sound behind me again and turn to look out into the mist. A shape is approaching. It is the size of an infant but walks like a man. Its silhouette begins to become an outline as it makes its way out of the fog and towards me.[11]

## A Video Game Arts Manifesto

1) It is time video games became more than simply entertainment.

2) The interactivity of games provides them with a unique potential to connect with their audience, possibly more deeply than any established art form. Recognizing that this interactivity creates a stronger emotional bond between player and character than between viewer and character or reader and character is essential to the medium breaking its current bonds. It is time this bond was exploited for generating a wider range of emotions than merely intense excitement.

3) Elements of story and character have to be given as much precedence as elements of gameplay and visual design. This will allow "interactors" to become more emotionally involved in the work and emotional involvement is at the heart of any important work of art. A great leap in this direction could be made by developers hiring writers to create these elements instead of continuing with the practice of the lead game designer also being the head writer. Tremendous strides have been made in this direction in the most recent games, but until this is common practice, it seems unlikely that games will be able to take the next step and transcend their current moniker. Returning to the film analogy, films had writers before they had directors.

4) Likewise the boundaries of visual design have to be pushed further in ways that are entirely unique to the designer—they have to be the designer's personal vision, not just imitations of other styles (e.g. graffiti, anime, French comic books). For video games to begin to function as art, their graphics will need to be original, personal visions of the world.

5) It should be more clearly recognized that the thematic maturity barrier no longer exists. As the very first video gamers grow older but continue to play games, there is now a sizable portion of the gaming population over thirty. These players already demand, and will continue to demand, games with mature themes, but this deman can and should be exploited for emotional and artistic purposes as well as the purposes of entertainment. Games are no longer

exclusively for kids, so where are the games designed exclusively for adults?

6) The cost of developing an artistic game must be accepted in the same way the cost of an independent film is accepted. The mainstream game market already functions on the Hollywood studio model—one megahit pays for all the games that lost money. Given the other linkages between film and video games, this economic resemblance should also be carried to its logical extreme, paving the way for independent, arts-oriented video games. Arts grants for games would be a welcome addition to the arts funding pool as would support from major hardware manufacturers who could assist independent game developers with favorable licensing deals, etc.

7) Finally, here is a challenge, issued by the Video Game Arts Manifesto to video game developers everywhere. Make someone cry. That is your challenge. Because the day a game makes someone cry will be the day we will have to call that game art.

# HIGH SCORES
## About the Contributors

**JIM ANDREWS,** the creator of *Arteroids*, is a digital artist, programmer, visual poet, writer, and audio guy. <Vispo.com> has been the center of his artistic publishing since 1995. It houses *Arteroids* and all his other work. He is the founder of *webartery* and co-moderates the *-empyre-* list devoted to discussion of new media art issues. He lives in Victoria, BC, Canada, where he is employed by the Canadian Foundation for Innovation as a programmer of interactive audio applications for performing musicians.

**SHANNA COMPTON** is a poet, freelance editor, and writer whose work has appeared in *Gastronomica, McSweeney's, Verse, Pindeldyboz,* and elsewhere, including her chapbooks *Down Spooky* and *Big Confetti* (which was cowritten with Shafer Hall). She is Associate Publisher of Soft Skull Press and the editor of *LIT,* the literary journal of the Creative Writing Program at New School University. She lives in Brooklyn, NY, with her husband, a Sony PlayStation II, an Xbox, a Nintendo, and an extensive library of CD-ROM games for Macintosh. She maintains a website and blog at <www.shannacompton.com>.

**KATIE DEGENTESH** grew up playing 8-bit games on the Atari 800. She now lives and writes in New York City. Her poems and reviews have appeared in numerous magazines, including *Combo, Arras, Fence, Shiny,* and the *Poetry Project Newsletter,* and in the anthology *Free Radicals: American Poets Before Their First Books* (Subpress, 2004). She has an M.A. from the University of California at Davis, and keeps a blog of local observations at <katied.blogspot.com>.

**DREW GARDNER** is the author of *Sugar Pill* (Krupskaya, 2002). His essays and reviews have appeared in the *Poetry Project Newsletter, Crayon,* and elsewhere.

**ERNEST HILBERT**'s poetry and criticism have appeared in the *Boston Review, LIT, Fence,* and the *American Scholar.* He is the poetry editor for Random House's online literary magazine *Bold Type,* <www.boldtype.com>, and edits <nowCulture.com>'s biannual print edition, *NC.* He is also on the core staff of the *Contemporary Poetry Review.* He received his doctorate in English Literature from Oxford University, where he earlier completed a Master's Degree in English Literature and edited the *Oxford Quarterly.*

**SHANNON HOLMAN**'s poems have appeared in *Crowd, Diagram, Good Foot, La Petite Zine, Lodestar Quarterly, Pierogi Press, Swank Writing,* and elsewhere. Her *Dope Wars* high score is $36,811,432.

Raised in New England and Mississippi, **J. BRANDON HOUSLEY** now lives in New York where he is an M.F.A. candidate in Poetry at the New School. He is also the Poetry Editor for *LIT.*

**SHELLEY JACKSON** is the authorof a story collection, The Melancholy of Anatomy, hypertexts including Patchwork Girl and The Doll Games, and several children's books. Her stories have appeared in the Paris Review, Grand Street, Conjunctions, Fence, and many other journals and anthologies, and she is a recent recipient of a Pushcart Prize. She is tattooing a story one word at a time on the skin of her readers. Visit her website at <www.ineradicablestain.com>.

**LUIS JARAMILLO** teaches at the New School Writing Program. His most recent short story was published in *Open City.*

H. THOR JENSEN was born in Maple Valley, Washington in 1976 and now lives in Queens. He works for a small video game development company in New York City. He wishes he could go back in time to warn his younger self about a variety of issues. His website, which showcases his cartoons and illustrations, is <www.shortandhappy.com>.

THOMAS KELLY is the author of *Payback*, which was adapted for the screen by David Mamet, and *The Rackets,* as well as a third novel, *Empire Rising,* to be published by Farrar, Straus & Giroux in 2004. He has worked digging the tunnels of New York City as a sandhog, as Advance Man for former New York City Mayor David Denkins, and is a frequent contributor to *Esquire* and other publications.

NIC KELMAN holds an B.S. from MIT and an M.F.A. from Brown. His writing and photography have appeared, among other places, in *Kenyon Review, Glamour,* the *Village Voice,* and *Black Book,* as well as various anthologies. His first novel, *girls,* was published in 2003 by Little, Brown and Company and was named one of the Best Books of the Year by the *San Francisco Chronicle* and the *New York Journal.*

ROLAND KELTS is a Tokyo-based writer from New York whose fiction, essays, articles, and reviews have appeared in numerous publications in the US and Japan. He was he winner of the *Playboy* College Fiction Contest and a Jacob K. Javits Fellowship award in writing. In addition to Manhattan and Tokyo, he has lived in London, San Franciso, Anchorage, and Osaka. His essay on Japan's generation gap appears in the new collection *Kuhaku & Other Accounts from Japan,* and his forthcoming novel is called *Access.*

MARK LAMOUREUX's chapbook *City / Temple* was published by Ugly Duckling Presse in the autumn of 2003. Another chapbook, *29 Cheeseburgers,* was published by Boston's Pressed Wafer in early 2004. His work has appeared in *Lungfull!, Jubilat, Fulcrum, Art New England, Shampoo,* and other publications. He lives in Allston, MA.

AARON MCCOLLOUGH's third book of poems, *Little Ease,* is forthcoming from Ahsahta Press in 2006. His other books include *Double Venus* (Salt, 2003) and *Welkin* (Ahsahta, 2002).

McCollough's poems have appeared in or are forthcoming in *Volt, Denver Quarterly, Slope, Colorado Review, LIT, American Letters & Commentary, Verse, Typo,* and other periodicals. He is a Ph.D. student at the University of Michigan. He edits *GutCult* and maintains a blog at <aaronmccollough.blogspot.com>.

**JIM MUNROE** lives with his wife in Toronto's Annex neighborhood above an ice cream shop and an income tax office, which would be convenient except that he is a vegan who does his own taxes. His fourth novel is called *An Opening Act of Unspeakable Evil.* He runs a monthly indie touring circuit called the Perpetual Motion Roadshow, writes a video game column for the alt-weekly *eye* (which also appears at <www.theculturalgutter.com>, and irregularly put out *Novel Amusements,* a DVD zine. He invites you to visit his website, which has do-it-yourself articles on book and video making and news about his latest projects at <www.nomediakings.org>.

**MARC NESBITT**'s collection of short stories *Gigantic* was published by Grove/Atlantic and in 2003. His fiction has appeared in *Harper's,* the *New Yorker,* and elsewhere. He received his master's degree in creative writing from the University of Michigan and has worked as a video game tester for two New-York based companies.

**DANIEL NESTER** is the author of *God Save My Queen: A Tribute* (Soft Skull, 2003) and *God Save My Queen II: The Show Must Go On* (Soft Skull, 2004). His work has appeared *Open City, Nerve, Black Book,* and *The Best AmerIcan Poetry 2003.* He teaches writing occasionally at New School University. He lives in Brooklyn, NY, and edits *Unpleasant Event Schedule* (<www.unpleasanteventschedule.com>). He also keeps a blog and maintains a website at <www.godsavemyqueen.com>.

**WHITNEY PASTOREK** is a writer, musician, and international star of stage and screen who currently works for *Entertainment Weekly.* She is the executive editor of *Pindeldyboz,* and has written for the *Village Voice, Surface Magazine, Time Out, San Francisco Chronicle, Utne Reader,* and *McSweeney's.* She once interviewed the White Stripes for NPR's *Morning Edition,* has appeared on a VH-1 game show about Vanilla Ice, and is alleged to have vomited on Fred

Durst. A complete list of everything is constantly in flux over at <www.whittlz.com.>

**RICHARD POWERS** has been the recipient of a Lannan Literary Award and a MacArthur Fellowship. He is the author of eight novels, including *The Time of Our Singing, Gain,* and *Galatea 2.2.* His piece in this anthology is excerpted from his novel *Plowing the Dark,* by his kind permission.

Legendary championship gamer, **TODD ROGERS** is "The King of Video Games" and holds more than 2000 record high scores for video games. For more information about Todd Rogers, visit his website at <www.beatthechamp.com>.

**LAUREL SNYDER** is a graduate of the Iowa Writers' Workshop and a Paul Engle fellow. She has published nonfiction in publications such as *BUST, Bitch* and *Utne Reader,* and published poetry in *Post Road, Gulf Coast, shampoo, Unpleasant Event Schedule, Beacon Street Review,* and elsewhere. She is an editor at large for the *Land-Grant College Review* and maintains her own website at <www.jewishyirishy.com>.

**BILL SPRATCH**'s fiction has appeared in *Pindeldyboz, Diagram, failbetter, LIT,* the *Mississippi Review Prize Issue 2003,* and elsewhere. His story "The Breakers" was a finalist for the 2004 *One Story* fiction contest, judged by Darin Strauss.

**MAUREEN THORSON** is a lawyer working in New York City with a degree from Georgetown University. Her boyfriend, in addition to working toward his Ph.D. in Molecular Physiology, works intermittently as a beta tester for video games. She can make balloon animals, which, if you squint hard, look kind of like Luigi. Kind of. Her work has appeared in *canwehaveour-ballback?* and is forthcoming in *Good Foot* and *Exquisite Corpse.*

**MARION WRENN** is the Editor of *Painted Bride Quarterly* and a Ph.D. candidate at NYU where she writes about "Smart Fans" and the pleasures of expertise. She also teaches writing, media criticism, and the history of consumer culture at NYU and Parsons School of Design. Her work has appeared in *American Poetry Review, AlterNet,* the *Philadelphia Inquirer,* and elsewhere.

GAME OVER

# INDEX

This partial index comprises a list of the video games mentioned in Gamers, with publisher and release date. Citations in the essays themselves may refer to different versions (for various home systems, etc.) than those listed here.